WHITE DRESSES

WHITE DRESSES

A MEMOIR OF LOVE AND SECRETS, MOTHERS AND DAUGHTERS

MARY PFLUM PETERSON

wm

WILLIAM MORROW
An Imprint of HarperCollins*Publishers*

HarperCollins books may be purchased for educational, business, or sales promotional use. For information please e-mail the Special Markets Department at SPsales@harpercollins.com.

FIRST EDITION

Designed by Diahann Sturge

Library of Congress Cataloging-in-Publication Data has been applied for.

ISBN 978-0-06-238697-7

15 16 17 18 19   OV/RRD   10 9 8 7 6 5 4 3 2 1

To my mother, Anne Diener Pflum.
She gave me everything. And then some more.

White. A blank page or canvas. His favorite. So many possibilities.

—Stephen Sondheim, *Sunday in the Park with George*
(among Anne Diener Pflum's favorite quotes)

Contents

Introduction

They had to be here.

They just had to be here. Somewhere.

But where?

Where?!

I felt the wave of panic wash over me and struggled to breathe. The smell, that horrible smell of the place, made my stomach churn. The air was heavy, steeped in the sickening aroma of a rancid barn that had been deprived of fresh air for the better part of a decade. I felt the vomit burn at the back of my throat.

Not now, I told myself. Not now! I could get sick back at the hotel. Now I had to find them. And I didn't have much time.

I struggled to move. But my feet were gone. I'd lost them between the front door and the landing of the staircase. They were buried somewhere beneath the mountains of *Milwaukee Journals*, the unopened mail and once-used cat leashes and the dozens and dozens of disposable cameras, some of them still wrapped in the yellow plastic Kodak packaging. She'd always loved to take the pictures but never wanted to look in the mirror.

How could I have failed to find a way to rescue her from this?

Slowly, I inched my way to the staircase. Up the stairs is

where they'd surely be. If, that is, they were still here. If she hadn't moved them. If they hadn't been destroyed.

I'd covered the stories of natural disasters many times. Too many to count. I'd spent more than a week in New Orleans after Katrina. I'd gone through Turkey's earthquake in 1999. It was a 7.8 that lasted forty-five seconds—an eternity in terms of earthquakes—and killed tens of thousands. Then, like now, there was rubble everywhere.

When disaster strikes, no matter where in the world, no matter what the circumstances of the destruction, be it fire or flood or wind, people behave the same. Young or old, rich or poor, people want to save their lives and the lives of loved ones first. And they want to save the little things second. The once seemingly big and important things like furniture and electronics—the shoes and dishes and appliances, even the cars and bikes they once spent months selecting and saving to buy—don't matter. No, after the lives, it's the family heirlooms—treasured rugs, handmade quilts, family Bibles, homemade cards and letters—that victims of disaster work desperately to salvage.

And so it was today. I couldn't have cared less about the furniture. Had no use for a car. I just had to save them.

We had never had any real family heirlooms to speak of. Not from my mother's side of the family, anyway. No, my mother and I—we had white dresses.

Like rings of an old oak tree, white dresses marked passages of time, our milestones in life. Both the good ones and the bad. The dresses were not just important. To us, they were sacred.

My mother was not a slave to fashion. But she did adhere to certain rules. Skirts were always to be worn with nylons or tights unless a girl was under the age of twelve or playing tennis. Two-piece bathing suits and halter tops were absolutely verboten for women of all ages. (When it came to swimming, my mother always said a one-piece was, without exception, the way to go.)

And white was to be worn only between Memorial Day weekend (formerly known as Decoration Day weekend) and Labor Day. Never was it to be worn in fall, winter, or early spring, unless there was a christening, First Communion, graduation, or wedding involved.

I openly called my mother's first two fashion rules ridiculous and spent the better part of my teenage years railing against them. But the last rule—what I came to refer to as the White Commandment—I not only accepted, but embraced.

My mother taught me to love all that white represents: cleanliness, innocence, simplicity, sophistication, and, above all, possibilities. And not just possibilities. In my mother's estimation, white represented Infinite Possibilities. For her, white—a blank canvas—was the embodiment of hope and the promise of new beginnings and good things to come.

On the happiest day of my life—my wedding day—my mother's White Commandment was in full effect. I wed Dean on Memorial Day weekend in a crisp white Vera Wang gown that had to be specially ordered since most modern brides, I was told, prefer ivory to true white. Not me. Not Mom.

Today the Vera Wang gown was safe. It lay in a sealed wooden box beneath the bed I shared with Dean, a thousand miles away in New York.

But the fate of the other white dresses? I didn't know. I only knew I had to save them.

For her. For me. For us.

My head spun as I struggled to mount the stairs. Still struggling to breathe, I saw spots. First yellow. Then black. They distorted my view of the staircase. Of what used to be a staircase. There were no steps in sight, just an enormous fabric slope. It looked as if a dozen washing machines had thrown up, spewing down the staircase stained blouses and old pants, long-forgotten scarves and mittens and towels and decades-old linens. I had to get out of here or I was going to faint, fall into one of the mountains of random stuff that was mixed in with the garments, with no rhyme or reason: the unopened boxes of baking soda and mangled cardboard eggs containing unworn panty hose; the discarded fast-food bags and dirty Styrofoam cups and Kleenexes.

I had to get to them before it was too late.

Using the banister for leverage, I pulled my way to the top of the staircase, hand over hand, and waded through more discarded clothes to my room. The first door on the right. It had always been my oasis, where I'd done all of my studying and playing and crying and dreaming.

"Oh my God," I gasped upon entering.

The entire space—once pink and ruffly and girly and light—had gone remarkably dark, covered now in a black sooty dust.

The heavy layer of grime had taken hold of everything, including cherished dolls whose blond hair was now gray and science fair trophies that had turned from golden to a yucky brown. The pink burlap bulletin board that still hung above my twin bed remained littered with faded photos and ribbons from a citywide track meet. Cobwebs hung from all four corners of the room. The lone window was covered in a murky film, allowing only a few rays of winter sunlight to stream in.

I shook my head in disbelief. It was gone. Virtually everything in the room as I had once known it was gone.

I took a deep breath. The second-floor air was a bit less noxious than that on the main floor. It was also considerably colder. That was because of the hole in the roof. The one my uncle discovered last year. That's how, they think, the bats got in. I cringed at the thought. Bats in the house.

Slowly, I made my way to the closet, covered by a now-sooty poster of Tom Cruise, copping his best badass look as *Top Gun*'s Maverick. Then I said a little prayer and slid the right-hand door open.

There, hanging on the long metal rod, I spied a familiar splash of yellow yarn. It was a shawl I'd worn to an Easter Sunday Mass when I was four. The once-bright yellow was now a dull yellow owing to all the dust. I reached to touch it then screamed as a long, leggy spider—what my mother used to call a daddy longlegs—made its way down the length of it.

Beside the shawl hung a fading aqua-blue Forenza camp shirt from The Limited that I'd used my babysitting savings to buy my junior year in high school. It wouldn't have looked so faded had it not been caked in the thick layer of soot that had swallowed the rest of the room.

My heart beat harder now. I felt the panic rise up again, like an impatient tidal wave. Please. Please! They had to be in here. Everything else could go—everything else could be torched—but I couldn't leave without them.

I reached past an old sleeveless peach dress—another Easter relic. Then an ivory lace cardigan. It was full of holes, half eaten by moths.

No—no—no—no white dresses.

But wait! There to the far right on the rod, pushed up against the wall of the closet, I saw It: my First Communion dress. It had hung there in a place of honor every day for nearly three decades and remained, somehow, impossibly white. The deep recesses of the closet had served as a sort of protective armor, shielding it from the storm that had engulfed the house. Miraculously, the long, semitransparent sleeves remained pretty, the lace on the bodice delicate and unspoiled. Even the pleats and long satin sash remained intact.

"Oh, thank God," I cried aloud, pulling the dress, hanger and all, off the rod and hugging it to me. "Oh, thank God!"

I had one white dress, one piece of her. One piece of us. Now if only I could find the rest.

Chapter 1

My Mother's Baptism

September 1935

On a sunny fall day in 1935, they stood, the three of them: Al, hand-some in his dark suit, his curly brown hair blowing in the wind; Aurelia, in the navy-blue drop-waist dress that she'd paired with a matching hat in a bid to mask a mop of disastrous curls; and their infant daughter, Anne. Anne Virginia Diener.

The baby—bald save for a little shock of dark peach fuzz—squirmed in the long white cotton dress enveloping her. The gown, a present from her grandmother Trudy—her father's mother—was beautiful, something Trudy referred to as "Sumptuous! Absolutely sumptuous!" Trimmed with lace at the bodice and the hem, it fea-tured mother-of-pearl buttons down the back and, when paired with a matching bonnet, made the baby look every bit the vision of the proper little girl Trudy had hoped for when she learned of Anne's birth.

Yes, it was the Depression, and money was terribly tight. But, Trudy reasoned, this was her first grandchild—her oldest child's baby girl!—and God knows those kids couldn't have afforded to buy such a thing. For goodness' sake, they couldn't even afford a proper crib. Not even a cradle! Much to Trudy's horror, the baby was sleep-ing in an old dresser drawer Aurelia had once used for sweaters, now lined with blankets.

Just four weeks old, Anne alternately cried and slept as her par-ents took turns holding her in the autumn breeze. An hour before, *she had managed to sleep through most of her own christening. It was only when the elderly priest, speaking Latin, doused her with water that she'd stirred, then fluttered open those big brown eyes.*

After the ceremony, Al and Aurelia had gathered with their new charge in a park not far from Trudy and August Diener's North Indianapolis home for an impromptu photo op. The threesome stood first this way, then that way. And while Al managed a few smiles, Aurelia remained largely subdued. She knew she was supposed to be happy, but this baby business was more than she'd bargained for. So far, she wasn't liking much of it at all. The baby demanded near-constant attention. She didn't have a moment to herself—and worse, barely a moment alone with Al. Before the baby, there'd been late-night dinners, time to read, time to write, and oh! those near-nightly explosions of passion that had made the baby in the first place.

Aurelia had wanted Al from the moment she saw him, had plotted to catch him when she spied him at that birthday party in high school. The gathering had been organized by a local ice-cream shop owner for his niece and nephew. Aurelia went to school with the niece, Al with the nephew. And when Aurelia saw Al, that was all she wrote. She wanted him. With all her heart. And then some. It hadn't been easy. Al came from a good family, old money rooted in a monument business that had been the best in all of Indiana and one of the most prominent in the Midwest. Aurelia came from nothing to speak of. She'd grown up the daughter of a brilliant but deaf father, who, unable to find work as an accountant during the Depression, was forced to take on odd jobs. At one point, he worked as a launderer, cleaning women's soiled undergarments among other things.

But differences aside, there were notable similarities. Al was Catholic and so was Aurelia. He was brilliant—valedictorian of his high school class. And she was brilliant—valedictorian of hers. She would win his heart, she vowed.

For years, they dated. Al tried to tell his parents it was a casual relationship. But it was anything but. In June 1934, the pair secretly wed.

Aurelia coaxed Al into the elopement using that deadliest of weapons: Catholic guilt.

"We can't live in sin forever," she'd told him one night, her blouse unbuttoned, her skirt hiked up over her knees after yet another session of heavy panting and petting.

Filled with a combination of guilt and lusty ardor, Al agreed and arranged to take Aurelia for a quickie marriage in a neighboring town where he'd called in a favor and gotten a bishop—a bishop!—to agree to marry them. For the better part of a year, they told no one except Aurelia's baby sister, Mary Jane, of the marriage. Eventually, they let their parents in on the truth. Trudy sobbed at the news, then shouted at the top of her lungs, then begged for an annulment. Didn't Al see that Aurelia would ruin his life? Didn't Al see the life in medicine that he'd dreamed of—that Trudy had dreamed of—would be doomed if he was with Aurelia? But it was too late. Anne was already on the way. Al opted to forgo medical school in favor of engineering in a bid to graduate, and score a paying job, more quickly. He did, after all, have a family to support.

Now there were dirty diapers, soiled burp cloths, and, in Aurelia's case, aching breasts. Aurelia tried for all of two days to nurse Anne before declaring she didn't have enough milk to give. Secretly, she knew she probably did. But she didn't need one more reason to be saddled with a screaming, red-faced baby. Bottle feeding gave her a freedom nursing wouldn't. Now she had the chance to drop the baby off at her parents', or, if need be, his. They didn't like her. Hated her for marrying their eldest son. For trapping him, they said. But Lord, how they loved that child.

Al had been smart, Aurelia realized, to insist upon naming her Anne. St. Anne, the mother of the Virgin Mary, was among Trudy's favorites. Anne was the saint Al had prayed to when Trudy was ill. The fact that Al had chosen to give the cherished name to his firstborn thrilled his mother no end, showing her that despite his taste in brides, the Catholic seeds she had planted within him as a boy had taken hold and blossomed. Anne was a blessing. She was their little Annie.

The entire family was smitten. Even Peg, Al's gorgeous dark-haired sister, who modeled professionally and was often mistaken for a film actress, fell head over heels for the infant.

All delighted in the squirming baby, save Aurelia. For her, Anne was more of a means to an end. With Anne's birth came a guarantee that now, at last, Al was hers. Forever. Never would he leave the mother of his child. That Catholic guilt would kill him.

After Al and Aurelia had their turns holding the baby and posing for the photos that autumn afternoon, Trudy and August and Peg took theirs, cradling her in their arms. Upon looking at Annie, their hearts melted, their eyes grew moist. There she was. A perfect little girl born out of a completely imperfect situation. Amidst the orange and red of the changing leaves that had begun to litter the park, against the vivid blue of that late September sky, the baby was a dream. Their little Annie. Their vision in white.

From the beginning, my mother, Anne Virginia Diener, was known for three things: a round, open face; deep brown eyes; and a boundless sense of curiosity. Within a year of her arrival home from the hospital, it was evident to all who knew her that Anne was anxious, almost desperate, to explore the world. She loved to put on performances on the front lawn of her Dunkirk, Indiana, home. She relished going for walks and greeting the neighbors, calling to those she knew by name. And she enjoyed dancing around the garden surrounding her house, committing to memory the names of the various flowers. There were rhododendron and hollyhock and the fragrant lilacs that sprang from stubby bushes. And in the spring, there were my mother's favorites: peonies. The big fat blooms that burst from those little buds fascinated her, as did the colony of bumblebees they attracted, each fatter and fuzzier than the last.

But as interested as Anne was in flowers and insects, she was most interested in getting to better know and understand her family. She was especially curious about, and desperate to please, her father. Possessing a deep voice and a brilliant mind, Al Diener was a strikingly handsome man whose eyes were just as dark and beautiful as hers. Standing five foot eight, he was wiry, tanned easily, and looked equally good in the dark suits he wore to Mass and the t-shirts he sported when he did yard work or indulged in a post-work cigarette. Al was something of a mystery to Anne. He left for work soon after she rose in the morning, reporting to Armstrong Glass, a gigantic glass factory, where he'd put his degree in chemical engineering to use as a plant manager. And often, he arrived home after her mother had put her to bed. It was only on weekends that she saw much of him. And a good part of that time was spent going to Mass.

Al Diener had three great loves in his life: his mother, Trudy; his wife, Aurelia; and the Catholic Church. And more often than not, the women took a backseat to the Father, Son, and Holy Ghost. In Christ, in the sacraments, in the words of the pope and the cardinals and the presiding parish priest, Al found life's meaning and order. And in that order—in those traditions and rigid commandments—he placed his undying faith. The church provided the structure around which all things, both personal and professional, revolved. So it was no accident that Al chose as the first home in which to raise his family a rambling gray house next to St. Mary's, the only Catholic church in Dunkirk.

For my mother, it became evident early on that if she wished to spend more time with her father, to find a way into his heart so that she could be certain he was thinking about her during at least some of those many long hours he spent away from her at work, she needed to do so through the church. Saying the rosary with Daddy, attending weekday masses with him, helping set the table when a priest was invited over for dinner, all scored her additional moments with her father, and, more importantly, additional doses of the love and approval she so desperately craved. She was intrigued by the stories her father told her about the saints, listened with rapt attention to the Gospels, and marveled, with a combination of fear and intrigue, at the robed priests who held court before the altar, engulfed in plumes of smoke that spilled out of their incense decanters.

But while embracing Catholicism was the clear path to reach her father, less clear to Anne was how to find an "in" with her mother.

Aurelia Arvin Diener longed to become many things as a child, but a good mother was not at the top of the list. As a child, in the wake of her father's devastating loss of hearing and her stern mother's growing arthritis, she had watched the family's fortune dwindle to nothing. One minute, they were living a life of teas and dance classes in Cincinnati. The next, the family was destitute. For years, Aurelia scrounged for coal along train tracks to keep the family's modest home in Indianapolis heated, worked on nights and weekends for a car dealer so that she could buy her younger sister a winter coat. She prayed that when she eventually married, she could exhale. But motherhood was anything but relaxing.

The constant penny-pinching and nose wiping that came with motherhood made her feel, more often than not, trapped. And it showed. She snapped often or retreated, burying her head in newspapers and cherished books instead of paying attention to the house or her children. To a young Anne, her mother's moodiness made her feel as if she were doing something wrong, as if she weren't the daughter she was supposed to be.

The level of stress in the young Diener home only intensified as my grandmother became pregnant again—and again—and again—in rapid succession. Fourteen months after my mother came another daughter, Mary, whom my grandparents would call Mimi. The delivery was so fast that the doctor dropped my poor aunt as she exited the womb. My grandmother winced as she heard the baby's head hit the table. Thankfully, she survived. Soon after Mimi came Patty, a curly-haired dirty-blonde who, almost from the day she was born, clashed with my mother for her parents' affection. Then came Kathy, a dark-haired beauty with a sweet smile and doe eyes. Finally, after four girls, my grandfather got the boy he'd always dreamed of: Albert Joseph Junior, a.k.a. Al Joe, a strapping boy who commanded his family's attention.

Dealing with five babies in six and a half years prompted Aurelia to turn into something of a robot. She approached childcare in an increasingly pragmatic fashion, seeming less interested in doling out hugs and praise than in managing chaos. Meals were served systematically at five o'clock. All the children—including my mother, the oldest—were in bed by six o'clock. In this way, Aurelia carved out time for what she really desired: being alone with Al. There was now no time for writing, for completing those novels she'd dreamed of penning as a teenager. And there was less and less time for reading. But Al? She would always make time for her beloved husband. By all accounts, he was what she lived for.

The house they dwelled in on Broad Street had two stories, but it was small. All the children were forced to share one room, the girls sleeping two to a bed.

To combat fuel costs, heat was limited to the downstairs. Consequently, during the winter months, the children slept in two or three layers of clothing and two pairs of socks at a time to ward off pneumonia.

"Oftentimes," my mother told me, "the house was so cold I could see my breath when I got dressed. And the sweaters on the drying racks became solid as blocks of wood."

Other times, she said, her mother's bottles of cheap perfume turned into fragrant ice cubes.

Aurelia displayed intermittent bursts of warmth during the difficult times. She treated the children to popcorn and Coke on holiday nights when finances allowed. She was a capable nurse when her brood came down with bouts of chicken pox and mumps and measles and whooping cough.

But for the most part, she ruled the house with something of an iron fist. For Aurelia, the implementation and enforcement of rules was a means of controlling the chaos engulfing—and sometimes drowning—her. That quest for rules reared its head when she decided it was time for a young Anne to be separated from her beloved childhood blanket, Pooh. For years, the blanket, tattered and torn, was my mother's one true constant through the changes of more siblings. She slept with it clenched in her chubby little fists at night, played with it alongside her dolls by day, even attempted to bathe with it.

"I loved my Pooh," my mother would later tell me. "It was more than a blanket, it was a friend."

But for Aurelia, Pooh was a problem. Anne was the oldest, and enough was enough. It wasn't proper for Anne to keep a blanket. That's what conventional wisdom told her, and that's what she'd adhere to.

One morning when my mother was out playing, Pooh disappeared.

"Where's my Pooh?" my mother asked innocently upon returning to her bedroom at lunchtime to seek out the comfort of the blanket.

"Pooh is gone," Aurelia responded curtly, snapping string beans in the kitchen sink, an apron tied around her waist.

"What do you mean, g-g-g-gone?" asked my mother, her eyes widening, her voice rising. She had begun to stutter when she spoke, and moments like these, when she was especially nervous, made her stuttering more pronounced.

"Gone," Aurelia replied firmly, placing a roast beef sandwich in front of her daughter. "I've told you before. You're a big girl now. Big girls don't need security blankets."

"But it wasn't a s-s-s-s-security blanket," cried my mother, confused. Her stomach churned. The tears started. She didn't even know what a security blanket was supposed to be. All she knew was that she loved her Pooh. She needed her Pooh. "It was m-m-m-m-m-mine."

She couldn't breathe. She tried to eat the sandwich in front of her, afraid to make her mother any angrier. But each bite made her feel sicker and sicker.

For hours, then days, she cried for her Pooh.

"You'll get used to life without Pooh," her father told her matter-of-factly that weekend before diving into the enormous to-do list of household chores Aurelia had compiled for him.

But Anne never got used to life without Pooh. For years, she kept one eye open for the tattered blanket, hoping against hope that it would turn up beneath a sofa cushion or at the back of a kitchen cabinet. It never did. And my mother's relationship with her mother was irrevocably altered.

The bedwetting episodes started soon after Pooh disappeared. Though she'd long been potty trained, Anne regressed, wetting her bed on a nightly basis. She tried to hide the soiled sheets from her mother but failed more often than not.

"You naughty girl!" Aurelia would cry, pressing her nose to the sheets before angrily stripping the bed. "You're the oldest! We don't have time for these things!"

The overarching result of all the chaos of the household was that Anne was shipped to her grandparents to stay for long stretches of time. Each time a new baby arrived, each time a crisis gripped the household, she was sent away for days, sometimes weeks, as her mother worked to get the new dose of chaos at home under control.

My mother loved both sets of grandparents, but it was her paternal grandparents—her Trudy and Dad Diener—to whom she became especially close and with whom she spent the greatest amount of time. The love Trudy had for her eldest son, Al, was passed on to my mother in great supply. Trudy took my mother to fine lunches in Indianapolis's LS Ayres tearoom, taught her how to set a table and place a napkin on her lap, how to properly eat her soup, tipping the bowl just so, moving the spoon away from her as she scooped. She purchased for my mother school supplies—colorful pencils and fancy notebooks—and pretty dresses that Al and Aurelia Diener could not afford. Most significantly, Trudy gave my mother a place to call her own in their North Indianapolis home.

At Trudy and Dad Diener's house, my mother developed, among other things, her love for the radio. August Diener, whose glaucoma and cataracts had eaten away his vision bit by bit, spent hours seated in front of the radio. And he passed that passion for the spoken word on to my curious mother. It was with August that my mother listened breathlessly to the speeches delivered by Franklin Delano Roosevelt as he worked to put the nation back on the road to recovery with his New Deal plans. Together, they listened enthralled to the cracks of the bats and the cheers of the crowds at his beloved Cincinnati Reds games. And as a family unit, they gathered to hear *Amos 'n' Andy* and *The Lone Ranger*.

"Your generation has television," my mother would tell me as I rolled my teenaged eyes. "Mine had the real deal: radio."

Radio, my mother said, soothed her to sleep during countless nights and offered hours of comfort as she suffered through childhood fevers and the mumps. The dramatic chords of the organ used to narrate *The Guiding Light*, the melodic strains of Glen Miller, and the jokes shared between Edgar Bergen and his dummy, Charlie McCarthy, between George Burns and Gracie Allen, all served to calm my mother and make her feel as if everything, even on the scariest of nights, was going to be all right. She was afraid of the typical things of youth, monsters beneath beds chief among them. And she was afraid of the issues gripping the adults of the nation, including a polio outbreak that was forcing public pools to close and children her age to live out their days in iron lungs. But the sounds of the radio took her mind off of her worries, if only for a few minutes. In radio, Anne Diener happily escaped.

"You haven't really learned how to imagine," she would later tell me, "how to really see a story come to life in your mind, until you've spent an afternoon just listening—really listening—to words."

While August Diener instilled in my mother a love of radio and the spoken word, Trudy Diener instilled in her a love of the arts. Decked out in a mink stole she'd been given long before the Depression struck and a pair of gloves that buttoned at the wrist, Trudy squired a young Anne to musicals in Indianapolis's finest theaters, ice shows featuring the figure-skating sensation Sonja Henie, and orchestral concerts at symphony halls. Over the course of months, then years, Trudy painstakingly introduced her young charge to Bach, Brahms, Beethoven.

"I'll never forget the first time I heard the Emperor Concerto," my mother used to sigh. "I felt as if I'd discovered something so special, so exquisite, I wanted to share it with everyone and with no one all at the same time."

And at night, Trudy introduced a young Anne to more music: lullabies. While Aurelia and Al were more often than not too busy to sing to their children at bedtime, Trudy was not. Sitting beside Anne in a darkened room after her eldest grandchild had completed a day of tree-climbing and radio-playing, Trudy sang song upon song: "Rock-a-bye Baby," "When the Fairies Sing," and my mother's favorite, an old Native American tune. Trudy belted out the plaintive melody to my mother as she tucked her into bed. My mother lay, both mesmerized and torn, not sure which she wanted more: to stay awake to enjoy her grandmother's performance or to retreat to a world of sleep.

"Trudy made me feel safe. Her voice, her song, they made me feel as if I mattered," my mother told me one night from the post of the rocking chair in my bedroom before breaking into her own version of the lullaby.

But almost as important as music to Trudy and my mother were movies. Every Saturday, Trudy accompanied my mother to the cinema. Oftentimes, they attended a double feature. They were nondiscriminatory and ran to whatever was playing, loving virtually all genres: romantic dramas, whodunits, adventure capers. The darkened theaters introduced my mother to worlds she increasingly longed to be a part of: far-off lands, mysterious castles, happy homes. She may not have seen as much as she would have liked of her parents in those early years, but she saw plenty of Shirley Temple and Cary Grant and Joseph Cotton and Fred Astaire. They became her heroes, her surrogate friends. For a few hours she forgot about her cold house and quarreling siblings.

If my mother loved one thing more than movies during her childhood, it was books. Her most treasured possessions in her early years were her hardbound editions of beloved classics: *Little Women*, *The Wizard of Oz*, *Tom Sawyer*, *Robinson Crusoe*. She additionally adored the Hardy Boys, Nancy Drew, and Bobbsey Twins series. Most of the books were gifts from Aurelia. Money strapped though the Diener family was, my mother often said her literary-minded mother would have let her starve physically before she allowed her to starve intellectually. Every Christmas, a brand-new beautiful book was among her presents. Other books in my mother's little library were given to her by Trudy and Dad Diener and her aunt Peg. All were kept in places of honor beside and beneath her bed.

"In books," my mother always liked to remind me, "anything— and I mean anything!—is possible: adventure, peace, stability. And love. Definitely love."

"When I read *Little Women* for the first time, I wanted with all of my heart to be Jo," she said to me years later, reflecting upon the classic tale's spunky heroine, one of four girls. "What I wouldn't have given to have had the love of Laurie. Then the professor. And Marmie."

"Marmie?" I'd asked, confused. Laurie, I knew, was the wealthy boy who lived next door to Jo and shared her sense of adventure and mischief. The professor was the man she'd fallen in love with in New York City over mutual passions for literature and theater. But Marmie?

"Marmie wasn't one of Jo's boyfriends," I said, gently correcting her. "She was Jo's mother."

"That's right," said my mother. At that point, a cloud passed over her face.

"Mother or not, Marmie was one of Jo's true loves. Every bit as important to her, if not more so, than men. Such a tremendous mother, don't you think? Loving her girls, taking care of each of them, encouraging Jo to write the way she did?"

I realized then that from the time she was old enough to read, Anne Diener had craved the affection and approval of a mother she couldn't seem to reach every bit as much as she did the unconditional love of a dashing suitor. Trouble was, she didn't have a clue as to how to go about obtaining either.

Chapter 2

First Communion at St. Mary's

Today was the day. Today was the day! Anne stood in front of the mirror in the house on Broad Street, admiring herself. The dress was all that she dreamed it would be. It was white. It was lacy. And best of all, it was new. She loved everything about it: the short puffed sleeves that reminded her of something Ginger Rogers might wear; the row of buttons down the back that her mother had to take the time to fasten, one at a time; the crinoline that made the skirt poof just so. But the best part? The veil. The lace-and-tulle confection that attached to her shoulder-length curls made her look and feel like the little princess bride she was. This was better than any dress she'd ever worn. In fact, this was probably as nice as or nicer than anything in Princess Elizabeth's closet.

Anne twirled on one foot to see if the dress poofed out even more when she spun. It did! She sighed happily. How lucky she was to be making her First Communion. She was one of only a few Catholic girls in the whole school. Everyone else was Baptist or Lutheran or Mormon or something her parents called Holy Rollers, and she was starting to get a lot of questions from her classmates about why her family went to St. Mary's. One of the boys even told her that the KKK chapter based in Jay County hated Catholics almost as much as they hated the Negroes. She'd asked her parents what that was supposed to mean. But they told her never to listen if anyone talked about the KKK again since everyone knew that Catholics and Negroes were good people.

Today all of that didn't matter. All that mattered was that she was making her First Communion. She'd been preparing for weeks, meeting with Father after Mass, memorizing the Hail Mary and the Our Father. Mimi had come along for the lessons since she was making her First Communion, too. Father said that as long as Anne was making her First Communion, they might as well do it for Mimi, too, especially since Mimi was just a year younger.

At first, Anne hadn't liked the idea of sharing her big day with her younger sister. It didn't seem fair. She'd had to wait a whole year longer than Mimi to receive the big sacrament, to don the dress. But in time she realized it might be nice to have someone up at that altar with her, just in case she got scared. And the whole point wasn't that there would be two of them—the point was the dress she got to wear. That new white dress. New! So many of her clothes these days were hand-me-downs. Friends and neighbors with older girls increasingly gave her mother their used clothes. Sometimes the dresses were nice. But sometimes they had holes in them. Or they had the kind of wrinkles that never seemed to come out, no matter how much her mother ironed them. Everyone knew that money was tight for the Diener kids. That's what Anne's parents said every time someone slipped them extra ration stamps after Mass or when they were at the grocery store.

But never mind the ration stamps or old dresses. Today she had only one thought: standing up there to accept Holy Communion, the body of Christ in wafer form, for the first time in front of everyone. In front of everyone—including Daddy. Her father was going to be so proud of her. His eyes would be glued to her. Mimi would be up there, too. And Patty and Kathy would be making their First Communions in a couple of years. But she was going to make her First Communion first and best. Today was her day. Hers and Daddy's. She was going to the best little Catholic girl in the whole wide world, and make Al Diener the proudest daddy in all of Indiana.

World War II was a frightening time for any child, especially for one as sensitive as my mother. As the boys in her town went off to fight the Nazis and the Japanese, the small Indiana community—and the entire Diener family—hunkered down around the radio, listening for updates, praying for peace. For Anne, who already lived in fear of contracting polio and living out her days in an iron lung, the war was one more real-world scenario that kept her awake at night. The bedwetting continued even as she approached the third grade. Exacerbating her struggles: the pressure to keep her fears hidden from her siblings, and especially from her mother. She was the oldest, and she was supposed to be the strongest. If there wasn't enough food to go around, she was supposed to go hungry. If the air-raid sirens sounded, she was expected to stand stoically when younger siblings covered their ears and cried. Trouble was, she wanted to cry out, too, just as loud as, if not louder than, the babies.

During the school day, Anne, like many of her friends, tried to brush off the war as something of an adventure. At recess and on weekends, the youngsters often played a game in which some of the children pretended to be Americans, some Germans, and some Japanese—hiding, seeking, chasing.

"We called the game 'War,'" my mother told me matter-of-factly, years later. "It's all any of us wanted to play."

But at night, when the games were over, Anne huddled in a fetal position in her bed, wishing she had her long-missing Pooh blanket and worrying about all of it. About the Japanese launching another Pearl Harbor–like surprise attack on U.S. soil. About Hitler and his team dropping a horrible bomb on Indianapolis, similar to the deluge of bombs he'd dropped on London that had killed dozens, even hundreds, at a time. About her beloved father being sent off to fight.

As a father of five, Al Diener was never considered a candidate for the draft, much to the chagrin of the patriot within him. In the eyes of Uncle Sam, he was already doing his part leading a glass factory and raising so many children. Still, Al worried about the toll a long war would take on his young family. The rationing of the war, which limited his family to only a fixed amount of food—some bread, some meat, some milk, but not much else—made him nervous. Yes, the town of Dunkirk was generous. Many parishioners at St. Mary's gave Aurelia extra ration stamps so that she could buy sugar for the children and gas for the car. But if this war continued, Al Diener feared that his children would starve. Literally. No—the only answer for him was to take matters into his own hands and plant his own crops.

Al had raised tomatoes and cucumbers and peas in the yard at Broad Street. But he needed space for a big garden: land to grow not just a little victory garden, but to start a victory farm to sustain his family, if need be, for years. He found his opportunity in a large plot of land a half mile up the road from the house on Broad Street. Inspecting the acres of trees and open space, Al decided he would take the little money he and Aurelia had managed to cobble together and buy his family a future. They would call it the Pine Patch.

But while Al scraped together the funds for the land, there was little left over for a house. The house, Al decided, was something he would have to build himself, using his engineering skills and the manual labor of friends and family, including that of his own small children.

"He had no real background in architecture," my mother would later tell me of the cobbled-together blueprints for the house. "But with Daddy, if there was a will, there was a way."

If my grandfather was the chief engineer and architect of the new house, my mother and my aunt Mimi were his lieutenants. In the morning before school, while their classmates slept in or ate breakfast, Al Diener's two oldest girls donned jeans and accompanied him to build their future family home. They wielded wheelbarrows, helped to lay cement, assisted their father in the fine art of plastering.

For my mother, the physical tasks that left her hands blistered, her fingernails broken, her hair streaked with cement in the early-morning hours were nothing to complain about. Quite the contrary. She was in heaven.

Away from her mother, who was home tending to the younger children, she had found a way, besides going to Mass at St. Mary's, to connect with her beloved daddy. Sure, it was messy. And her father was a sometimes impatient taskmaster who demanded that his instructions be followed explicitly. But my mother wouldn't have traded that time with her father for anything in the world.

"It was such a special time," she said. "Out there in nature. With just Daddy.

"Sometimes he yelled. We never seemed to do things quite right. And it was always either too hot or too cold. But it didn't matter. It was Daddy time."

Slowly, the house took shape. And by the time my mother was ready to enter high school, it was ready for move-in. At first, the dwelling was extraordinarily small, consisting of just a front room, a living room, a kitchen, a bathroom, a laundry room, and one very large bedroom for all. Additional rooms would come in later years. But in those early years, the six rooms would suffice. And so would the land. The sizable plot featured an apple and pear orchard, a gargantuan vegetable garden, and a pond to swim in during the summer and to ice-skate upon in the winter.

My mother became a capable young skater during those early years at the Pine Patch. For hours after school and on weekends, she perfected her figure eights and spirals. Her favorite time to skate wasn't in the light of day, but instead after the sun had set on the shortest days of winter, beneath a full moon.

"It was the best feeling," she would later tell me. "I was free. Skating out there I could think and dream. It was magical."

Soon after my mother's home address changed, so too did her family unit. Just shy of her fifteenth birthday, Mimi decided to enter the convent. She was inspired by a book entitled *You're Called to Be a Nun* that my grandmother had left out on the living room coffee table.

"I think my parents put the book out on display as a hint to all of us girls," my aunt Mimi would later recall. "And I was the only one to take the bait."

During a summer of babysitting for her aunt Peg's children in Indianapolis, Mimi, reading the book and its message, wrote a letter to her parents, informing them that she was thinking about becoming a nun. When she returned home, without ever bothering to discuss the idea with her, my grandparents packed her things and drove her to the St. Joseph Academy and Convent in Tipton, Indiana. They bade goodbye not only to their second-eldest daughter, but also to her name. Within the walls of the convent, she relinquished "Mimi"—her entire Diener identity—and became Sister Mary Gertrude.

In later years, it was revealed that both Aurelia's and Al's parents were outraged by the sudden decision, arguing that it was premature and that young Mimi should at least have been encouraged to graduate from high school in Dunkirk alongside her peers and siblings before entering any convent. But Aurelia, perhaps actively working to reduce the number of mouths to feed, was undeterred. If her fourteen-year-old daughter thought she heard a calling, there was no need for discussion. Off to the convent she would go.

My aunt Mimi remembers her departure as a virtual nonevent in the Diener household. "There was never really a discussion. There were never any questions." Perhaps most surprising, and most troubling of all, she said, there were never really any tears.

Was she homesick? I would later ask. "Yes, of course," she said. "There were times when I was extremely homesick. But as far as your grandparents were concerned, the decision had been made. Now I belonged not to them, but to the sisters and the church."

My mother had a different take on the decision. "It was child abuse," she told me when I was in college. "They didn't know it was child abuse. But it was."

Mimi's calling was a source of intrigue and confusion for my teenaged mother. Anne had always fancied herself the good Catholic. She was the oldest. She had been the first of the Diener children to memorize the prayers of the rosary, the first of the siblings to be confirmed. If God wanted a Diener girl in his fold, shouldn't he have tapped her first? Was she doing something wrong, she wondered, to have not yet heard the calling? Why had Mimi been the one to take and read that book? Was something wrong with Anne that she preferred *Wuthering Heights* and Nancy Drew to *You're Called to Be a Nun*?

"I wanted to impress Daddy," my mother said, shaking her head once at the memory. "So I just prayed harder to be better. I tried so hard."

For my mother, Mimi's departure left a significant hole. It marked the first time in nearly a decade that the family had only six members. That meant there was one fewer sibling with whom to quarrel and with whom to vie for her parents' attention, which remained in short supply. But in spite of Mimi's absence, the headache of sibling rivalry was far from over. Indeed, in the wake of Mimi's departure, the war continued, and intensified, particularly between my mother and her greatest rival at the time, her sister Patty.

With Mimi out of the way, Patricia "Patty" Diener became sandwiched—some might say smothered—between my mother and their youngest sister, Kathy. As the eldest, my mother was Trudy and Dad Diener's unmistakable favorite grandchild. And as a straight-A student, she was also a class leader. That meant, for Patty, my mother cast a mighty shadow in both the school and the town. Kathy, meanwhile, was both the baby girl and the designated sweetheart of the family.

Kathy earned the sweetheart title through a now-famous story within the Diener family. When my mother and her siblings were deemed naughty, Aurelia often resorted to sending them to the kitchen pantry and locking them in the closet area usually reserved for baking supplies. All the children railed against the draconian punishment—except Kathy, who went willingly to the kitchen closet with a sweet smile upon her face. My grandmother was initially surprised at this reaction. But eventually, her surprise turned to suspicion. Her hunch that something was amiss was spot-on. It turned out Aunt Kathy was keeping a little silver spoon in the large bag of sugar stored in the pantry and was only too happy to be punished so that she could indulge in spoonfuls of sugar for uninterrupted swaths of time. Her philosophy: something good could always come out of something bad.

For Patty, the unenviable position that placed her squarely between an older award-winning sister and a younger beatific sister was often too much. My mother later admitted it was a no-win situation.

"Patty was stuck in the middle," my mother said.

Patty was bright and earned good grades. But Anne's academic achievements—her straight A's and involvement in a plethora of extracurricular activities—had set the bar extremely high. "Even if I won an award or went out for a club, it was often something Anne had already won or done," Patty told me recently. "And with our grandparents, especially our father's parents, it was clear during our childhood that she was the favorite and could do no wrong."

The strain of trying to find a place of distinction in the family took its toll. Arguments increasingly broke out not only between

Anne and Patty, but also between strong-willed Aurelia and equally strong-willed Patty. A young Al Joe witnessed the friction.

"Patty was the first of the Diener kids to question why things were done in the home the way they were done," my uncle Al would later tell me. "But she certainly wasn't the last."

There were plenty of rules to rail against. The bedtime routine my grandmother had put into place for her children had made sense when they were still in diapers. But as my mother and her siblings reached adolescence, the six P.M. bedtime began to feel exceptionally unfair for healthy, growing children who had friends and ample energy.

"We would go to bed and it would still be light out," my mother told me sadly in later years. "Not just a little bit light. In the summer months, when the sun didn't set until nine o'clock, it was very light. The worst sound in the world when you're small and healthy and well behaved is hearing all of your friends laugh and play outside while you're being told to go to sleep. The sound of their laughter carried into the room. It was like salt in the wound."

The enforcement of rules coincided with my grandmother's diminishing looks. The once relatively trim figure my grandmother had sported when she'd met my grandfather had grown thicker. Her hair became even more of an afterthought. The biggest telltale sign of her discontent: her eyes. Most of the photos my mother has from the 1940s and 1950s are of her and her siblings sporting cherubic smiles. But in photos where my grandmother's image can be found, her eyes appear increasingly tired and preoccupied, sometimes listless, as if she's willing herself to get through both the picture taking and the day.

A multitude of miscarriages was almost certainly part of the problem. While doctors told Aurelia to stop having children after she birthed Patty, she continued to get pregnant.

"Catholic or not, I would have gone on the pill if it had been available to me," my grandmother told me years later, as she not so subtly encouraged me to embrace the birth control pill when I came of age. "But since it wasn't, I didn't. And sometimes you reach a point when you just can't stop."

Translation: in the words of my mother, the sex between Aurelia and Al "must have been pretty amazing."

But the unprotected sex came with a price. Beginning in 1942, shortly after my uncle Al's birth, my grandmother suffered miscarriage after miscarriage. Often the miscarriages were fast and kept from the children. But other times, Aurelia was unable to hide the losses. By 1951, she'd suffered at least five miscarriages.

"I helped Mother with one of them," my mother told me once. "She screamed for me to bring her towels. I remember there was blood. So much blood. I thought she was going to die."

Aurelia didn't die physically. Instead, she faded away emotionally, becoming less and less available to her children. Increasingly, she sought to escape through words, just as she had as a child. And while the children left her with no time to write, there was time to read. She buried herself between meals in Agatha Christie novels and periodicals of the day like *Time, Life,* and the *Saturday Evening Post*. The *Indianapolis Star*, the leading paper of Indianapolis, was for her a veritable bible. My grandmother read the newspaper from front to back, keeping tabs on global and domestic stories of the day. But interested though she was in news, without doubt her favorite section was the *Star*'s society page. She pored over the page, her children would later tell me, as if cramming for a test, committing to memory the names of the movers and shakers of Indianapolis's social circle. In subsequent months and years, the names served as secret weapons my grandmother kept at the ready, sprinkling them into conversations with friends and neighbors at cocktail parties and church socials and Al's business gatherings in a bid to suggest that those well-heeled couples were Al and Aurelia's old friends. Seldom did listeners question her actual connections to Indianapolis's elite or doubt that she really exchanged phone calls and holi-day cards with them. Family members say Aurelia was so keen to convince neighbors that she actually rubbed elbows with the upper crust of the Midwest that she took to memorizing portions of the phone book so that she could tick off various socialites' numbers and addresses as she spoke of them in conversation. If the well-to-do world that Aurelia Arvin had dreamed about since she was a teenager wouldn't come to her, she would create it for herself, one tale at a time.

"Aurelia Diener was happiest when she lived in a fantasy world," my uncle Al told me. "It wasn't who she knew that mattered. For her, it was all about who she claimed she knew."

According to him, if she'd been half as committed to the notion of motherhood as she was to convincing onlookers that she really was Somebody, she would have been Mother of the Year.

But while my grandmother disliked many of the trappings of domestic life, she continued to adore my grandfather. She rose early to see him off to the factory, then in the afternoon, she smoothed her hair, changed her dress, applied a splash of per-fume just before he arrived home from work. She laid out his pipe, smoothed out the wrinkles of the newspaper she'd already devoured, turned on the radio, and waited.

Once, when Al Diener was particularly perplexed that a pear tree he had planted in the front yard refused to yield any fruit, Aurelia surprised him by taking pieces of string and hang-ing a collection of fruit from the fruit bowl on the branches of the tree. As my grandfather approached the front door after a day's work, the tree greeted him, teeming with bananas, apples, peaches, and plums she had saved to buy at the grocery store. My grandmother stood waiting inside the door, smiling and laugh-ing as she saw his frown turn into a grin. A hearty laugh sprang from his belly, a giggle from hers. A moment later, she was in his arms.

"It was magical to see him laugh like that and her laugh in return," my mother would tell me years later, after both of her parents had died. "We kids watched her surprise him from upstairs. She worked all afternoon on that tree. And it paid off. It's like they were teenagers."

But it was my mother—not my grandmother—who was approaching teenhood.

On the surface of things, Anne Diener was the typical schoolgirl of the 1940s and 1950s. She wore sweater sets and Peter Pan–collared blouses and loafers to school. She donned blue jeans that cuffed at the ankles when she performed chores around the Pine Patch. Now, in addition to the radio, she enjoyed records, especially show tunes, which her beloved aunt Peg bought for her. Al's only sister, who had since married a dashing soldier-turned-insurance-executive named Fritz, continued to dote on my mother and view her as her special project. She took her shopping for things my grandparents couldn't afford, including cashmere sweaters and her first poodle skirts.

My mother appreciated Peg's attention. But even with her beautiful aunt, she felt as if she never quite measured up. Peg, with her to-die-for cheekbones, her trim waist, her ability to capably apply makeup, looked as if she'd walked straight out of the pages of *Vogue*. My mother, by comparison, felt forever gangly and awkward. Her curls were unruly. She had no clue how to apply makeup. And she was developing acne on her forehead and chin. Making matters worse: her mouth. Dentists said it was too small and was contributing to the crooked teeth that jutted up and out. They tried time and again to correct them with the help of braces, with little effect.

It was Anne's teachers who became her cheerleaders, patiently taking her under their wings and encouraging her to push herself ever harder and to reach ever higher. With the exception of math and physical education, her grades were stellar. And her ability to write was unparalleled. She penned her first musical at the age of fifteen.

The score to the girl-dreams-of-boy-then-winds-up-with-boy romantic comedy was lost in later years, but my mother never forgot the lyrics. She sang them to me once when I was in the sixth grade, in the process of writing and directing the first of my own plays for a class project.

"Who can think of dishes when you're dreaming about kisses?" she sang.

A beloved English teacher, Mr. Wilcox, encouraged my mother to send the script to New York for consideration. But she never did.

"Why not?" I asked her when she revealed this nugget of information. "Why not send it to New York if your teacher thought it was good enough?"

"Because my parents never told me it was good enough," she said with a shrug. "If your parents don't believe in you, it's hard to believe in yourself."

One silver lining that my mother clung to throughout even the darkest of times was Pete, her first dog. She'd been presented with the springer spaniel shortly after moving to the Pine Patch. Within days, the dog was my mother's whole life, her source of endless pride and joy.

"He filled a hole in my heart I never knew was empty," my mother explained.

All the Diener children wanted to think of Pete as theirs, and according to the family friend who had given the Dieners the dog, he was supposed to belong to the entire family. But even my mother's siblings admit Pete was always Anne's dog. Wagging his tail, panting softly, he kept her company as she did her homework. He lifted her spirits when she quarreled with her siblings or vied for the attention of her parents. And each night, he slept in her bed, watching for her to fall asleep before he fell into a deep slumber of his own.

Pete, a hunting dog by nature, was happiest when he went with my mother to explore the grounds of the Pine Patch. One night, he surprised her during a stroll by retrieving three baby bunny rabbits. He carried all of them carefully in his mouth, depositing them at my mother's feet. My mother and aunts raised the bunnies to adulthood before releasing them into the wild.

"Pete was just the best dog," my mother would later tell me. "He loved me like I'd never been loved."

Anne included Pete in her nightly prayers to God. At last he had given her something to love that loved her just as much in return.

But as much as Anne loved Pete, Aurelia disliked him. The dog was work, she lamented. More work than she wanted or felt she needed to take on. He was literally and figuratively one more mouth to feed. He smelled. He made messes. And he was loud, frequently barking. At birds. At squirrels. Even at the priest when he came to Sunday dinner.

The night that Pete took a bite out of young Kathy was the final straw.

"That dog is an inbreed and more trouble than he's worth!" Aurelia shouted at Al.

In the heat of the moment, with Kathy still bleeding and frightened, Aurelia Arvin Diener begged my grandfather: Do something about the dog.

A resigned Al agreed.

"He started to dig a hole," my uncle Al later explained. "I asked him what he was doing and he said that Pete was sick."

My uncle watched in horror as my grandfather called for Pete to get into the hole. That's when he pulled out the revolver and shot him, execution-style.

My mother was inconsolable.

"You k-k-k-k-killed Pete," she sobbed, her stutter returning, the way it always did when she was under duress.

She never managed to recover from the loss of Pete. In a way, she ached for him for the rest of her life, stopping decades later to pet English springer spaniels she spied on the street, always remarking upon what a special breed they were.

As much as Pete prompted her to fall in love with dogs, it also made her swear off owning—or loving—dogs forever. For years, it was a decision I failed to understand.

"Why can't I have a dog?" I would cry, begging her birthday after birthday for a beagle like the one my friend Jenny Stancer had or a golden retriever like the one our next-door neighbors doted upon.

"We have a house. We have a yard. We have the room," I would argue. "We need a dog!"

Usually, my mother would remain quiet during my wails and whines and pleas, waiting for me to finish before changing the subject.

Only once did she respond directly to my request. As we drove through town on our way to church one Sunday morning, her knuckles whitened around the tan vinyl wheel of our old Chevette before she drew in a sharp breath.

"You know why you can't get a dog?" she asked

"No," I said, shaking my head.

"Because eventually a dog dies or gets taken away. It's one of the worst losses you'll ever know."

I thought I spied her crying that morning during Mass. In later years, that wasn't entirely unusual. But that morning, I suspect, the tears were shed for Pete.

Chapter 3

White Dress, White House

June 1953

Anne Diener took a breath and studied herself in the Pine Patch's one and only floor-length mirror. Her curls wouldn't lie flat. That she could blame on the muggy nature of June in Indiana. Still, she liked what she saw. More specifically, she liked what she wore. She wasn't sure which screen legend her gown was the embodiment of—Grace Kelly or Ingrid Bergman. But she was pretty certain either actress would have looked at home on the cover of a movie magazine in the all-white sateen dress with the cinched waist and the full ball skirt. She loved the dress. Loved the clean lines. Loved the red rose pinned to it. Most of all, she loved how the gown made her feel. Today she was a grown-up. Today she had arrived! All that was missing was a golden Oscar statue to clutch in her hands. Who cared if all the other girls in the class were going to be wearing the same gown? In the Diener house, today was her day. Her Day.

Everyone had come to Dunkirk for the occasion. Trudy and Dad Diener and Grandma and Grandpa Arvin had made the trek from Indianapolis. So had Aunt Mary Jane and Uncle Bob. Even Peg had come down from her new home up in Winnetka, Illinois, dressed to kill in a brand-new gray fitted dress, handpicked from the designer section of Chicago's Marshall Field's. All were there to see Annie—their Annie—graduate from high school.

The only noticeable absence was Mimi. Immersed in her life of duty at the convent, she was unable to break away. But in her place was a new *Diener* sibling: Michael Francis. He was just a few months old, and Anne knew her baby brother would be squirming and likely squawking on Mother's lap during the ceremony. She wouldn't have it any other way. After all of those miscarriages, all of that loss, all of those tears and sadness and emptiness and unbearable silence of the past few years, Baby Michael's squawks were music to Anne's ears. A blessing from the Lord our Father, whom Anne prayed to mightily every morning, noon, and night.

What was his will? she wondered, turning to study her backside in the mirror. What in the world did God want from her? She wished she knew. She had some ideas. But still no clear direction. No vision. No direct orders or signs of the kind that she felt certain Mimi must have had before joining those Irish nuns. She knew she loved him, as she'd always been taught to love him. But where he wanted her to go next, what he wanted her to do, she wasn't certain.

Trudy and Dad Diener thought maybe Anne's future lay in politics. How she wished they were right! It sounded so—well—so exciting. The trip to Washington last summer—meeting President Truman in the Rose Garden, shaking his hand, posing for photos with him—it had all been such a thrill. It had been front-page news in Dunkirk. The photographer did a whole photo shoot at the house with just her. Just her! She posed on command, smiling playfully with her loving cup trophy.

So yes, Anne thought, nodding in silence, maybe her beloved grandparents were right—politics just might be in her future. Politics or journalism. Anne still loved to write. She'd loved editing the school newspaper. Loved putting pen to paper to write most anything. She'd even written a special history of the class for each of her fifty-nine classmates, personalizing tales of their individual journeys through senior high.

Now the class of sixty would enter that auditorium, graduate as a unit, and go their separate ways. Some were getting married. A few were going to work for Anne's father at the Armstrong Glass Factory in town. And a select few, including Anne, were college bound. Ball State

University, in nearby Muncie, Indiana, beckoned. For Anne, it had been an easy choice: it was close—just forty minutes away by car—and it offered a wealth of liberal arts opportunities.

For the class of 1953, the future was theirs. At least that's what they liked to think. Even their class motto said so. Anne had memorized it and recited it often these past few months: "Forward forever, backward never. Within ourselves our future lies."

"Anne!" called a voice, breaking Anne's moment of vanity in front of the mirror. "Anne Virginia Diener, come right now! You'll be late for your own graduation! You know your father doesn't like to be late!"

Anne sighed. It was the unmistakable cry of her mother.

What was the future? Anne Diener wasn't certain. But smoothing her skirt, adjusting her glasses, she took a deep breath and answered.

"Coming, Mother!"

My mother took to the academic and social demands of high school like a duck to water. Indeed, her recollections of her high school years suggest that, for her, late adolescence provided some of the happiest moments of her life.

"Our school was small. Our town was small. I tended to mix with nearly all of my classmates," my mother wrote not long before she died in a journal she devoted to memories of her childhood. "We did things together."

Her grades remained stellar—nearly all A's. And, in the capacity of school newspaper and yearbook editor, and as class secretary, her popularity soared. Among her favorite activities were Friday and Saturday night basketball games. "I tried to attend all of our high school basketball games," she wrote. "This was what held our small town of Dunkirk together. I would dress in a white Peter Pan–collared blouse, with a green plaid skirt and bobby socks. I would yell and scream at the games. Mom would have hot chocolate for us when we got home."

But while she had many close friends, and though she was a

pretty young woman with a slim figure, shoulder-length hair, and soulful brown eyes, she had no high school boyfriends. No real dates. She attended the senior prom, but only as an organizer. Part of this lack of dating stemmed from religious differences: my mother was a Catholic girl in a non-Catholic community during a time in history in which religious differences mattered. And part of her lack of boyfriends stemmed from the police state in which she lived. Her bedtime on nights when she didn't have a school event remained as early as seven thirty, depending upon her mother's mood. That left her with little to no time to socialize, particularly with boys.

"It was cruel," my mother would later reflect. But it was a form of cruelty that my mother felt powerless to fight, let alone overcome.

Dating, my mother told herself, would come later. Her immediate concern was to get good grades—good enough, anyway, to enable her to escape the fate that had befallen her own mother. Anne Diener was determined not to become a young woman who had to marry in order to succeed in life. She would use her brain and talents to do something of her own making.

Anne took a monumental step in that direction the summer between her junior and senior years of high school when the local American Legion selected her to represent Dunkirk at Girls State, a weeklong summer camp that assembled Indiana high school girls deemed academic leaders in a mock government setting at Indiana University. My mother adored the experience. It was her first time away from home or family, and she loved every moment of it: living in a dorm, meeting girls from all over, staying up late. Her enthusiasm was infectious. She quickly became known for her "chatterbox" ways. She served as a lobbyist, toured the Indiana senate, and spent seven days discussing at length the nation's mounting post–World War II issues, notably budget concerns, fears of Communism, and Cold War angst.

By the end of her week at Girls State, Anne Diener was a more confident and worldly young woman. And she was something more. She was bound for Washington, D.C. She had been elected by her peers the "Model Citizen" of the week. More than five hundred of the brightest girls in Indiana had assembled for the week. And Anne Diener alone was awarded the top prize. The reward: a meeting with the president at the White House.

For the sleepy town of Dunkirk, my mother's feat was more than a newsworthy event—it was the biggest of events. A local girl from a hardworking family had put the community on the map. A day after my mother was awarded the golden citizenship cup, her face was plastered on the Dunkirk paper's front page with enthusiastic headlines: *Local Girl Wins Top Prize! Diener Bound for White House!* In one picture, she stands with the loving cup, playfully hoisting it atop the family mantelpiece at the Pine Patch. In another she proudly holds the trophy to her heart. The Muncie and Indianapolis papers additionally penned articles about her, referring to her as a future state leader.

The trip to Washington was beyond my mother's wildest dreams. For years, she had been told by her parents that vacations were things that other families took. And the few trips she had taken—to Indianapolis, to Cincinnati, to Winnetka to see Aunt Peg—typically required her to ride sandwiched with three other siblings in the back of a car that was decidedly over- or underheated, depending upon the season. Now she was riding by train in a luxe sleeper car, staffed with uniformed valets who wore starched white shirts and neat black vests. And she was doing it without any parents or siblings in tow. A female chaperone from the state chapter of Girls State served as her designated guide and joined her as she ate for the first time in a formal train dining car. Anne Diener drank fresh-squeezed orange juice and piping hot coffee. And she feasted on warm bread, served with copious amounts of creamy butter. If this was the world waiting for her outside of the Pine Patch, she couldn't wait to be a part of it.

In Washington, my mother's love affair with the outside world continued. She met Girls Nation delegates from each of the forty-eight states, young women who, much like her, were academically bright, socially conscious, and armed with boundless amounts of enthusiasm. Together in their nightgowns, they stayed up late at night in the dorm rooms of George Washington University, sharing hopes and dreams. Many came from families of privilege: households with more than one car, even vacation homes. My mother was in awe.

The highlight of the week in Washington, D.C., came the afternoon my mother met face-to-face with President Truman in the Rose Garden of the White House. Pictures show her wearing a starched hat that Trudy had bought for her, looking on in awe at the president as he spoke to the young women, comparing some of them to his own beloved daughter.

In Washington, my mother thrived and dared to dream of a future beyond Indiana. But once back home, her dreams of the future took a backseat to the familiar longing to win the attention and approval of her parents. For a busy Al and Aurelia, who had long preached the importance of humility and modesty, Anne's meeting with the president was noteworthy, but soon all but forgotten amid the chaos of a full house. Anne realized she needed more than the White House to find a means of carving out more time with, and attention from, her parents. She found that path by taking a summer job in her father's factory, Armstrong Glass.

Al Diener's place of work had always been a source of intrigue to my mother. For as long as she could remember, she'd longed to know how he filled the hours that he spent away from the family home. Anne knew from the locals who greeted him warmly at church and Elks Club gatherings that he held a position of considerable power and that he was largely loved and revered. But she'd never seen him in action. Working in the factory allowed her and her alone—not her siblings—to be close to her father during those previously off-limits business hours.

Every morning, Anne donned blue jeans and a plain white blouse and gamely trekked a mile and a half to the plant. Once there, she clocked in and took her position in the row of box makers, most of whom were women more than twice her age. Their task: to assemble the cardboard boxes that would ultimately house the glass jars and bottles made at the factory.

The work was hard, the hours long. There was no air-conditioning in the factory, and the breaks were brief. Making matters worse, the work was painful. "My fingers would bleed and bleed," she later told me, wincing as she recalled the deep paper cuts.

"Couldn't you have done a different job?" I asked. Her father did, after all, run the factory.

My mother smiled, shaking her head. "No. Daddy wanted me in that position. He wanted to make clear to everyone else who'd been working there for years that his daughter would get no special treatment. And I wanted to prove to him that I could do it."

Her favorite moments came when her father made his way through the factory floor to inspect his troops each day. "When he made his rounds, the whole factory would work harder and begin to whisper, 'Diener's coming! Diener's coming!' I was so proud. They were talking about my father."

While Al became focused upon expanding his role in the factory, Aurelia remained focused during my mother's high school years upon expanding her role, and visibility, in the larger Dunkirk community.

By the time Anne entered high school, Aurelia had founded a community research club in which the women of Dunkirk came together on weekday afternoons to discuss books and research timely topics. She'd also developed a reputation for being charitable to the poor. She was known by area hobos as the go-to woman in town, willing to provide spare bread and leftover food when they stopped by the house. Aurelia even started a Nature Club aimed at conservation, a precursor to today's environmental movement.

But the compassion Aurelia displayed toward outsiders and global causes often failed to make its way to her own children, with whom she was often short-tempered. Part of this, my mother believed, stemmed from Aurelia's ongoing cycles of pregnancies and subsequent miscarriages.

When Aurelia became pregnant for the twelfth time and made it successfully to the third trimester, there was quiet cause for celebration. It was my mother's sophomore year of high school. The pregnancy had been a difficult one for Aurelia. The doctor, conscious of her previous miscarriages, confined her to bed rest for the bulk of the pregnancy.

As her due date approached, the doctors announced that they thought it best for Aurelia to undergo a cesarean section. Together with Al, they picked a date that seemed suitable, at what doctors then thought was at or around the thirty-eight-week mark in the pregnancy.

But the doctors miscalculated. Aurelia was not at the thirty-eight-week mark when the C-section was performed. Almost as soon as they made the incision, the medical team realized they had made a grave error. The baby boy was premature, his lungs not yet fully developed. He was blue and eerily silent upon delivery. For two days, he managed to cling to life, but by the third, Kevin Walter was gone.

Aurelia's previous miscarriages had come and gone with no discussion and few tears. But this one was different. Kevin was a fully formed baby boy. He had arrived with an adorable nub of a nose, a perfectly round head, porcelain skin. My mother and her siblings had visited him in the hospital, said prayers for him. This time, the loss could not be ignored. My mother sobbed, as did her siblings. A full Catholic funeral Mass was held and a tombstone erected.

For the first time, my mother saw the frailty of her mother in full. "Mother was inconsolable," she later told me. "I heard her tell Daddy, 'I so wanted this baby!'"

Al responded by breaking down in tears alongside his wife.

A pall fell over the house. The loss was not discussed. But the grief could not be ignored.

"It was so unbearably sad," my mother would later say. For the rest of her life, she was haunted by Kevin's passing, speaking of him any time she learned of the loss of an infant among friends and neighbors. "He was so very perfect. I wonder so often what he would have been like had he had the opportunity to live."

More than a year passed before Aurelia became pregnant again. And when the happy discovery was made, she was again confined to bed rest. This time, she was even more serious about following doctor's orders. My grandfather did his part, going to Mass daily to pray for his unborn child, escorting the priest back to the house to deliver Communion to Aurelia.

My mother and her siblings tiptoed around the house, afraid that any noises or disruptions could cost their mother yet another pregnancy. And when word came that this was to be another C-section delivery, together, as a family unit, they worked with the medical team to determine the baby's birthday.

"We picked February twelfth," my mother would later tell me, "because it was Abraham Lincoln's birthday. We reasoned nothing tragic would happen on Lincoln's birthday."

As it turns out, they were right. On February 12, 1953, Michael Francis Diener was delivered by cesarean section. He entered the world with red-brown hair, a strong pair of lungs, and a ready-made place in the Diener house as an answer to a family's prayers.

The entire Diener family rejoiced. My grandfather jumped

for joy and wept before heading to church to light candles with which to give thanks to his Lord. And Aurelia breathed a huge sigh of relief. After all of those miscarriages, at last she'd managed to again deliver a healthy baby. For weeks, my grandfather forced the entire family to don surgical masks, so afraid was he that they would once again lose a baby. But beneath the masks, the family—especially my mother—sported broad grins.

For Anne, Mike's birth was a source of tremendous pride and joy.

"He was the baby all of us had dreamed of," she explained. "He wasn't just Mother and Daddy's baby. He was all of ours."

Seventeen years older than Mike, Anne was old enough to be his mother. And many times, she and her sisters tended to Mike as if he were their own child. They changed his diapers, fought over who got to hold him, warmed his bottles, bundled and swaddled him.

The good news of Mike's arrival coincided with the joyful end of my mother's senior year of high school. On the heels of Girls Nation and becoming a big sister again, she was filled with joy. She organized unescorted trips with her girlfriends to Indianapolis to see hit musicals, including *South Pacific*. Later, she helped coordinate a class trip to New York City. "It was magical," she would later tell me of her first time in the Big Apple, her eyes glistening. "We were all from little tiny Dunkirk, and all of a sudden, we were staying at the Mayflower Hotel in New York City."

Among her activities: a trip to see *The King and I* and a trek to see the then brand-new United Nations. "I couldn't get over it," she told me decades later, visiting the city when I was a college student. "World War Two was so big, so horrible. And here was this gleaming new building that looked like something from the future. White and modern and designed to prevent any more wars."

The travels did much to bolster my mother's confidence as she prepared for commencement.

"It was such a special time," she would later reflect. "It was such a neat class." She was happy for her girlfriends who were engaged to be married, encouraging of those classmates who would soon go to work full-time in her father's factory.

Filled with hope, Anne left the Pine Patch in the summer of 1953 for Ball State University. And when she arrived on campus, she hit the ground running. Rooming with three other girls in a cramped dorm room, she made friends quickly and threw herself into campus life, including its Greek system. She also remained true to her Catholic roots, attending Mass regularly and becoming actively involved in Ball State's Newman Club, an organization devoted to young Catholics.

It was in the Newman Club that she was introduced to a handsome underclassman named Bob Mings, a blond-haired, blue-eyed fellow Hoosier. Few on campus actually called him Bob. Instead, he was famously referred to by his fraternity nickname: Bongo. Like my mother, Bongo was intellectually curious and active in the Greek system. Also like my mother, he was a devoted Catholic. Soon, the two were inseparable, my mother attending a host of dances on his arm. There are scores of photos of the two of them together. In some, they're dressed in formal attire, she in a white evening gown, he in a white dinner jacket. In all the photos, my mother appears luminous: her face glows, her hair—pulled back—shines. Her smile is big and broad, her laughter leaps through the lens.

"Bongo was dreamy," my mother would often reflect over the years when talk would turn to college life. "And kind."

Among my mother's favorite tales, one that she would regale me with for decades was of the time after a college formal when she and Bongo piled into his old convertible, which he'd nicknamed The Rivet, and took a drive. My mother loved the car and even wrote Bongo an illustrated poem about it.

It gave her a sense of freedom, of importance, of magic, she would later tell me, to ride in that car with the top down alongside a dashing suitor. During her high school years, she'd been on the outside looking in when she'd seen the girls in Dunkirk squired about on dates in convertibles. Now it was her turn.

"Bongo drove that Rivet into a dark alley that night after the dance and then"—my mother paused, sighing at the memory— "he saw them: roses. On a trellis. Someone in Muncie had planted them, cared for them, clearly worked on them. Bongo got out of The Rivet and climbed—*climbed!!*—that trellis."

At this, she would stop and sigh again.

"And then he plucked by hand, rose by rose, a beautiful bouquet for me. Just for me. Thorns and all."

Bongo was soon invited by my mother to the Pine Patch. He met her brothers and sisters, took part in family dinners, spent entire weekends with the family. They seemed the perfect match, my mother's siblings tell me. Anne and Bongo were bright and witty, young and fit and attractive. And, it seemed, they brought out the best in each other.

"He made me laugh," my mother told me.

"She made me a kinder person," Bongo later told me, referring to my mother and her do-gooder ways as his own personal moral compass. "She was so good about keeping me in line. If I wasn't kind enough, patient enough, or was being sort of a jerk, she let me know I could do better. And she was right about those things. Without fail, Anne was a truly good person and knew how to encourage me to be the same."

Among those praying for an Anne-Bongo marriage was Aurelia. Life was humming along back at the Pine Patch, now more smoothly than ever. With my mother at Ball State and Mimi in the convent, there were only four children at home. And with Patty preparing to head to college, soon there would be only three. Al was doing well at Armstrong Glass. There was financial light at the end of the tunnel, especially if Anne wed. Soon, part of Al's paycheck might reach a savings account, maybe even a stock portfolio.

Anne wasn't sure what to think. She knew her feelings for Bongo were stronger than his for her. But as young woman after young woman in her sorority was "pinned" by a fraternity man— essentially engaged to be engaged—she couldn't help but wonder if her time might be coming, too. She wrote Bongo notes when they weren't together, leaving them for him on the windshield of The Rivet. The notes were eager, enthusiastic, and clearly penned by a young woman with a serious crush. They asked about his day, invited him to Patty's high school graduation, told him how her baby brother Mike—whom Bongo had met during visits home to the Pine Patch—was growing.

In the spring of 1956, Bongo dropped a bombshell on my mother: "I'm leaving Ball State," he told her. "I'm transferring to Indiana University."

Bongo had decided to study geography—and not only a little bit of geography, but geography at the PhD level. Ball State didn't have the sort of program that he needed for what he wanted to do. He'd be leaving Muncie for Bloomington in the fall, he told her.

The news was devastating on more than one level for my mother. Not only was Bongo leaving Ball State, he was also leaving behind whatever there was of a relationship with her.

The news drove my mother into the first major depression of her life. The summer after Bongo announced his plans to leave Ball State, my mother stopped eating. Her clothes began to hang on her. Her hair fell out in clumps. Circles formed beneath her eyes. She alternately slept, then cried, for hours before experiencing periods of insomnia that lasted up to two days at a time. Bongo, who would later explain he'd always viewed my mother not as a girlfriend, but instead as a "very good, dear friend" with whom he liked to go to dances, knew nothing of my mother's deeper feelings for him, nor of the depression she fell into.

"When I left, I thought I was just saying goodbye to a dear friend with whom I'd stay in touch," he later explained to me.

Back in her childhood bedroom in Dunkirk, my mother lay in bed, the blanket pulled to her chin, rereading the class motto written upon her high school yearbook: "Forward forever, backward never. Within ourselves our future lies." Facing a life without Bongo, my mother saw for herself no future and utter darkness where there had been light.

Chapter 4

Bride of Christ

Mirrors were frowned upon at Oldenburg, as they were at most convents, so Anne couldn't be sure how she looked. But from what she saw of what she wore—the white cotton wedding gown that puffed slightly at the sleeves and cinched at the waist and fell into a full skirt—she knew she looked pretty. A white lace veil was attached to the back of her nearly shoulder-length hair with a pair of hairpins the sisters had helped her with. It fell past her elbows, just the way it had for Aunt Mary Jane when she married Uncle Bob and for Grace Kelly when she married Prince Rainier.

So this is what it felt like to be a bride. A bride of Christ, that is.

It still felt surreal. Had it really been less than five years ago that she'd been at Ball State, living in a dorm, going to fraternity dances, driving in The Rivet with Bongo? How drastically her life had changed.

Back at Ball State, her biggest challenge was carrying those loads of books from the bookstore back to the dorm, studying for an exam, finding the right dress to wear to a dance with Bongo. Her Bongo. Now her challenges were many: identifying God's will, doing God's will, and, above all, obeying and pleasing the other sisters. There were so many of them to please.

In a few minutes, she'd enter the chapel, march down the aisle, take her place at the altar, become an official nun. She'd been preparing for this moment since she'd arrived at Oldenburg last year.

And she'd been thinking about it, toying with the idea, longer—even before Mimi became a nun. She'd always wanted to become one with her Lord. And now she really would be. And Daddy would be there, front and center, to watch.

He'd nearly cried when she told him that she wanted to be a sister. She thought he'd be so proud, so impressed, so in awe. But instead of pride, there seemed to be something else in his eyes when she'd sprung the news. Surprise? Hesitation? She thought he'd be ecstatic. Wasn't this what he'd always wanted?

Trudy and Dad Diener and Grandma and Grandpa Arvin had been against the idea. Anne only knew of some of the squabbles, questioning why their Annie, their bright shining star, was signing herself up for a life of solitude and childlessness at such a young age, at a time when she seemed on the verge of accomplishing so much. She'd been to meet the president! they'd argued. "Tell her she's making a rash decision that can't be undone!" they'd begged.

But Al and Aurelia were resolute. They'd been twice blessed, they told their parents. First Mimi and now Anne had been called to become official members of the church. They'd done their jobs well. In the eyes of the truly devout, they were parents to look up to. Their daughters wished to devote their lives to Christ.

Anne had prayed mightily to the Blessed Virgin prior to announcing her decision. The prayers had been long, often filled with tears. She'd had no vision, not the way she'd hoped. But at the end of the day, she'd decided it was the right thing to do. More right, certainly, than graduating from college with no boyfriend and no clear idea as to where she was headed.

No, at Oldenburg, she hoped to feel again the way she'd felt at her happiest at Ball State, before that awful summer after Bongo had left, before those strange two years at Marian College. Mother and Daddy thought she'd find herself if she transferred to Marian. It was a Catholic college. It was in Indianapolis. And at Marian, she wouldn't be surrounded by memories of Bongo. But Marian had made her lonelier,

*more confused. The only thing that didn't confuse her was her despera-
tion to please her family, to become one with God. So here she was.*

*Outside the neat brick building that served as the Novice House,
the dorm in which the nuns-in-training lived, the sun shone brightly,
and Anne heard birds singing in the enormous sycamore trees. It was a
beautiful day in Indiana. Her family must be here by now, gathering
in the chapel: Mother and Daddy and little Mike. And Aunt Mary
Jane and Uncle Bob and her cousin Bobby and all the grandparents. It
was the first time they'd all been together since her college graduation.
They'd come to watch her get married to Christ. Afterward, they'd all
pose for photos and celebrate with cake and punch.*

*Surely the gorgeous weather was some kind of sign for her and her
fellow nuns-in-training—her eight classmates—who were also to
become brides of Christ today. Surely it meant God in his heaven was
smiling at her decision.*

*All brides, Anne remembered reading, had moments of doubt on
their wedding days. If that was true, she thought, adjusting her lace
veil once more and letting out a long sigh, today she was a very normal
bride.*

I did not discover my mother had been a nun until I was nine
years old. And even then, it was an accidental discovery. It was
a cold gray Sunday in November, and my best friend, Kim Swanberg, and I, unable to go outside to play, declared for all the world
to hear that we were bored. So bored that we decided to spend
the afternoon going through a paper bag filled with old photos
we'd found in the back of the guest room closet in my house. Sitting cross-legged atop the bed, we examined the pictures closely.
There were several of my mother with her brothers and sisters in
their early years in Indiana. There was a picture of my teenaged
mother standing in the Rose Garden of the White House, posing
beside President Truman. And then, sandwiched between some
old photos of my parents on their wedding day and of me the day

I was baptized, we found *them:* a curious collection of old black-and-white photos of my grandparents standing on either side of a young woman in a nun's habit.

"What's that?" Kim, who was raised Lutheran, asked, bending to look more closely at the nun swimming in the enormous black-and-white garment.

I tried to explain to her what a habit was, but that's not what she meant.

"No—*who's* that?" she demanded.

I remember staring at the photo. The face that stared back at me was strangely familiar, but I couldn't place her.

Kim studied the photo and posited a theory. "I think it's your mother."

My mother—the nun? It couldn't be.

Or could it?

I took the photo to my mother, who was down in the kitchen that Sunday night, preparing dinner for my brother and me. She was visibly shaken, I realize now, as she stopped stirring the boiling pot of macaroni and turned her attention from the stove to the picture I clutched in my hand. Pale and flustered, she looked as if she'd seen a ghost. I guess, in a way, she had. She stared at the photo. After a beat that lasted close to a minute, she spoke.

"Yes," she said sadly, awkwardly. "That nun in the picture was me."

Entering a convent is by no means a small transaction. From the moment Anne Diener passed through the doors of Oldenburg in August 1957—a full year before she would don that wedding dress and say her vows—her life was turned upside down. For much of the nation, the 1950s were a time of great consumption: shiny new cars, state-of-the-art appliances, sleek clothing. But for Anne Diener, the era was all about the shunning of material things.

The vow of poverty my mother took as a nun meant that she

was no longer entitled to anything of consequence: no clothing, no makeup, no personal clothing or record albums. Within weeks of her making the decision to become a nun, the few things she had cherished as a child—her books, her journals, her clothing, her records, her beloved movie magazines, even yummy taffeta dresses she had worn to the sorority balls—were given away by her parents at the instruction of the sisters. Her identity went with the possessions. Upon entering the convent at Oldenburg, she was no longer Anne Diener. As was the case with her sister Mimi, she was given a new name: Sister Aurelia Mary. Now she bore the name of the mother she'd tried so desperately for all of these years to know. The name had been the convent's choice, not hers. And my mother's vow of obedience meant she had no choice other than to accept it.

My mother's decision to enter the convent perplexed virtually all who knew her. Her grandparents cried. Her aunt Mary Jane openly questioned her about her choice. Even Bongo was stunned by the announcement.

"She wrote me a letter one day and said, 'I have news,'" he recalled of the letter she sent him after his transfer to Indiana University. "She said she was going to enter the convent. In all the time that I'd known her, there'd been no signs she was leaning in that direction. It was very out of the blue."

Her sister Mimi, who by this time had been in the convent for eight years, was similarly shocked.

"Did you see it coming?" I asked.

"Hardly." My aunt laughed. "She called one day and asked me if I thought it was 'all right' in the convent. And when I told her it was fine, she told me she had decided to enter the convent, too. I was so stunned I didn't know what to say."

Anne reached the decision during her time at Marian, the Catholic, mostly women's college she'd transferred to after Bongo left Ball State. The transfer to Marian had been Al and Aurelia's idea. After my mother's summer of insomnia and weight loss and fits of sobbing in 1955, they reasoned she needed a change of scenery.

But Marian didn't eliminate Anne's depression. If anything, the new environment—more rigid, less lively than Ball State—exacerbated the situation. While there are hundreds of photos to be found of my mother's days at Ball State, as well as scores of souvenirs, ranging from pennants and yearbooks to corsages pressed into books between layers of wax paper, there are virtually no artifacts that remain linking her to Marian. Certainly no happy ones. The pictures that do exist show her with a furrowed brow, shorter hair, and an increasingly gaunt, almost skeletal, figure.

Marian in the 1950s was primarily for serious young Catholic women, a few of whom decided to enter the convent each year. My mother, depressed and directionless, was influenced by the not-so-subtle pressure to consider a life of prayer. As a nun, her education could be put to good use, she was told. And as a nun, she could travel the nation—even the world—tending to the poor, doing the work of the martyrs and saints she had spent a lifetime reading about. At a time in which her world felt hopelessly unstable, the absoluteness of a life of prayer made sense. More sense, anyway, than any of her other options. If Bongo wouldn't have Anne, maybe God would. And unlike Bongo, God wouldn't transfer to another school, leaving her behind. If anything, God would bring her closer than ever to the parental love that had always eluded her. It seemed, particularly in Anne's depressed state, a logical and noble move.

The convent my mother chose to enter in Oldenburg, Indiana, was founded and presided over by the Sisters of St. Francis, an order long associated with the education of children. It had long been populated by a number of Marian graduates. Situated in a picturesque valley amidst rolling hills dotted with apple orchards and horse farms in southeastern Indiana, the convent—

even now—is the kind of place that time seems to have forgotten. Street signs remain labeled in German, the native language of the town's founders. And the only real distinguishing features of the burg remain the spires of the convent's chapel and its accompanying Catholic school.

It made sense in so many ways for Anne to gravitate to Oldenburg. It was relatively close to Dunkirk—just over an hour's drive—and its legacy of educating was in keeping with her own love of learning. Above all, the order was consistent with my mother's goal of helping others. Members of the order branched out from the Mother House to far-flung areas of the world, ranging from inner-city New York to South America. They were educated women helping to educate the young, feed the poor. What, wondered my mother, wasn't admirable about that?

For the new sisters, the schedules were grueling. Days began at five A.M. First came morning meditation, then morning prayer and morning Mass. All of this came before any food was ingested. Following breakfast with the other nuns in the dining hall, there were chores and work. In my mother's case, that meant a day of teaching at the academy. At noon, there were more prayers. And in the evening, more prayers, more Mass. Then came dinner. Following dinner, there was an hour of recreation, then an hour of study and preparation for the following day. At nine P.M., it was lights-out. Talking after hours was strictly forbidden.

The nuns with whom my mother cohabitated were to become her new family, her whole world. The convent sought to cement this notion by keeping a novice nun's contact with family and friends from her former life to a bare minimum. In Anne's first years at Oldenburg, no home visits were allowed, and visits from family and friends were limited to a few hours on weekends. Contact with family members was maintained largely through letters. But even the letters were closely monitored. It was not uncommon to have packages that were deemed inappropriate seized, and letters read, shared, and even destroyed prior to reaching the intended recipient. My mother was not aware of this practice and was caught off guard when her Mother Superior summoned her to her office one day.

"Sister Aurelia Mary, there is something I have been meaning to ask you," said the Mother Superior sternly. "Who's Bongo?"

My mother's jaw dropped open. She looked at her leader, stunned. She hadn't uttered Bongo's name to anyone at the convent, had tried to prevent herself from even thinking about him. And Bongo had not visited. The last time she saw him was shortly before she entered the convent, when she was still at Marian, and when he was happily entrenched at Indiana University. With his new girlfriend. Was this the work of God—or something else?

"Bongo?" asked my mother, convinced she had misheard.

"Yes, Bongo," answered the Mother Superior impatiently. "Who is Bongo?"

"He's an old friend," my mother answered, still confused. "How do you know who Bongo is?"

"The Lord works in mysterious ways," the Mother Superior told her curtly before dismissing her.

Years later, my mother would learn that Bongo had written to her several times at the convent over the course of a few years, but each and every one of the letters was intercepted before my mother had a chance to read it.

"Why didn't you write back to me?" he would ask her a decade after she'd made her vows. "I wrote you all those letters."

"I never got them," my mother told him, sadly shaking her head.

The seizing of my mother's letters was one of the many things the sisters of Oldenburg viewed as a means to an end. Their goal: to develop a band of women wholly committed to the church and to a life that put uniformity and conformity before all other things. Even, at times, before God.

Everything the sisters did, they did together. There was no time for privacy, save for brief visits to the restroom and moments stolen away in the chapel. They were together for meditation, together for Mass, together for meals. At night, they gathered as a group to listen to a communal radio situated in their shared living room. For my mother, at least this part of convent life was reminiscent of her childhood, of those evenings with her blind grandfather, listening to all of those speeches and baseball games and *Amos 'n' Andy* shows. As a group, the sisters listened to newscasts and papal sermons. For nearly four entire days in November 1963, they gathered, struggling to digest the news of the assassination of President Kennedy, the nation's first Catholic president.

The sisters also gathered in the common living space after dinner to enjoy books as a group, taking turns reading aloud a pair of chapters before bed. Among my mother's favorite times in the convent were these reading episodes. She particularly liked *Mr. Blue*, a novel by Myles Connolly exploring what would happen if a wealthy man like Jay Gatsby had embraced the pauper life of St. Francis of Assisi, and Steinbeck's *Travels with Charley*, in which the famous author chronicles his road trip across America with his beloved dog.

"I'll never forget the chapter when Steinbeck stopped at a diner and no one was there. I thought for days, for weeks, for years about that diner. About where the people might have gone. About that trip. About just driving, just going the way he and Charley did, without any plan other than to be together."

By all accounts, my mother threw herself into her new existence as Sister Aurelia Mary. She didn't want to be just a nun. Family members say she wanted to be the best nun that she could be. She wanted to be not only a sister, but The Sister, a sort of alpha nun. Just as she had always thrown herself full force into building the family home as a girl, and helming high school and campus projects as a student leader—striving for the approval from her father, the A from her teachers—now she strived to do the same at Oldenburg. If she had to give up her life of independence, her clothes and movie magazines and Girls Nation trophy, then she wanted to make her sacrifices count for something. She wanted to be a model nun, recognized by her superiors.

A friend of hers from Marian, Marian Robinson, had entered Oldenburg at the same time, and observed my mother's passion for her new surroundings. "Anne never did anything wrong. Ever. She followed the rules of the convent to the letter of the law."

A case in point, she said, came at the close of the recreation hour at night. "When the hour was up, a bell was rung," Marian explained, "and you were to stop everything and go absolutely silent. If you were in the middle of the sentence, you weren't to finish that sentence. Or else. Most of us ignored that rule and finished saying what we had to say. Not Anne. When that bell rang, she was absolutely silent."

But hard as she tried, her siblings and cousins saw that my mother's life as a nun was one that didn't seem to agree with her. The Diener family concurs that Anne fit into the convent about as poorly as her frame fit into the enormous black habit, which swam on her.

"I just remember going to see her and thinking, 'This is not a happy camper,'" my mother's youngest brother, Mike, would tell me in later years. "She didn't smile during those Sundays when we drove to Oldenburg and visited her. She looked so sad, sitting on the lawn of that convent, like that habit was eating her alive."

There was much to be sad about. For one thing, she was constantly hungry. Among the primary things Anne and her fellow sisters were expected to forgo in the name of Christ was food. For young nuns, fasting was a way of life. Numerous times throughout the year, notably during the long stretches of Lent and Advent, a sister's level of devotion to Christ was measured by her ability to shun food for hours and days at a time. The presiding nuns made clear that the less a nun ate, the holier—and in turn, the closer to God—she was.

My mother did her best to comply with the strict diet, but her body was ill equipped. Since childhood, she'd suffered from low blood pressure and low blood sugar. The problems only got worse at Oldenburg. On more than one occasion, she passed out between meals, infuriating some of her superiors, who ordered her to "pray harder, eat less!"

The only times the nuns could eat in excess were on holidays. Easter Sunday and Christmas Day were times of gluttonous, day-long feasts, in which, my mother reported, nuns ate from dawn to dusk, starting each of the mornings with pans full of sticky buns and rounding out the days with plates laden with roast beef, baked hams, mashed potatoes, homemade bread, and copious amounts of cookies, pies, and cakes.

"I ate until I got sick," my mother would later say. "We all did."

The endless cycle of fast-then-feast destroyed Anne's relationship with food. For the rest of her life, she gorged herself on rich food, eating big Danishes and butter-laden bread and plates of meat ravenously, as if any of it might be taken away from her at a moment's notice.

Compounding the lack of food in the convent was the heavy attire. The white dress my mother wore when she made her vows was light and airy. The habit she donned as a nun at Oldenburg was the opposite: dark and heavy and made entirely of wool. Sister Aurelia Mary wore the classic penguin costume parodied in film. A white yoke engulfed her face and neck, leaving only a tiny window for her face. The black veil that extended from the yoke was massive, ballooning up into a rigid rectangle atop her head before falling down well past her shoulders.

The entire ensemble was so heavy, my mother would later tell me, that it sometimes caused her head to throb and her back to ache. Making matters worse, the heavy material trapped in the heat, which proved problematic in summer months. There was no air-conditioning in the convent and only a few fans. My mother attempted to stay cool, but on more than one occasion she passed out.

"Pray harder, Sister Aurelia Mary," her superiors told her before instructing her to take salt tablets.

And then there was her hair. Even though Anne could easily have kept her pretty waves and curls beneath her enormous veil, in a barrette or a bun, the supervising sisters commanded her to cut all of it off. The mandatory haircut reduced my mother's nearly shoulder-length hair to a closely shorn crooked bowl cut that left parts of her head bald. The drastic cut robbed her of what was left of her youth and beauty. Before the haircut, Anne appeared her age of twenty-three, if not younger. Afterward, she appeared an aging spinster, as did her classmates, who had been subjected to similar hackings.

"But I don't understand," I told my aunt Mimi during a conversation about convent life in the 1950s. "Why would anyone care what a sister's hair looked like underneath the veil? If the veils hid the hair, who cared how long the hair actually was?"

Aunt Mimi chortled at my ignorance. "In order to understand that, you must first understand the goal of the convent. Nuns were to look and to feel as sexless and unattractive as possible. No one was to look at us as anything other than servants of God. No one was to look at us at all. The goal was to make everyone forget we were women."

The push to make my mother and her fellow sisters at Oldenburg unattractive was further helped by the inability to bathe regularly. There were no bathtubs. Showers were permitted, but only at night and not every day. My mother told me showers at Oldenburg were typically short and unpleasant.

"The water was cold," my mother once told me when I was in

college. "I think it was done on purpose. They didn't want us lingering in the showers—or to have the opportunity to look at each other naked. They didn't want us to get any ideas."

It was the only time my mother would hint at the sisters' efforts to prevent lesbian relationships. But it wasn't only lesbian relationships that were frowned upon. The forging of close alliances, even the simple act of confiding in each other or sharing a private conversation, was also verboten.

"Relationships of any kind," Aunt Mimi told me, "were not tolerated."

She had endured this practice, accepted it as the norm for her twenty years of service to her convent, until she left.

"You mean you couldn't have any friends?" I asked.

My aunt paused and thought for a moment. "You could, but you had to be careful. You couldn't let anyone know you mattered to anyone or that anyone mattered to you. Eating too frequently with the same sisters, even laughing too loudly, wasn't allowed. If you started forging friendships, the Mother Superior broke them up."

"We could never gather as a group of two," my mother's fellow nun Marian told me. "Groups of three or four? That was okay. But groups of two were an absolute no-no. They didn't want any illicit relationships to take place. And they didn't want anyone to have a confidante."

Sisters who failed to conform to the strict standards were reported to management. In my mother's first years, that manager was the novice mistress, the sister who oversaw the new class of nuns who, like my mother, had yet to make their final vows. The novice mistress at Oldenburg in the latter part of the 1950s was a stern, unsmiling woman who was difficult to please. Unfortunately, the woman—who liked few nuns to begin with—took a particular dislike to my mother. She loathed my mother's intelligence as well as her growing popularity among the young students at the academy where my mother taught. She also took particular issue with my mother's frequent questions about why certain things were done the way they were at Oldenburg.

"I couldn't do anything right," my mother once told me sadly. "Everything I did, everything I said, was wrong."

When my mother good-naturedly asked whether the sisters might consider doing additional community outreach in the area, whether they might be able to read some different books on communal reading nights, whether the sisters could possibly consider conducting dinners differently or implementing new recipes, the mistress balked.

"This is the way we do things at Oldenburg, Sister Aurelia Mary," the mistress said with a click of the tongue. "This is the way we have always done things."

Change was not an option, the mistress told my mother. The role of a young nun was not to question why—her role was but to serve or die. Posing questions was viewed as a challenge to authority and a direct violation of the vow of obedience.

"They wanted to keep things as they'd always been," said my mother's nun friend, Marian. "I asked once why, if we were to embody the values of St. Francis, couldn't we go to Goodwill and get our clothes there, instead of wearing habits. St. Francis was all about modesty and the clothes from Goodwill would have made sense for us to wear. When I asked that, the sisters in charge looked at me as if I was crazy. Then they said, 'If we went to Goodwill, we wouldn't all look alike.' And to them, uniformity was what it was all about."

Punishment for perceived acts of insubordination was swift. In my mother's case, it came in the form of additional chores, the relinquishment of certain privileges, and, worst of all, being forced to remain silent for additional hours, even days, on end. My mother was told that the punishments were for her own good. In truth, they were a means of maintaining control and rendering a highly intelligent woman powerless.

The one thing that sustained her throughout the period of transition was the young students she'd been assigned to teach. The more restrictive and oppressive things became within the order, the more my mother clung to the spirit and energy of the students she taught in sun-dappled classrooms in the academy. The academy was technically part of the convent, but within her classroom, my mother had a freedom that she lacked anywhere else at Oldenburg. And in her students she had a reprieve from the stern and judgmental stares of her fellow nuns. The boys and girls were her window to the outside world she had given up, telling her of their hopes and dreams, bringing her apples, talking to her about movies she was no longer able to see, music she couldn't listen to on the convent's communal radio.

· My mother enjoyed her students' company, often staying after class to help those struggling, or lending an ear to those who needed to talk about problems at home.

"One young man didn't want his mother to remarry," she recalled. "The girls worried about the mean girls in the class."

She relished every moment she spent with her students. The children accepted and loved my mother for who she was instead of imploring her to pray harder, do better.

When my mother was gifted with presents of handmade cards, there was trouble.

"You smile too often, Sister Aurelia Mary!" the novice mistress hissed. "You enjoy their attention entirely too much. You are failing. Have you forgotten the need for humility?"

After a series of warnings and admonishments, the novice mistress doled out the ultimate punishment: she reassigned my mother to a post outside of the school, away from the students.

"I d-d-don't understand!" my mother cried to the novice mistress when she heard the news. Her heart raced. Her stuttering returned. "I'm a g-g-g-good teacher. What have I done wrong?"

"Your services are needed elsewhere," said the novice mistress.

"Do you not recall that you took a vow of obedience? Questioning me and my decision will only make matters worse."

My mother shook her head in disbelief. "But I'm a good teacher!"

Students' grades had improved dramatically under her tutelage.

"Can I at least say goodbye to the children?" my mother asked. Her heart broke at the thought of the boys and girls coming into the classroom and not finding her there to greet them, to listen to their problems. She needed to say goodbye, to give them closure, for their sake. And hers.

"Goodbyes, Sister Aurelia Mary, will only make things more difficult," sniffed the mistress. "Great damage has already been done," she continued, referring to the senior sisters' belief that my mother's open, happy ways in the classroom—the ones that had encouraged her young charges to speak their minds and to express their feelings—were at odds with Oldenburg's long-held belief that children were to be seen and lectured to, not heard.

"You are dismissed from your teaching duties effective imme-diately," repeated the novice mistress. "We will tell the children goodbye for you."

At this, she sent my mother to her room. My mother wept uncontrollably, stopping only long enough to vomit before crying some more.

She had prayed so hard that summer after Bongo left for a sign of what God wanted from her, where he wanted her to serve him. She had thought for certain that Oldenburg was the answer. On paper, at least, it had all seemed so right. But could it be? Could the answer really be a lonely existence among rigid women who seemed to care so little for the children they were supposed to be educating?

The new assignment my mother received at Oldenburg seemed to her something akin to solitary confinement. Instead of a teacher, she was now the equivalent of a maid and secretary, spending hours on end cleaning and doing the bidding of the novice mistress. At times, this meant remaining on her knees and waxing a marble floor until it shone. At other times, it meant attending to convent correspondence.

Her lowest moment, my mother told me one night, was the afternoon a group of her former students came to the front door of the convent. There were five or six of them, she said. They climbed the stairs of the main house and rang the bell. My mother, cleaning the floors at the time in an upstairs hallway, recognized their voices and approached the main hallway.

"We've come to see Sister Aurelia Mary," said the young lady leading the group. Her voice was soft and timid, likely daunted by the frosty reception of the old nun who answered the door.

"Please, we miss her," said another.

My mother's heart skipped a beat. She had visitors! She longed to run to them, to throw her arms around them. But no sooner was her spirit buoyed than it was crushed again.

"Sister Aurelia Mary does not wish to see you," replied the nun tersely, motioning the children away from the door. "We've work to do. It's best you leave. Now."

And with that, the door was closed in the children's crestfallen faces.

My mother described the moment as not only one of the lowest in her life as a nun, but in her entire life.

"I didn't know what pain felt like until then. I'd never hurt so much. They told them I didn't want to see the children. That was the furthest thing from the truth. They made it sound like I chose to leave them. They wanted them to think I was as cruel and uncaring as the rest of them."

Anne was sinking in the rising tidewaters of a life of cruelty and loneliness, and the one lifeboat she'd had—the children—had been taken away. She prayed for a miracle, for a sign that she hadn't stumbled down the wrong path. Her prayers were answered in the form of one of the few men among the sea of Old-enburg's sisters: Father Vincent.

Father Vincent was a priest at the church affiliated with the convent in Oldenburg. The priest, with dark hair, kind brown eyes, and an easy smile, had taken an immediate shine to my mother. He offered her smiles when possible, brightened at the insightful compliments she paid him for his sermons.

In time, he invited her to the rectory, engaged her in conversation. He told her about his large family, his close relationship with his mother, whom he often visited on holidays. They talked about their mutual love of poetry, their shared loves of St. Francis and St. Augustine, their thoughts about different Gospel readings. Sometimes they even talked about music and politics.

The sisters, particularly the novice mistress, were incensed at the development of such a close relationship between my mother and the priest.

"What is she doing in that rectory?" they whispered. "Who does she think she is, spending time with him instead of us?"

But in the 1950s, the Catholic Church remained a patriarchal system. If a priest—a male leader in the parish community—deemed it necessary to visit with my mother behind closed doors, there was nothing the nuns could say or do to stop the visits. She was forbidden from confiding in just one other nun, owing to the rules they had in place against female friendships. But a friendship with a priest? That was out of their control.

What they could do was mete out punishment when my mother returned to the convent after a visit with Father Vincent—namely, the turning of an increasingly cold shoulder toward her. There were as many as nine hundred nuns at Oldenburg when my mother lived there. But she felt as if few, if any, of the many sisters were friends.

"So many of us wanted to better know Anne," Marian would later tell me. "But she was so quiet. When they told her to talk to no one, she took it very seriously. She didn't confide in any of us. She was very secretive."

The growing frostiness of the nuns took a considerable toll on Anne. The flicker of light that had once shone in her eyes dimmed. Her fair skin grew paler. And beneath her robe, her body began to waste away. Increasingly, it was racked by unbearably painful abdominal cramps that often forced her to double over in anguish. The sisters—notably her novice mistress—turned a blind eye.

"Pray through the pain," she instructed Anne.

For a time, my mother did as she was told, spending hours on her knees, a rosary at the ready. Even her journals show her intense, and at times disturbing, devotion to prayer. At her lowest, she filled entire notebooks with handwritten Hail Marys, obsessive pleas to a higher power and beyond to right the ship she was sinking upon.

But eventually, the physical pain in her abdomen became too much, making it all but impossible for her to get out of bed in the morning or to move up and down the numerous flights of stairs. My mother credited Father Vincent with saving her life.

Increasingly concerned about my mother's gaunt frame, Father Vincent implored the hierarchy of the convent to get my mother medical help.

"Sister Aurelia Mary is sick, I tell you," he barked one day at the Mother Superior. "Really sick!"

"We're handling the situation," the Mother Superior told Father Vincent, motioning for him to keep his voice down. "This is a private affair involving the sisters. There's no need for you to get involved."

"Handling the situation?" Father Vincent asked, incredulous. "The girl is wasting away and you're telling her to pray it off? This is the twentieth century, not the Dark Ages. She needs a doctor!"

Reluctantly, the Mother Superior agreed, sending Anne to a local physician under the watchful eyes of a pair of nuns who had been asked to drive the car. Sisters were never allowed to do anything on their own—even seek medical care, Marian explained. "We were always chaperoned and always watched," she said.

Nuns who said they weren't feeling well, Marian added, were often viewed with skepticism by the hierarchy.

"They would say nuns who felt sick just wanted attention," Marian said. "I remember one poor sister complained and complained she had a headache. She told the sisters in charge for weeks, months, that something was wrong. They never took her seriously. By the time she finally got them to take her to St. Vincent's Hospital in Indianapolis to see doctors there, it was too late. They took a biopsy from the roof of her mouth and discovered cancer. It was everywhere. A big portion of her brain and a large section of her face had to be removed. It was horrible."

Fortunately for my mother, her condition was caught in time. Horrified at the shape he found her in—he described her as a "bag of bones"—the first doctor my mother saw sent her to a hospital in a nearby city. The diagnosis: a tipped uterus, which explained the abdominal pain, and a case of myasthenia gravis, an autoimmune neuromuscular disorder, which explained her extreme fatigue. Emergency surgery was necessary. Without it, she was told, she could die.

My mother lay listless in the hospital bed, self-consciously touching a hand to her badly cut hair, now exposed for all the world to see since the hospital had replaced her habit with a hospital gown. She made two requests before her surgery: She wanted a rosary with which to pray. And she wanted to send a note of gratitude to Father Vincent.

"Tell him thank you," she told the nurses.

When Anne regained consciousness after the surgery, her uterus was fixed, and medication was prescribed to bring her myasthenia gravis under control. But while her body was on the mend, her spirit was not. Sometime during the recovery period in the hospital is when the tears started. Perhaps it was because she was out from under the crushing pressure of the convent walls, or maybe it was because of her weakened physical state and the pain of the surgery itself. Whatever the reason, the tears started, and she couldn't stop. It was her second major bout of depression. This one was even worse than the summer after Bongo left Ball State.

Al and Aurelia drove from Dunkirk with young Mike to be by Anne's side. Perplexed by her tears, they hoped she'd feel better when she finished recovering from her surgery. But they were worried. In those days—the mid-1960s—new situations were arising called "nervous conditions." Aurelia prayed that this wasn't what was wrong with Anne, but it certainly sounded like those conditions she'd read about. To her, it appeared that her heaving, sobbing mess of a daughter had suffered a nervous breakdown.

The nuns of Oldenburg concurred.

As official "property" of the Catholic Church, my mother couldn't seek out just any help for her frayed nerves. Instead, she was assigned a church-appointed psychiatrist. In southeastern Indiana, that psychiatrist was Dr. Countryman.

Dr. Countryman was a learned man whom family members would later describe as a consummate egghead. When my mother was discharged from the hospital, he listened in an austere office as my mother recounted her feelings of inferiority in the convent, her quest to be the perfect nun, her fear of falling short and disappointing her family and, in turn, God. Dr. Countryman prescribed "nerve" medication for my mother. But the tears continued. And the frosty treatment on the part of my mother's fellow nuns intensified.

Ultimately, it was Father Vincent who again came to my mother's rescue. Following her return to Oldenburg, Father Vincent kept watch over her, inviting her again to visit him in the privacy of his residence at the rectory. There he prayed with her, talked with her, and perhaps most importantly, he listened to her, not with the analytical ears of Dr. Countryman, but instead with the compassionate ears of someone who adored her. During those long talks, he began to call her by her given name, Anne. He also offered her that most scandalous of things: human contact. Taking her into his arms, he held her as she cried and confided in him her innermost fears.

"His hugs were the best," my mother would tell me years later, closing her eyes as she momentarily relived the memory. "He was the best."

In addition to hugs, Father Vincent presented my mother with gifts, notably an intricately carved pewter crucifix. Some eight inches long, the cross remained among her most treasured possessions. Decades after leaving the convent, she kept it in a large jewelry box with her valuables, next to a brooch from her grandmother Trudy and cherished letters from her parents. I saw it for the first time when I was having a particularly difficult time in high school.

"Hold this," my mother told me, handing me the crucifix. "Pray on this, and everything will be better."

"What's so special about this?" I'd asked, confused.

"It's too difficult to explain," she'd said. "Just know that the man who gave it to me was as saintly as they come. This got me through my darkest times. It will help you with yours."

Time and again, my mother turned to Father Vincent in the safety of the rectory and asked with pleading eyes, "What should I do?"

Life within the convent had gone from bad to worse. The sisters wouldn't let her back in the classroom, and now they used her medical issues and growing friendship with Father Vincent as reasons to further ostracize her from the group. Any hopes she might have harbored of eventually moving up the convent totem pole had been summarily crushed. At most, she might be able to hope for a transfer to another arm of the order. But attaining a position of leadership within the convent? Her reputation for being a "problem nun" deemed those "promotions" highly unlikely, if not impossible.

"Should I stay?" she asked Father Vincent. "Should I leave? What do I do?"

Father Vincent's answer was nearly always the same. "When in doubt, pray," he would gently instruct her, cupping her face in his hands. "Pray on it."

And so she did. My mother prayed, she would later tell me, with all of her heart, all of her might. She prayed for a sign, one of biblical proportions: a bolt of lightning, a message from God. She prayed in the chapel. She prayed in her narrow bed. She prayed in the shower.

Eventually, she told me, her prayers were answered in the form of a vision.

"A vision?" I asked her, my tone skeptical. I was sixteen when she recounted the story and had been pressing her for an explanation as to why she had named me Mary.

I never much cared for my name. In fact, I'd never liked my given name at all. I wanted something less Catholic and more glamorous sounding, so I'd asked her one night over dinner why she couldn't have named me something more fun, like Linda.

Her response?

"I named you Mary because I made a promise."

The promise, she said, was made in response to a vision she'd had—from none other than Mary. *The* Mary. The mother of Christ herself. After weeks of praying, my mother told me that Mary appeared to her at Oldenburg and told her it was time to leave the convent, that she was destined to better serve the church and the world outside of the convent walls.

Whether this vision came in a dream or appeared to her during her waking hours, I'm not sure. My mother spoke of the apparition only once, and when I doubted the validity of her words (I was, after all, only sixteen and a typical eye-rolling teenager), she abruptly changed the subject. But in any case, the vision from Mary, she said, was the sign she'd been waiting for. So relieved was my mother for the sign from Mary that she made a vow: if she were to eventually bear a daughter, she would name the baby after her.

If the vision from Mary wasn't enough to convince my mother it was time to leave Oldenburg, there was one thing more to bolster her decision: a rapidly changing world. Though the sisters of St. Francis remained largely sequestered, there were two events that even the church hierarchy could not shield them from: the growing women's movement sweeping the nation, and the approach of Vatican II, the mini-revolution that would fundamentally banish Latin masses and elevate the role of laypeople within the church. The two seismic shifts meant that the life Anne Diener wished to lead—one that involved teaching and helping others—was not exclusive to nuns. Educated women looking to change the world could increasingly do so out from under the heavy burden of a nun's habit. And thanks to the growing women's movement, they could opt to do so without the assistance of any church at all. For Catholic and non-Catholic women in the 1960s, the sky was the limit.

My mother knew nuns had left Oldenburg before. One, she would tell me later, she would never forget: a pretty young woman from a wealthy family in Indianapolis who sent her sweet-smelling bath soaps and hand lotions that my mother envied. Soaps were among the few possessions the upper echelons of the order wouldn't take away. My mother distinctly remembered the woman's kindness and enjoyed her company in chapel and the dining hall. One day the young woman was an active part of convent life. And the next she was gone, spirited away in the dark of night after the lights went out and the sisters were ordered to bed.

"That's what they would do," my mother told me sadly. "The sisters who left would just disappear with no notice. Their beds would be empty and in the morning, at breakfast, no one would know where they'd gone. No one could say goodbye."

When my mother attempted to ask what had become of her friend, where she had gone, she was silenced by the presiding sisters, and, worse, ignored. It was as if her friend had never existed. The young sister had deigned to leave and had therefore been erased. While nuns were welcomed into the fold of the church amidst grandiose displays of pomp and circumstance, those who opted to leave were forced to exit under veils of secrecy and shame far heavier than any habit they'd been forced to wear. To leave the convent was to seek a divorce from a way of life. In a way, it was the equivalent of seeking a divorce from Christ himself.

"They always said the same thing," Marian would later tell me of the nuns' reactions to the women who had left the fold. Marian would leave the convent some four years after my mother, and, leading up to her own departure, she watched more than a dozen sisters leave the order, as Oldenburg's nun population began its gradual decline.

"In the morning, when everyone discovered so-and-so had left the night before, they'd click their tongues and shake their heads and say, 'Oh, she just didn't have the calling,'" Marian recalled. "The sisters who remained never said, 'Hmm, I wonder what happened.' For them, it couldn't be the convent's fault that someone had left. They assumed the person who left was the one with a problem."

When my mother announced her decision to leave the convent to her Mother Superior, the effort to erase her from the Oldenburg community began almost immediately.

First came the instruction to keep the decision to herself.

"You must tell no one of this decision," instructed the Mother Superior. "No one, Sister Aurelia Mary. Do you hear me?"

Failure to cooperate would be met with stiff punishment, she was told, not the least of which would be the inability to leave the convent with full dispensation, church lingo for an honorable discharge from the order. My mother desperately wanted the full dispensation. That's what would allow her to continue to receive the sacraments, including Communion, and to eventually marry in the church.

The letter from Rome would come to the Mother Superior, my mother was informed. And if she wanted that letter, she needed to tell no one of her plans to leave.

Then, a date was decided upon. In my mother's case, her departure was scheduled for September 25, 1965.

Finally came the exit.

A nun leaving a convent in the 1960s was something akin to a prisoner leaving the penitentiary, my mother later told me. A departing prisoner often has nothing to wear the day he gets out of jail other than the clothes he wore as an inmate, and nuns in the years preceding the reforms of Vatican II faced a similar fate. The clothes my mother had worn all those years ago upon entering Oldenburg had long since been given away. All that she'd had in the way of a wardrobe for nearly a decade consisted of the veils and tunics and robes and wimples that were the property of the Catholic Church. Penniless—as she was obliged to be, thanks to her vow of poverty—she had no civilian clothes to call her own. She literally had nothing to wear back out into the real world.

In the dark of night, after the others had gone to bed, the supervising sisters at Oldenburg stripped my mother of her habit and threw at her feet a collection of ill-fitting rags.

"Put these on!" the two nuns overseeing her departure hissed.

Still mired in her vow of obedience, my mother did as she was told, slipping on a badly stained blouse—some of its buttons missing—and an ill-fitting skirt that smelled. The shoes she was given to wear were equally ill fitting. Not only were they two sizes too small for her size 10 feet, but they were mismatched. The left shoe didn't match the right. One was navy blue. One was black.

Making matters worse: my mother's hair. Without the veil, she could not hide the bad haircuts she had endured for nearly a decade. She was nearly bald in places and her hair was uneven throughout. She had no bangs to speak of and no real part. Just a jagged series of cuts above her forehead. It was an unmitigated disaster. It hadn't been washed in days and hadn't been properly brushed in years. Sister Aurelia Mary had not owned a hairbrush since 1957 and was offered none the morning of her departure.

My mother was frightened. She trembled and had to hold tight to the railing of the stairwell to keep from careening down it headfirst as she was led downstairs.

When she asked a presiding sister where she should go, what she should do, she was silenced. Family members speculate she was physically assaulted in those final hours in the convent, perhaps with a hand, perhaps with something else. My mother would never confirm or deny the story. Not to me, anyway. But facial bruising was evident when she arrived back at the Pine Patch.

"They really did a number on your mother," my uncle Mike would tell me, shaking his head at the memory of seeing his oldest sister hours after her departure. "Someone just did her in. She looked like she'd been in a concentration camp when she got out of there.

"She looked like a dog. A sick, mangy dog."

At the appointed time of departure, my mother was led down a corridor of the main level of the Mother House and told to kneel.

"They left me alone and told me to wait until exactly four o'clock," my mother would later recount to my father. "At exactly four, I was supposed to go through a door and receive my next set of instructions."

My mother did as she was told, crying in silence, still shaking in fear.

As the clock struck four A.M., she walked through the door, expecting to find nuns waiting for her with new instructions. Instead, she stumbled into a dark alley where a car sat idling. To my mother's astonishment, it was her father who had come to collect her. Al Diener was alone, seated behind the steering wheel. There were no nuns to see her off. No one to wave goodbye.

The setting for her exit from Oldenburg was the same as that of her entrance. Anne Diener was still on church property, still surrounded by spires and steeples and lofty crosses. But the circumstances surrounding those final moments were so different. On September 25, 1965, there was no cake, no punch, no pealing of bells. Just the waiting arms of her father, standing by to rescue her. Nearly a decade before, my mother had entered the darkest chapter of her life in broad daylight, a blushing bride dressed in white. Now, amidst her divorce from the church, she fled in the dark of night, wearing nothing but rags.

Chapter 5

Bride of Dale

Anne Diener gingerly ran the back of her hand across the bodice of the satin gown that hung over the full-length mirror. It was so rich, so heavy. Trudy would have called it sumptuous. It was sumptuous to be sure.

She'd loved it the moment she saw it in the LS Ayres bridal look-book. The ivory sheath gown featured sleeves that fell just past the elbow, cloth-covered buttons that cascaded down the back, and, best of all, glorious touches of lace. Not just any lace. But the heavy stuff that bordered on being a brocade. The lace was in all the right places—a dash to line each sleeve, some at the hem, lots at the rear of the train that extended five feet when it wasn't bustled. The lace was so rich and added such dignity and class to the gown. How could it not, when the name of the lace was Queen Anne's lace? Queen Anne's lace for Anne Diener's wedding day.

Her favorite part about the gown: its simplicity. Other gowns she'd looked at had cinched waists, low-cut tops, and excessive amounts of tulle. Some were so short they weren't so much bridal gowns as minidresses. She knew it was 1968, but she remained a traditionalist at heart. A traditionalist who still sometimes marveled that she was again wearing civilian clothes and that she was getting married in the Catholic Church.

Just three years ago, she'd been a nun, a bride of Christ. And *today she was a bride of Dale. Dale Edmund Pflum. She couldn't quite believe it.*

She'd had so many questions when he'd proposed. In fact, she'd had so many that the first thing she blurted out after he asked, "Anne, will you marry me?" was "Can I think about it?"

And thought about it she had. For a week. While she consulted her gut. And Father Vincent. Her darling Father Vincent. He hadn't wanted her to marry Dale. He'd told her so in letters. He'd told her so to her face. But he'd supported her decision. He would be here today. She'd even arranged to have him sit beside her at the reception. They'd be together, the three of them, Father Vincent on one side of her, Dale on the other.

He'd encouraged her to wait for the right man. But she was thirty-three. All of her classmates and most of her younger siblings—Kathy and Patty and even Al—were married. She didn't want to wait any longer. If she wasn't cut out to be a bride of Christ, at least she could be someone's bride. That was his will, wasn't it? God's intent? For those women who didn't serve him in the church to serve him as wives and mothers?

They'd make things work, she told herself, fingering now the long lace veil her sister Kathy had lent her for the big day. It was the same veil Kathy had worn when she married Joe Boland in Dunkirk's St. Mary's Church just a few months ago. Anne and Dale had thought about marrying there, but had ultimately settled upon the chapel at Ball State in Muncie, where they'd met. Anne so loved Ball State. It held for her so many fond memories. Of life in the dorm. Of her pre-convent days of carefree confidence. Of Bongo.

Dale was no Bongo. For one thing, he was much taller. At nearly six foot six Dale was a full foot taller than Anne. And unlike Bongo, Dale was into business, not geography. Dale was—well, Dale was Dale. Who was she to judge how a marriage should feel? All brides surely must wonder about what life will be like with their grooms. Her feel-

ings of insecurity were natural, she told herself. They must be. They just had to be.

"Anne, sweetheart, do you need any help getting ready?"

Anne turned to Kathy. She wore the floor-length blue bridesmaid dress Anne had picked out for her the same day she'd picked out her wedding gown. Kathy would be her only attendant today. Mimi would sing with her fellow nuns in the choir. Patty would oversee the guestbook. Only Kathy would stand up with her at the altar. She'd help her through the day.

"I'd love the help," said Anne, smiling at Kathy. "Today I can use all the help I can get."

For the majority of women, the most significant white dress they wear in a lifetime is the gown they wear on their wedding day. That wasn't the case for Anne Diener. For her, the white dress she wore the day she wed my father ranked, at best, a distant second on the list of Most Important White Dresses. Maybe it came in third. In fact, I'm not sure she would have counted the gown among the top four or five most important white dresses of her life.

It's not that she didn't like the dress. Indeed, she often remarked upon her fondness for it when I was growing up, particularly when she spied a wedding gown that she believed to be too, in her words, "over the top." While I delighted in the dresses sported by my favorite soap opera characters of the 1980s, my mother was typically scandalized. Among her least favorite wedding dresses of my childhood: the lace and sheer silk concoction Hope from *Days of Our Lives* wore when she wed Bo. My mother was horrified by the "unladylike" look of Hope's dress, which showed off the actress's ample bosom, and which was topped off with a gaudy, spiky headpiece that made it appear as if the actress and the tufts of tulle atop her head had been electrocuted.

"Wedding gowns should leave something to the imagination," my mother would say, making it clear that if I was interested in one day donning a gown cut down to *there*, I'd probably be better off eloping.

One of my favorite things to do as a little girl was to look at the two wedding albums my mother kept at the base of our living room's coffee table. I would sit on the olive-green couch, my legs too short to touch the ground, with the albums spread out on my little lap and pore over the photos.

After careful consideration, I made a mental list of what I liked about my mother's wedding day: 1) how she looked in a white dress with white snow on the ground in the pictures snapped of her leaving the reception on that chilly November day; 2) her bouquet, a breathtaking spread of gardenias and ivy; and 3) her dessert course (there was not only cake, but also a delectable-looking sugar cream pie).

Then I made a list of what I didn't like about my mother's wedding day: 1) the cut of the dress (to me, it looked like a tent); 2) the lack of contact lenses (I couldn't believe my father wore glasses on a day so important); and, above all, 3) the expression on my mother's face. Even at age five I knew my mother lacked the look of elation I'd seen on the faces of so many other brides. Yes, my mother smiled in some of her wedding photos. But in so many others, she didn't. She looked pensive, tired, on edge. There was something in her eyes—sadness, I realize now, or perhaps a nagging doubt—that seemed to suggest this wasn't one of the happiest days of her life, and actually might have been just the opposite.

It was a sad few years that followed my mother's departure from the convent. Letters show that leaving Oldenburg may have removed her from the realm of the cruel and unsupportive sisters, but the exit also placed her back in the world of her overwhelmed parents, who were often at a loss as to how to give her the support she desperately needed.

Within hours of her return to the Pine Patch in Dunkirk, my mother was a bundle of uncontrollable sobs and sighs, and my grandparents were at their wits' end.

"She was such a mess," Uncle Mike would later tell me, shaking his head. He had been frightened by the reappearance of his big sister, stripped of her habit.

For my devoutly Catholic grandparents, who had taken enormous pride in successfully placing two of their daughters in the church's fold, my mother's decision to quit the convent presented a problem.

"Anne's departure," her first cousin Bob would explain, "was a tremendous embarrassment." The situation was perplexing. No books had been written on the subject. What should—or shouldn't—they tell people about Anne?

For my grandmother in particular, who increasingly relished her role as small-town club leader, and as the respected Al Diener's wife, this was a worrisome matter. My mother's return was an unwelcome addition to her nearly empty nest and a blemish on her household, according to family members. Should she address the subject head-on or not say anything about it at all? What should she say if someone asked her point-blank why Anne had left Oldenburg?

My mother sensed the discomfort in her parents and retreated even further into her already-fractured shell.

"She was just awkward to be around when she returned," Bob explained, referring to the first extended family gatherings with my mother post-convent. "She used to wear the habit. And now she had none. She felt awkward. And Aurelia clearly felt ashamed, as if she'd just as soon hide her in a back room when company came if she could. No one knew what to say or do."

Making matters worse was the erosion of my mother's relationships with her beloved grandparents. It's not that Trudy and Dad Diener didn't love her. They would always love their Annie.

But while she had once been the apple of their eye—the grandchild who had met the president and could do no wrong—she now had become more complicated to love and, in turn, to be around. Like her parents, they weren't sure what to tell friends about Anne, how to explain that she had quit the convent. And they were at a loss as to what to do when she broke down into gut-wrenching sobs, often with little or no notice. Theirs was a generation that had weathered a Great Depression and two world wars. For them, when life got tough, one was supposed to throw one's shoulders back and soldier on. When Anne failed to do this, they were at a loss for words. She felt awkward in their presence, and they in hers.

"Anne had always been the favorite grandchild before Oldenburg, the one who got the most attention and the special treatment," her sister Patty would later explain to me. "But after she got out of the convent, there was a noticeable shift."

It wasn't just the grandparents whose attitudes toward Anne had changed. The aunts and uncles who had once doted on her, including her father's beautiful sister, Peg, now treated Anne differently as well. In Peg's case, much of this had to do with the erosion of her personal life. Married to a successful business executive who had moved to New York without her, Peg now lived in a big lonely house in Winnetka, Illinois, unable to help herself, let alone her lonely niece.

Even my mother's brothers and sisters were at a loss as to what to say or do. Mimi remained a nun, busy teaching in her own convent. Kathy, Patty, and Al Joe had all graduated from high school and were busy with their respective young-adult lives. Only Mike remained at home, and he was too young to know what to say to his older sister, whose appearance, he says, made him feel sad and uncomfortable.

"It was a really rough time for her," he explained.

Back at the Pine Patch, away from the strict order and routine of convent life, my mother flailed about in search of a sense of safety and stability that was not to be found. For years, she had lived according to a strict, orderly structure, in which every minute of the day was accounted for. Now she had no schedule to speak of. She was no longer a nun. But she also no longer felt like a citizen of the world. The world she'd known and understood when she entered the convent back in 1957 had vanished. In its place was a strange new nation.

It was now the mid-1960s. Hemlines were shorter, waistlines more defined. With the advent of Elvis and the Beatles, music had changed dramatically, as had haircuts, attitudes, even vocabularies. Anne Diener didn't understand this world. What's more, she had forgotten all the little things—what it was like to handle her own money, how to make her own decisions about what to read and where to go.

Anne's dramatically changed world pushed her further into the pit of depression she'd fallen into at the end of her days at Oldenburg. She sobbed uncontrollably in her bedroom at the Pine Patch, and even during meals with her parents. For Aurelia, the strain of the mood swings was often too much to bear.

"Snap out of it this instant!" she'd yell at my crying mother.

But Anne didn't know how to snap out of anything. She felt like a failure on a multitude of levels.

One afternoon not long after my mother's return, Aurelia, unable to take the strain anymore, did the unthinkable: she slapped Anne across the face. Hard. A stunned Mike, home at the time, witnessed the encounter.

"I'd never seen anything like it before," he told me years after the event. "I'd never seen my mother hit anyone like that."

After the altercation, it was Anne who apologized to Aurelia, not the other way around. Later she retreated to her room to cry and convulse some more.

Just as troubling as her crying spells were her sleep patterns, which were all over the place. Sometimes she slept for twelve hours. Other times, she was up all night. With sleeplessness came an increase in the stuttering that had plagued her since childhood. She was often unable to get her thoughts out to her parents without stopping and struggling to start her sentences again and again.

"I-I-I n-n-need t-t-t-to use the t-t-t-telephone," she'd stammer. "C-c-c-can I p-p-p-please b-b-b-borrow the c-c-c-c-c-car?"

Only one light remained in her darkened world: Father Vincent.

Anne may have left the convent, but she had hardly abandoned her relationship with the Oldenburg priest. At Father Vincent's instruction, she phoned him daily, sometimes two or three times a day. Without fail, he took her calls. His letters to her spelled out his schedule, letting her know when he would be away. When he was sent to New York for several months, he made certain she knew where and when to find him there as well.

"You are never alone, Annie," he told her. "I will always be there for you."

Conversations between the two remained focused on Anne's future. Father Vincent alternated prayers and lighthearted banter with pep talks. "Take one day at a time. Remember to pray. Remember you are not alone. Remember the Lord is with you."

In time, Anne's hair grew back. She managed to return to an increasingly normal sleep schedule. And, thanks to her sister Patty, she embraced a new wardrobe that was in keeping with the times.

By this time, Patty Diener had moved to the greener pastures of Beverly Hills, California. She'd gone there in her early twenties, in part because of her friendship with her college roommate: Linda Hope, entertainer Bob Hope's eldest daughter. Linda and Patty had become fast friends as undergraduates. During college, Patty brought Linda home to the Pine Patch on weekends, where the Diener family taught her how to bake a cake. Linda, in turn, took Patty home to Beverly Hills. When it came time to decide where to use her nursing degree, Patty opted to leave the Midwest for the warmer and more exciting world of California.

Just as Patty's mailing address changed in the 1960s, so did her attitude toward Anne. A girl needed options, Patty told her older sister. And she also needed good clothes. So when Anne left the convent, it was Patty who turned to her own closet and to the closets of her girlfriends to organize a quasi clothing drive.

"Anne always said she had nothing to wear until Patty came to the rescue with the boxes of dresses she sent to her," my father would later tell me.

From Patty and Patty's California girlfriends my mother received her first miniskirts, minidresses, sleeveless shifts, polyester vests, paisley scarves. They were hand-me-downs, to be sure, but they were better than the scant offerings my mother had. Patty, who had once dreamed of getting out of her sisters' shadows, had now officially done so. She was no longer following. She was leading.

Aunt Patty didn't stop with clothes. She also introduced my mother to men, including the gentleman she arranged to escort Anne to her own wedding at the Beverly Hills Hotel. Patty had gotten to know several men during her years in Hollywood, but the man who ultimately stole her heart was a successful psychoanalyst she'd met while working at the Los Angeles veterans' hospital. He was learned. He was older. And he was something more: Jewish. When Patty informed her family that she was not only marrying a Jewish doctor, but that she was also converting to Judaism, it was a shock, particularly to Al and Aurelia and their strict Catholic beliefs.

But the family rallied, agreeing to stand by Aunt Patty on her big day. Al Diener gave Patty away. Kathy served as maid of honor. My mother was an invited guest, looking on with a mixture of awe and confusion as her now platinum-blond sister wed beneath a chuppah. My mother's hair looked more beautiful than ever on the day of the wedding. Its body and sheen were returning. Thanks to Patty, she'd had it set into a nice series of waves and frosted to a lighter color that turned her brown to a deep dirty blond. She wore a sleek blue shift that accentuated her narrow waist. And beside her stood a handsome escort, tall and dark.

The date had been carefully selected by Patty. A German immigrant, he had escaped from East Berlin in 1961 by swimming through waters not far from the newly constructed Berlin Wall.

"He told me they tried to shoot him as he swam, but the bullets bounced off the water," my mother told me years later as we watched a documentary about the building of the wall.

"Was he handsome?" I asked.

"Yes." She smiled sheepishly. "Very."

My mother would talk about her date for years, always noting what an "intriguing" and "fascinating" man he was. But she wasn't sufficiently intrigued to see him again after the wedding. In those fragile months following her departure from Oldenburg, Father Vincent remained the only man outside of the family in whose company she felt safe.

Back in Dunkirk, my mother continued to question who she was, where she was going. The struggle to readjust reared its head on a near-daily basis, including the day the IRS called and informed her she was being audited. After years of being off the books, my mother's reemergence as a citizen of the world made the federal government think something was amiss.

"Thankfully, the man who audited me was so nice, so gentle," my mother would later say with a laugh. "He sat down at the dining room table to go over my papers with me and was so amazed. He kept telling me he had never met a former nun."

As she slowly readjusted to civilian life, one thing became increasingly clear: she had to escape from the Pine Patch. The tension with her mother was palpable. As a child, Anne had had no choice other than to put up with Aurelia Diener's bouts of aloofness. But now Anne was a bona fide adult. She was old enough to know when she wasn't wanted, to know when her mother was ashamed of her and wanted her out of her sight. She was old enough to make the decision to leave.

With the help of Father Vincent, Anne secured a teaching job at a Catholic high school in Cincinnati and moved into an all-women's hotel called the Fontbonne. The downtown hotel provided her with the sort of camaraderie she'd sought at Oldenburg but that had long eluded her. Ironically, the Fontbonne was a Catholic hotel, overseen by a group of nuns who imposed strict curfews and glared at young women they deemed unsuitable. But the Fontbonne's nuns were a far cry from those my mother had known at Oldenburg. At the Fontbonne, Anne did not have to fast and wasn't punished for sleeping late or for asking simple questions. More importantly, the young women she encountered at the hotel were almost without fail a friendly bunch with whom she felt comfortable. Most hailed from the Midwest and, like my mother, were in need of a place to stay as they navigated careers and single life in the city of Cincinnati.

They joined my mother in eating breakfast in a communal dining room each morning before heading off to their respective jobs as secretaries, teachers, actresses, even models. Then they came together again at night, back at the hotel or at local coffee shops and restaurants nearby, for dinner and to celebrate birthdays, job promotions, even engagements.

In eating and shopping with these new neighbors and friends—only some of whom were Catholic—my mother learned what it was like to laugh and trust again. For years and decades, she would reminisce about the women she'd met and the lessons they'd taught her.

"They were such a neat bunch," she would later tell me. "They showed me that independence was fun and that life didn't have to begin and end with the Catholic Church."

That's not to say that Anne abandoned her Catholic roots. During her time in Cincinnati, she still attended Mass daily. She still visited Father Vincent when time permitted and continued to write and call him at least once a week. But now she counted Lutheran and Jewish and even agnostic women among her closest friends. What's more, thanks to new friends at the Fontbonne, she even learned how to curse.

"It felt so good to say 'shit' for the first time," my mother recounted, "and know that it might not send me straight to hell. I never knew one word could feel so good."

She laughed as she told me this one day when I was thirteen, not long after I'd had spinal surgery. I hurt so much that I didn't know what to do with the pain.

That's when she told me about the power of one well-placed curse here and there.

"Sometimes words like 'darn' and 'dang' and 'geez' just don't cut it," she said, surprising me with her candor. "Sometimes only a really good 'shit' makes you feel better."

I would wonder years later if she regretted not knowing how to curse—or curse her superiors out—during her days as a nun. My guess is she did.

At the Fontbonne, Anne kept a rosary tucked in her purse and prayed the novena frequently. And perhaps the most telling sign of her ongoing relationship with the church: after receiving Communion, she spent an inordinate amount of time making her way back to her pew, as nuns in the 1950s had been taught to do. Moving too quickly suggested that one wasn't taking the sacrament of Communion—the acceptance of the body of Christ— seriously. Even after marriage, my father would tell me, my mother remained loath to move faster than a few paces a minute after accepting her Communion wafer.

"It was really something to see," my father would tell me years later. "Everyone in the church would stare and wonder who in the world your mother was."

Still, the positive results of leaving Oldenburg were unmistakable.

Within a year, Anne had gained weight, and color had returned to her cheeks. Now she was ready to take the next big step in her life: graduate school.

In entering the master's program in speech pathology at Ball State University, my mother had several goals in mind. She wanted to continue to attend Mass every day. She wanted to attain a graduate degree that would enable her to help those who, like her, suffered from stuttering and its sometimes debilitating effects. And, back on the campus where she had met Bongo all those years before, she wanted to begin to date again.

The first two goals were easily attainable. The third, she knew, would require some work, particularly since she had dated so little in her life, and the majority of the men she'd had any real contact with since Bongo were, like Father Vincent, unattainable men of the cloth.

Anne was cautiously optimistic. And when she was introduced to Dale—a tall, gangly, bespectacled farm boy from Connersville, Indiana—not long after rejoining the Newman Club, she was both curious and vulnerable.

Anne Diener met Dale Pflum in the fall of 1966. My father was on campus to get his master's degree in business. Together, he and my mother bonded over the excitement of Vatican II and bringing aspects of it to the Ball State campus under the guidance of Father Jim Bates, a then young Catholic priest and college chaplain who would become a lifelong friend to them both.

For Anne, Dale was a nice companion. He made her laugh. And on many occasions, he made her think. They both had doubts about the Catholic Church. They both loved their Indiana roots. They both loved their families and said they wanted families of their own. At the end of the day, she enjoyed his company. He was no Bongo. But he was good company. And that was a start.

Dale, for his part, thought Anne was nice and respectable.

"She was the kind of person I think I thought I was supposed to be with," my father told me years later.

Together, they began to frequent Muncie pizza parlors and attend house parties held by their fellow grad students at which they drank cheap wine and ate fondue atop trunks that had been transformed into makeshift coffee tables.

While my mother was initially hopeful about the relationship, there were signs of trouble early on. As time went on, Dale showed a moody side, she would later explain, and seemed increasingly noncommittal.

"He seemed more interested a lot of the times in his friends than in me," she would tell me when I was in high school.

Sometimes he was jovial and lighthearted, and other times he snapped at her, pushing her away.

She craved warmth and at least a hint of romance, but more often than not, he was most comfortable giving her sisterly pecks on the cheek after an evening out, or ribbing her the way he'd joke with a pal.

She wanted a commitment. He wasn't sure what he wanted.

The trouble was noted a year into their relationship in a letter from my mother's beloved Father Vincent.

"*I know you are disappointed in Dale and to that extent I am too,*" Father Vincent wrote. "*But let me tell you, you are talking my language when you say that you want to mean something special—EVERYTHING—to the man that is to be your life's companion.*

"*Personally, I would not want one for a life's companion who does*

*not know what he wants, or who cannot make up his mind, or who
cannot give a full quotient of love for the love he receives."*

As it turns out, the source of my father's indecisiveness was not
an overarching love of freedom or adventure, nor of cigars, alcohol, or other women. No, the source of Dale's inability to commit
to Anne—almost certainly the source of that pained look on my
mother's face on their wedding day—was something far more
scandalous in the 1960s. My father was gay.

Dale told no one, including, of course, my mother. Still, Anne
must have sensed something was wrong early enough in the relationship to prompt her to tell him when he eventually proposed
marriage in 1968 that she needed some time to think over his
offer.

"I told him big decisions require lots of time to think," she
told me.

Even as a little girl, I knew that didn't sound right.

But the truth of the matter was things weren't right. After
years of reading about the love affairs involving her literary hero-
ines and their dreamy partners, in which hearts pounded and lips
quivered, my mother had hoped she would find a man breathless
with excitement at the very thought of her. But with Dale, those
moments never came. Not only was there little passion; moments
of intimacy, or the pressure to have intimacy, often brought out in
Dale bouts of terrifying rage.

My mother told me she knew the marriage was in trouble as
early as the honeymoon.

"When things didn't go quite right," she told me one night
after dinner, looking off into the distance to a place only she could
see, "he chased me."

"Chased you?" I asked.

"Chased me," she repeated. "I knew I had to run."

"Run?" I asked, still incredulous. My mother despised exercise. A gym teacher she'd had back in Dunkirk during elementary

school—some woman she later described as "monstrous"—had scared her out of ever wanting to have anything to do with physical exertion after publicly shaming my poor mother on more than one occasion for failing to execute a somersault. If my mother had run—and run on her honeymoon!—the situation must have been extreme.

"He was so angry," my mother said, still looking at that far-off place. "I knew whatever I did, I couldn't let him catch me."

The thing was, though my mother was the one afraid of getting caught, my father was the one who felt trapped.

Dale Edwin Pflum was born June 10, 1941, in southern Indiana to a young farmer, George Pflum, and his even younger wife, Bernice.

George and Bernice were farm kids who met and fell in love at a barn dance when my grandmother was just seventeen. As a child, I would stare for hours at their wedding photos. Unlike the photos of my parents' wedding, those of my father's parents showed a young, beautiful couple very much in love.

After a one-night honeymoon at an Indianapolis hotel, George and Bernice threw themselves headfirst into the task of making their new farm a resounding success and raising a family to help them achieve the task. First came Richard, my father's older brother, born in October 1938.

Three and a half years later came my father.

And four and a half years after my father's birth came the tragedy that would shape my father's entire life and my parents' entire marriage.

It was February 1946. After a day of errands, my grandmother headed back to the farm with my father to greet Richard, then a first grader, as he got off the school bus. They were running late, my father later told me. As my grandmother approached the drive to their farm in Rushville, Indiana, she spied the school bus—and something more.

My father would later recount that there is one sound that will never be erased from his memory, no matter what kind of dementia might eventually set in: the sound of my grandmother screaming with maternal intensity and urgency as she ran toward that bus, "Richard's hurt!"

Richard was getting off the school bus and crossing the road to reach the farm when a car driven by a prominent Rushville woman who lived in town failed to brake. Apparently in a hurry, she hit the gas and, in the process, killed an uncle I would never get to meet.

Studies have shown that the death of a child is the most stressful thing a married couple can ever expect to endure as a unit. And so it was with my grandparents. The death of Richard, a handsome boy with a mischievous grin, silenced the once-happy home and drove my grandmother into a deep state of depression she would wander into and out of—often for months at a time—for the remainder of her life.

More children would eventually come—two girls. But the sadness of Richard's loss remained. He was the son forever mourned, a ghost whose presence was forever felt. Richard's clothes and school books were cherished and saved. A kitchen window he'd broken with a baseball the week prior to his death was never replaced. Instead, the crack was taped over with Scotch tape, then retaped as the tape grew old. Decades later, I used to eye it curiously when I went to the house and helped to wash the dishes after a holiday meal, knowing even then that the window held some sort of special power over my grandparents and great-grandparents; that it was as sacred as any stained-glass window in any church. The cracked window would remain in place until well into the 1980s, some forty years after Richard's death.

When Richard died, he left a hole that would never be filled. And my father did what so many surviving children attempt to do: He worked to fill that hole at all costs. Even at the cost of denying his sexuality.

In later years, my father would tell me he always knew he was gay. As a small boy, he longed for the times when both parents were out of the house so that he could dress up in my grandmother's dresses, even putting on her faux pearls. And though he was tall—climbing to nearly six foot six—he preferred the world of theater and pageantry-filled operas to the Indiana basketball that other boys in his school embraced. But coming out during or shortly after his childhood would not only have been socially unacceptable—it also would have added to the anguish in the family home. My grandparents had already lost one son. Bearing witness to my father's coming out of the closet would have caused them to lose their lone surviving son, not to mention their reputation as a respectable family within a closed, conservative community.

So, my father said, he did the only thing he felt he could do at the time: "I wanted to become the man Richard would have been."

To that end, he developed into an affable young man. He earned good grades. He was popular in school. He won multiple blue ribbons showing cattle and chickens at the county fair. He took attractive girls to the prom and joined a fraternity at Purdue University, eventually moving into the Alpha Gamma Ro house and assuming positions of leadership within the campus Greek system. His secret—that big, dark, awful secret—was meticulously hidden.

No one knew of the secret world he was embracing, the one involving liaisons with other young men he would meet in the university library and who followed him home to various dorm rooms with a mixture of excitement and shame.

"One of the guys I met in the library forced himself on me. I liked it," he would later confess.

When Dale eventually met Anne, she stirred something in him: thoughts of his deceased brother.

"Your mother was exactly the kind of woman I thought Richard would marry," he later told me. "I felt like I needed to marry her because I felt like that's what Richard would have done."

He proceeded to tick through the reasons he felt certain Anne and Richard would have been a fine couple: "She was six years older than I was, which would have made her close to Richard's age. And she was kind and smart and down-to-earth."

The fact that my mother was a former nun seemed to only add intrigue to the picture. For years, my father had thought the priesthood might be his destiny. As an altar boy, he loved the drama of the Mass, the pageantry of the frocked priests. During the year he lived in Italy as part of an exchange program in college, he had spent time at the Vatican, reveling in its rich history and tradition. To Dale, the idea of the former nun marrying the almost-priest seemed oddly appropriate.

My mother, of course, knew nothing of my father's line of reasoning when she finally agreed to marry him. Nor did she know about the conversation my father had shared with a priest in the months leading up to their wedding day. Apparently feeling a bit guilty about the way in which he was misleading my mother, and questioning his decision, my father turned for help to a man of the cloth in a hushed conversation in a parish rectory.

"Father, I've become engaged to a Catholic woman. She's good. She's kind. And we're to be married in November."

"All sounds very well, my son," responded the priest. "Whatever is the problem?"

"I have thoughts, feelings, often about—" started my father.

"About?" asked the priest.

"About other men," my father at last confessed.

At this, the priest took a sharp breath.

"These things are normal. Natural."

My father, the priest assured him, was not gay. His solution: my father should marry my mother.

So Dale threw himself full force into his marriage to Anne.

Anne never knew of Dale's doubts or of his secret longings and desires. She knew that her parents were comfortable with him and she with his parents. She knew that with Dale at her side, she would officially be able to move past the long shadow that had been cast by Oldenburg. She would no longer be Anne the Former Nun. Now, she'd be Anne the Wife. Most significantly, Anne knew that with this very tall, sometimes charming farm-boy-turned-businessman, she might have a chance of starting the sort of family she'd always dreamed of having.

"I wanted to be a mother more than anything," my mom would tell me when I was a teenager. "I just knew that's what I was supposed to be."

But by agreeing to marry my father she effectively moved from one abusive relationship—the one she'd had with the convent—to another, more intense one.

Perhaps sensing the sad road she was heading down, Anne seated herself at her own wedding reception squarely between my father and Father Vincent. It's as if on what should have been one of the happiest days of her life, she was already reaching out for reassurance, a guiding hand who could manage to make right things that felt all wrong.

Looking at those wedding photos—at the somber expression on my mother's face, the sadness in those big brown eyes, as she ate her wedding dinner in that beautiful white dress—it was clear: serious Catholics though she and my father might have been, desperately well intentioned though they were, my parents' marriage never had a prayer.

Chapter 6

My First White Dress

Anne stood over the infant, her hands shaking. It was after nine o'clock, and Mass started in under an hour. They were running late. Dale hated to be late. Especially when his parents were in town. Bernice Daniels Pflum was a good woman, but nothing if not a perfectionist. She equated tardiness with cardinal sins as unseemly as unswept floors and undusted tabletops. They just had to be on time. Especially today.

The infant squirmed as Anne struggled to fasten the buttons on the back of the long white dress. The gown, nearly a century old, was growing yellow in spots. Dozens of Daniels and Pflum children had been poured into the gown in their first weeks of life. Some had not reached adulthood, but most had, including Dale.

"Anne, are you ready?" Dale called impatiently from his post at the foot of the stairs.

Anne bristled. If only her family were here. If only Mother and Daddy lived closer. They'd come after the baby was born, making the drive from Dunkirk to Wisconsin in the span of one very long day. Her mother had been so helpful, rocking the baby to sleep at night, helping her with the laundry. But they had to get back to Indiana. It was only Dale and his family who would be there to witness everything this morning.

Anne felt the familiar flutter in her stomach. The one that made her feel as if she were about to throw up or, at the very least, fly into a fit of dry heaves. But she willed herself to do what Father Vincent always told her to do. She took a deep breath, closed her eyes, and said a little prayer to St. Francis. She'd get through this. She had to. If not for her sake, then for the baby's. Today her infant daughter was going to be baptized. And not just baptized. But baptized in public. For the first time in the history of Beaver Dam's St. Peter's Church, a baby was going to be baptized during Mass. Public baptisms were all part of Vatican II. Babies had once been privately baptized after Mass, away from other parishioners; now they were brought into the light, welcomed to a community by priests who spoke English, not Latin. A new generation of Catholic children was emerging, a generation that would be seen and heard. And Mary Elizabeth was going to be part of that generation.

Anne smiled now at her newborn. Mary Elizabeth was such a pleasant baby. Anne still couldn't believe that she had a girl. Birthing Anthony two years ago had been a tremendous joy. He had been her first. But Mary Elizabeth's arrival was special in a different way. It symbolized the fruition of that vision she'd had all those years before at Oldenburg. She'd told the Blessed Virgin that should she have a daughter, she'd name her Mary in her honor. And here she was—Mary Elizabeth—the living, breathing, kicking fulfillment of the promise.

The doctors had classified Anne's pregnancy as high-risk. There'd been frequent visits to the top hospitals in Madison, an amniocentesis—a then relatively new procedure. They'd been fearful that the medication Anne had been taking for myasthenia gravis, that nervous condition that she'd first been diagnosed with at Oldenburg, would affect the fetus, render the baby physically or mentally handicapped. But they'd been wrong. Tipping the scale at nearly nine pounds, measuring nearly twenty-three inches, Mary Elizabeth had entered the world big and pink and extraordinarily healthy. She'd dwarfed the other babies in the ICU where she'd been placed while doctors ran tests to double-check her blood work.

Now, home for several weeks, the baby was faring better than her mother. Anne's hands continued to shake as she struggled to fasten the tiny mother-of-pearl buttons that lined the back of the christening gown. A residence filled with tension was something she'd grown used to during her years at Oldenburg. There, she'd feared the admonishment of the elder nuns. Here, at the two-story house in Beaver Dam, Wisconsin, she feared the admonishment of a force almost as scary as the sisters: Dale. Sometimes he was in a jovial mood. On good days, he laughed, smiled, might even hug her unprompted. But increasingly, he was on edge, unfurling explosive bouts of anger with little or no warning. A sink full of dirty dishes, towels that were hung crooked in the bathroom, even calling him "honey" or "sweetheart"—all were grounds for criticism or, worse, the pounding of fists, a raised voice, a flying coffee cup. She didn't know which was worse, when he was home or when he was away and unreachable for hours, even days at a time.

When they'd left Indianapolis last year, Dale had convinced her that the move to Wisconsin would be a good one. She'd been reluctant. She didn't want to leave her parents—not when they'd established such a wonderful system of weekly visits to Dunkirk, regular meals that felt, at last, relaxed and not forced. Dale had been insistent, promising her they'd settle into a warm community, grow closer as a family and as a couple. But twelve months later, their marriage was arguably more strained than it had ever been.

In his new capacity as a sales representative for Eli Lilly's animal pharmaceuticals, Dale was on the road several days a month. Sometimes he called when he got to the hotel at night. But other times he didn't, blaming dinners that started and finished late. Anne didn't know what to believe. She did know that she was determined to make this marriage work. She just had to.

She turned Mary Elizabeth from her little tummy to her back and smiled at the baby. The big beautiful newborn was a gift from God. Who would have thought back at Oldenburg that Sister Aurelia Mary would birth a baby as beautiful as this one?

"Anne!" barked the voice. "Anne!" it cried louder.

"Dale, we're coming!" cried Anne. The gagging started anew. This time it wasn't a false alarm. She felt the burn of vomit in her throat. Grabbing a diaper from Mary Elizabeth's changing table, she threw up into the Pamper.

"Please, God, please, St. Francis, please, Mother Mary," she whispered, struggling for air. "Please help me through this."

Taking Mary Elizabeth into her arms, she held the infant to her, trying to comfort herself as much as the child. "Please, Father in Heaven, help me through all of this."

The first white dress I wore in my life was the white gown I was baptized in the month after my October birth. It was a family heirloom—one of the few that I have on either side of my family of Western European immigrants. The gown was first worn by my father's maternal grandmother, Katie O'Connell. She was one of a dozen children born to Irish immigrants. Her parents, like so many, had sailed from County Cork in the late nineteenth century to escape from the ravages of the potato famine and from a poverty-stricken existence.

How my great-grandmother's family managed to scrape together the money to assemble the beautiful lace gown—long and white, rimmed with a lovely silk ribbon that tied at the front and extended down the length of the dress—I'm not sure. And how the gown came to be passed down to my great-grandmother and her sister Margaret rather than to their many other siblings, I perhaps will never know.

But I do know that the gown went on to be worn by all four of my great-grandmother's children, including my grandmother, and, in turn, by every single one of her grandchildren and great-grandchildren as well as a multitude of her nieces and nephews.

Legend has it that the gown was nearly destroyed twice, once by my father, who, at birth, tipped the scale at ten pounds and all but tore the fragile dress to shreds when he was squeezed into it in a manner befitting a sausage.

By my family's calculation, I was the sixtieth baby to wear the gown, in that first public christening at St. Peter's Church in downtown Beaver Dam, a rural burg in southeastern Wisconsin. Prior to my christening, babies at St. Peter's were typically baptized on weekend afternoons, away from the prying gazes of other parishioners.

But my parents wanted to have their baby publicly sworn into the Catholic fold. Funny that this couple who beamed so publicly in presenting their newborn daughter to both their parish and God were working feverishly to hide so much about the rest of their lives.

From the beginning, the marriage of Dale and Anne, my father says, was in horrific shape.

"I couldn't perform on the honeymoon," he told me. "I couldn't come close to performing."

My mother, who had taken a perverse pride in remaining a virgin for more than thirty years, even during the free love era of the 1960s, was devastated that her wedding night didn't go at all as she'd planned. Half naked, half dressed in the negligee she had carefully selected from the lingerie department of LS Ayres, she cried in the hotel room they shared in the quaint resort town of French Lick, Indiana.

"Is it me?" she asked her new husband, her tone desperate. "Did I do something wrong?"

Was it her lack of sexual experience that was ruining things? she wondered. She'd made out with boys in her days before Dale, necked and petted, but had never gone all the way. Maybe the "fast" girls had been the smart ones. Maybe they'd learned to master things in the backseats of cars and in the bedrooms of fraternity houses that she'd only read about.

"What can I do?" my mother asked, pleading for direction from my father.

My father, rather than come clean, grew angry. He yelled. He screamed. He pounded his fists. He hit walls. On more than one occasion during those first days of the honeymoon, my mother told me, he caused her to bolt for the safety of a locked bathroom.

Three days into the honeymoon, with the marriage still not consummated, my mother struggled to find a means of saving her flailing marriage. Her solution: "Why don't we visit Father Vincent?" Her tone, my father said, was bright, hopeful, as if it were perfectly normal for a blushing bride to want to visit a favorite priest in the middle of her honeymoon.

But Anne had her reasons. If her honeymoon had started out on a bleak note, Anne rationalized that it could end on a good one with the help of her longtime rock, Father Vincent. She couldn't turn to her parents in her hour of need. She could never discuss her sex life with her father, Al. And while most women would have turned to their mothers at a time like this, Anne feared that her mother, Aurelia, would never understand. If Aurelia had slapped her days after she left the convent, when she needed her most, what would she do with this bit of unspeakable information? No, Anne needed someone who would be there for her. That person had been Father Vincent for nearly a decade. If anyone would know what to say, what to do, it would be him.

Unable to come up with a better solution, Dale complied and packed the car. Together, they checked out of their honeymoon lodging and headed to Oldenburg, the site of my mother's wedding to Christ a decade before and, more recently, the site of her shameful departure.

Upon their arrival that evening, Father Vincent greeted my mother warmly, wrapping her into his arms in a giant bear hug. To Dale, he was more reserved, cautiously extending his hand with which to perform a perfunctory handshake.

Taking a seat behind his desk, narrowing his eyes, Father Vincent looked my father up and down. "So, Dale," he said. "What seems to be the problem?"

My father took a deep breath. "The marriage to Anne isn't working out," Dale said, his voice trembling.

"Why?" demanded Father Vincent, his tone one part concerned and one part angry. What in the world, wondered the priest, had his Annie gotten herself into when she married this man? Hadn't he warned her in those letters?

"I can't," Dale stammered. "I can't—"

"Can't what?" demanded Father Vincent. The priest kicked himself now. He should have been even more direct with Anne when he'd had a chance to talk her out of the marriage. She would have listened if he'd ordered her to run away.

"I can't perform," my father said, his voice barely above a whisper.

Surely, Dale thought, the statement would lead his new wife's beloved priest to begin the talk of annulment. Surely that was the rightful out for all of them.

But much to his surprise, Father Vincent did not bring up annulment.

"You mustn't give up so easily," Father Vincent commanded. "You must work to fix this."

"But the church is clear," my father stammered. "If we can't consummate the marriage, the marriage is invalid."

"And the church is also clear," countered Father Vincent, "that the man and wife should strive to save the marriage at all costs. You've not even been married a week. Are you really trying?"

At this, Father Vincent leaned across the desk and looked Dale squarely in the eye. "You made your vows to stand by Anne. The onus is on you to keep those vows and to save this marriage."

Father Vincent didn't like Dale. He had made that clear to Anne on numerous occasions. But a marriage was a marriage. It was a commitment. The church, the Bible, all were clear about this. His Annie, God bless her, had already failed at her marriage to Christ. He would do what he could to save her marriage to this man. Dale wasn't good enough for her, Father Vincent believed then, had always believed. But Anne had made her choice. The deed was done. Now it was time for Dale to step up to the plate.

Dale nodded, agreeing. He would work to save the marriage. He believed in the church. And if the church said he was in the wrong and needed to fix things, he would listen.

Anne, for her part, was committed to helping in any way she could. She knew that Father Vincent would come through for her. It was Father Vincent to the rescue yet again.

After a brief overnight stay and a teary goodbye—Anne again taking comfort in an enormous Father Vincent hug—Dale and Anne made their way out of the rectory and into their new life in Kalamazoo, Michigan, where my father was stationed as a sales representative for Eli Lilly and Company.

In Michigan, they quickly settled into life in a comfortable home. Dale did well as an Eli Lilly sales rep. Anne found work at Western Michigan University, working as a receptionist for a professor. They filled their evenings, making casserole dishes, shoveling snow-filled driveways, and dreading time alone in the bedroom. Indeed, the first months of marriage remained a sexual disaster.

My mother told me years later that she tried everything to seduce my father. She went to the beauty parlor frequently to have her hair set so that she would look like the pretty women she saw in magazines, who seemed to have no problem with men. She invested in new perfumes, fancy soaps. When it came to lingerie, she tried it all: lace, then velvet, then silk. Nothing seemed to work. Her husband was positively unexcitable.

It was not until her grandfather, devoted husband of Trudy, beloved father of Al, died that things began to turn around.

Back in Indianapolis on the night of the funeral, while attempting to comfort Anne, Dale was surprised at what he felt: aroused. He was even more surprised when his level of interest in intimacy increased instead of waning, as it had countless times before.

At last he was able to not only sustain the erection, but ejaculate and, at long last, consummate the marriage.

Dale was relieved. Anne was ecstatic. Her daily prayers had finally been answered.

"It was nice," my father would later recount. "For both of us. It was nicer than I'd ever thought it could be."

Dale's first time with a woman pointed the couple in a new direction. The marriage remained largely passionless—more a friendship than a romantic relationship, my father said—but now, once a week, Dale found a way to perform his husbandly duties. My mother longed for more—for the two and three and four times a week that the characters in her favorite romance novels enjoyed, and that women's magazines increasingly implied was "normal" for the lovemaking-loving sixties—but for now, once a week would do. That's all she needed, she hoped, to secure what she longed for more than anything else in the world: a baby.

Anne's wish came true shortly after their weekly lovemaking began. In March 1970, not long before my father learned he was to be transferred back to Eli Lilly's headquarters in Indianapolis, my mother discovered she was pregnant.

And on December 1, 1970, Anthony Richard Pflum entered the world.

My mother took to mothering like a duck to water. For her, the baby and the sleepless nights that came with him were far easier to navigate than marriage to my father. At least, she reasoned, the baby, even amidst his bouts of colic, truly wanted her. Anne quickly developed routines: morning baths; an hour devoted to watching the then new public television show for kids, *Sesame Street;* afternoon strolls around the neighborhood. On weekends, she visited her parents, sometimes taking the baby for overnight trips. During this time of new motherhood, she reconnected with other members of her family as well. She frequently dined with her aunts and uncles in Indianapolis. She flew to see her sister Patty in California. She paid a visit to her baby brother, Mike, who was now in school at Notre Dame.

Both sets of grandparents welcomed the baby with open arms. For Anne's mother, in particular, Anthony's arrival was a source of tremendous relief. Aurelia Diener had worried about Anne and Dale in those early days of the marriage. She'd fretted that the wan, worried look on Anne's face signaled that the union was over before it'd begun. She didn't know what she would do if Anne's marriage failed so soon after her departure from Oldenburg. Leaving the convent was one thing. But being a childless divorcée—particularly in a family so Catholic—what could Aurelia possibly come up with to tell family and friends? And what would she do if Anne moved back to the Pine Patch again? With Mike at Notre Dame, Aurelia was finally getting the alone time with Al she'd craved since she was a teenager. The last thing she needed was a depressed daughter back home. No, with the arrival of Anthony, Aurelia's fervent prayers for Anne and the well-being of Anne's marriage to Dale had been answered.

Of course, things were not all right with Anne and Dale. But they were right enough. The new baby smoothed things over in a way that nothing else could. In Anthony, they at last had a common goal. He gave them something to talk about, to laugh about, to uniformly fret about.

But for Dale, in particular, life continued to implode. The corporate life of Eli Lilly that he thought he could embrace quickly turned into a tension-filled nightmare. He loathed the growing pressure to host and take part in couples-themed dinner parties with his straight colleagues, who invited him for rounds of golf and encouraged him to look at ever-more-expensive houses in the desirable neighborhoods of Indianapolis.

"I didn't want any of it," my father later explained regarding what he called "corporate culture."

He wanted a life that was not his to live. A life unlike the one he increasingly felt he'd been forced into.

In 1971, in a bid to escape from the growing expectations of straight bosses and colleagues, Dale requested and was granted another transfer from Eli Lilly, this time to Wisconsin.

"Are you sure?" sobbed a devastated Anne. "Don't you like Indianapolis? I don't want to leave."

"I need to be away from corporate headquarters," he said with conviction.

"Can't you just look for another job here?" she asked. "Or maybe Cincinnati?"

She'd grown accustomed to, addicted to, weekly visits with her parents, particularly with her beloved father, whom she'd fallen even more deeply in love with since leaving Oldenburg. Now that he had more time and fewer children to worry about, her visits with him and her mother had been enjoyable, leisurely. They played cards, cooked up dinners of steak and breakfasts of eggs and sausage, attended Mass together. She was in heaven.

She was finally approaching the happiness that had eluded her for a lifetime. She had a home. Friends. A baby. The sex wasn't great. But surely, she told herself, that would come.

"No," Dale told Anne with conviction. "If you want me—if you want us—I have to get out of here."

Anne knew what he meant. If she wanted this marriage to survive, she had to do as he said. Just as she had been beholden to a Mother Superior, she was now beholden to Dale. And he'd made up his mind.

The transfer job to which Dale was assigned was as a regional sales representative for Elanco, an animal health division of Eli Lilly. The job was a perfect fit for Dale. It combined his rural upbringing—his understanding of and fundamental respect for farmers and farm animals—with his gift of gab and astute business mind.

After mulling over where to live for the better part of two months, my parents ultimately settled on Beaver Dam, a small town of fourteen thousand that rested in the heart of Dodge County, a rural county known for its many dairy farms, about an hour's drive from Madison.

My mother sobbed intermittently throughout the move. In all her life, she had never lived so far from her beloved Indiana. Even at the women's hotel in Cincinnati, even during her year with Dale in Michigan, she'd never lived more than two hours from the Indiana state line.

"It's not so far," Dale would tell her good-naturedly. "It's only Wisconsin."

But for Anne, it might as well have been Mars. When the sadness overcame her in those first weeks after he announced the move, she clung to Baby Anthony, stroked his soft tufts of blond hair and his chubby legs. Sad though she was, she'd made those vows to stand beside Dale. She'd pledged her devotion to him before God. Before her parents. Before her darling Father Vincent. She wasn't going to go back on her word now. If Wisconsin was what Dale wanted, then this was what God must want, too.

In the end, Dale and Anne settled on a two-story red house that sat on a full acre of land on the outskirts of Beaver Dam. It stood at the end of a street populated by a dozen other homes in a new subdivision called Sunrise Acres. Cornfields lined two sides of the yard. For my parents, the house's setting was a perfect blend of country and city living. My father saw in it the opportunity to start life anew.

And shortly after the move into the home, that opportunity seemed to multiply a hundredfold when my mother discovered she was pregnant with me.

From the moment she found out I was on the way, Anne threw herself with renewed gusto into the task of building a proper nest for her growing family in Beaver Dam. She became an active member of Beaver Dam's Newcomer's Club, volunteered to help lead the local chapter of the American Association of University Women (AAUW), encouraged my father to sign up for the Lions Club, where he went door-to-door selling oranges in a bid to raise money for the vision impaired. They attended Mass at St. Peter's, volunteered for weekly church gatherings. My father lectored at Mass. My mother oversaw bake sales and book sales. Together, they helped organize annual neighborhood picnics.

As my mother's belly grew, as the phone started ringing with more and more invitations from newfound friends to come to dinners at local supper clubs and barbecues in backyards, Dale was conflicted. On the one hand, he was relieved. The risk he had taken in moving the family hundreds of miles away from their home state and from both of their families had paid off. They were fast becoming pillars of a growing young community, where no one knew of his desire for men, or of how long it had taken them to become husband and wife in a biblical sense.

On the other hand, he was sadder and more desperate than he'd ever been. The wife and child and career and house that were supposed to make him happy and cure him of those impure thoughts and desires had failed. He was still miserable. If anything, he felt more trapped than ever.

It was around that time in August 1972—two months before Anne was due to give birth to me—that Dale spied the article: in the pages of *Time* magazine, he read the story detailing the burgeoning gay movement in the United States. Homosexual men, the article said, were increasingly finding friendship and much more in bathhouses in urban areas.

"I read the article again," my father told me. "And again and again and again."

There were no bathhouses in Beaver Dam, of course. But, he realized, there might be in some of the cities he visited on his business travels.

Shortly after reading the article, Eli Lilly sent him to Minneapolis for a business conference. On his first night there, Dale called my mother early in the evening, then set out on an adventure he would later call "life altering." His destination: the city's then infamous gay neighborhood.

"I was nervous at first," my father would later tell me. "But after a while, I somehow felt at home."

Stumbling upon a bar called the Gay 90's, Dale says he was immediately enthralled. Behind the large windows lay what appeared to be a wonderland: there was an ornate antique wooden bar, an old-school piano, and beautiful old lamps that, my father said, his antique-loving mother would have coveted.

"I knew I had to stay and have a drink," he told me.

Without another thought—without any fear of being spotted by colleagues—my father stepped inside and took a seat at the bar. Within five minutes, he'd ordered his first drink. Within a half hour, he'd made his first new friend. He and the man, someone my father described only as a "Minnesota native and nice looking," talked for the better part of an hour. They spoke about Minneapolis. About life.

The next night, after a day of business meetings, my father sprinted back to the Gay 90's for more. This time, he made a pair of friends with whom he ate dinner. Delighted to learn that Dale hailed from the hinterlands of Indiana and Wisconsin and was new to their world, they took him out barhopping that night to Minneapolis's finest gay bars. At night's end, Dale hesitantly asked about those bathhouses he'd read about in *Time* magazine.

"You don't know of any place like that here in the Twin Cities, do you?" he asked, half hesitantly, half hopefully.

"Do we ever!" They laughed and pointed him in the direction of Minneapolis's most famous bathhouse, located just down the alley, behind the Gay 90's bar Dale had been drawn to.

"It was like fate," Dale says.

He had a wife and one baby at home. He had another on the way. He was a born-and-bred Catholic who had long been lectured on the sins of a man thinking lustfully about another—particularly another man—when one was already very married to a very devoted wife. But none of that stopped Dale Pflum that night from marching confidently and knowingly down the alleyway to the bathhouse.

Dale spent more than an hour in that bathhouse. In the end, he says, he emerged a changed man. For decades, he had been struggling with who he was. Since college, he'd wondered if those brief liaisons with young men in university libraries and dorm rooms meant anything, if his interest in men was a passing phase or illness that, as that priest had suggested, could eventually be quashed. After that night in the Minneapolis bathhouse, there was no longer a question. His interest in men was there to stay. His interest in my mother, on the other hand, was what he realized had been temporary, passing, and ultimately a mistake.

My father returned from his business trip as he returned from most business trips: exhausted. Quiet. Preoccupied. My mother had grown used to the mood swings, had learned not to ask him too much about what was wrong or what he was thinking about.

Too much probing would draw him into a rage, which increasingly included the hurling of spoons and coffee cups and lit cigarettes, which he now consumed two packs at a time. No, especially at this late stage of pregnancy, Anne knew to tread lightly. There was a baby on the way. A kicking little creature that she hoped and prayed would unite them and make him want to stay home more often, not less.

Dale kept what happened in Minneapolis entirely to himself, concentrating instead on putting the final touches on the little nursery he and Anne were creating on the second floor of their new home. But as he wallpapered what would become my room, set up the crib, adjusted drapes at the bedroom window, his mind wandered back time and again to Minneapolis and to when he might be able to schedule another business trip there.

A few weeks after Dale's visit to the bathhouse—at 2:08 in the very early hours of October 25—I was born at St. Mary's Hospital in Madison, Wisconsin. It was a Catholic hospital, and it was a Catholic nun, Sister Mary Cloud, who served as the delivery room nurse that night, taking turns holding hands with my frantic mother and my nervous father.

My father was the first to hold me, wrapping me in his arms moments after my mother pushed me out. As he looked at me, he says, he breathed a tremendous sigh of relief.

"We had a boy. And with you," he told me, "we had a girl. We were done."

On paper, at least, they had the perfect family. There was no need for any more sex. And when the doctor announced that my delivery had wrecked my mother's already-fragile uterus and recommended a hysterectomy, my father breathed an even larger sigh of relief.

"I'd done my husbandly duty," he explained to me matter-of-factly. "I was finally off the hook."

Now all he had to do was raise that family. Put on a smiling face.

And a few weeks later, he did just that at St. Peter's for my very public baptism. There he was, in a nice suit, a new tie, standing proudly holding my brother as I squawked and squirmed in my baptismal gown for all the world to see.

"She's so gorgeous," the parishioners cooed to my mother as they gathered around to congratulate her after Mass.

"She's so long," they enthused to my father's parents, commenting upon my remarkable height for a newborn, a full two feet.

"Welcome to the community," the presiding priest, a stern man, said to my father, shaking his hand. He had been reluctant to do this whole public baptism thing, but had grudgingly warmed to the idea as he observed the positive reactions of the parish.

"Tell us," said members of the parish council to my parents, eager to welcome a new family to the parish fold, "is your move to Wisconsin all that you hoped it would be?"

My father was the first to answer this question. Looking at Anne and his new baby daughter, then thinking of his recent life-altering visit to Minneapolis, he took a breath.

"I'd say that the move has been all that I'd hoped for. And more."

Chapter 7

A First Communion in Beaver Dam

"Meow. Meeeeeowww."

I awoke on the morning of May 4, 1980, to the sound of my cat, Blackie, meowing outside my bedroom door. Straining to push the dirty-blond hair out of my face, I saw first the familiar pink of the ruffled bedspread that took up most of my twin bed. Then I spied the rocking chair situated beneath the room's sole window, piled high with my favorite dolls and stuffed animals. Finally, out of the corner of my eye, I saw It. My heart skipped a beat. It was even more beautiful than I'd remembered. This was no ordinary day. This was The Day. After waiting for a full year, at last the time had come to put on the white dress of my dreams—my First Communion dress.

Ever since Anthony's First Communion the May before, I had dreamed of this moment. All through that Mass, I'd studied not the priest, nor my own brother up there at the altar, but instead the dresses the girls in Anthony's First Communion class wore. I loved every single one of them. The ones with lace and the ones with silk. The ones with short sleeves and the ones with long sleeves. The dresses with long sashes and those with no sashes at all. The collection of those twenty-five white dresses was the most beautiful thing I had ever seen and I vowed that if I was fortunate enough to get my mother to buy me a white dress like the ones I saw on that altar, I'd never, ever take it off. Not even for a bath.

"Meow," Blackie persisted, pawing again at the door. "Meeeeee-owwwww."

Crawling down to the foot of the bed, where the twin bed met the door, I reached to turn the doorknob, enabling the cat to enter. Blackie meowed appreciatively before jumping up on the bed to join me. I hugged Blackie to me, pulling him onto my lap so that we could stare at It together. I blinked once, hard. Then a second time, harder. I wanted to make sure I wasn't dreaming. But when I blinked hard for the third time and still saw It when I opened my eyes, I knew the morning had really come.

Hanging from the dresser that stood between the bedroom door and my closet, the long-sleeved polyester-and-lace dress with its high square neckline and semitransparent sleeves was just as beautiful as I remembered. The sales tags still hung from the sleeves. Atop the dresser, in a small white plastic bag, was the simple lace veil, anchored by a hair comb covered in a trio of faux roses, that my mother had selected. And at the foot of the dresser rested the lily-white Mary Janes my mother had bought for me at Beaver Bootery, the best shoe store in town. Mom had repeatedly begged me to keep them clean prior to today. Twice I'd been busted trying to wear the shoes to attempt a Shirley Temple–inspired tap dance in the driveway with Kim, my best friend from next door.

"Mary Elizabeth, get those shoes back in the house right now or I'll ground you for a week!" Mom had screamed.

I had done as she asked, putting the shoes back in their box. But today the shoes were mine to wear as I pleased. And so was the veil. And best of all—so was that dress.

Everyone would see me wearing it. Pop and Grandma Pflum. And Great-Aunt Sis. And Dad's sisters, Mary Jo and Sue Ann. And lots of cousins. And Dad, of course. He was back. For now, at least.

He'd even slept at the house last night—the first time he had done so since Anthony's First Communion last year. It was strange to have him home. Nice in some ways, but hard in others. Never mind his mood swings. I'd grown pretty used to those. What I couldn't get accustomed

*to was Mom and her tears. He made her happy one moment and sad—
really sad—the next. One minute she'd be laughing, and the next she'd
be standing over the kitchen sink, looking out the window and staring
at something way off in the distance that always seemed to make her
cry. She'd cried a lot this past year. Besides the kitchen sink, her favorite
places to cry were downstairs in the basement, huddled over the ironing
board, usually with a can of spray starch in one hand and a wrinkled
shirt in the other, and on the phone when Aunt Kathy called to ask how
she was feeling.*

*But she cried in other places, too. Sometimes she even cried when
she drove. Whenever that happened, she always made up an excuse,
like that the sun was hurting her eyes, which worked. Except for when
the sun was behind a cloud, which it often was in Wisconsin, especially
in the wintertime. Still, Mom's tears aside, I was glad to have Dad
home. His visit and the visit of all the other relatives made the house
feel happy again. And clean. Cleaner than it had been in months. Mom
had picked lots of things up. Thrown away the newspapers that were
usually stacked up around the living room. Pulled the vacuum cleaner
and Windex out for the first time in months. She'd even mopped! I'd
forgotten what the mop looked like.*

*Even if Mom did cry today, even if Dad yelled or threw something,
which he liked to do when he was mad, I knew the day couldn't possibly
be ruined. There was just no way. Even if everyone cried and yelled,
I'd still be wearing The Dress. That really incredible white dress. And
today that's all that mattered.*

My childhood was not what I would call particularly happy. It
was largely confusing and lonely, and, as a rule, filled with
significantly more tears than laughter. But a day that was an exception to that rule was the one on which I made my First Communion.

Unlike my mother—who, owing to her days of climbing trees
and swimming in muddy ponds at the Pine Patch, considered

herself a bit of a tomboy—I was a girly girl. I had never met a dress I didn't love. From the time I was old enough to walk, I delighted in the swish of a dress's skirt, the tie of its sash. I spent hours wishing I had been born in another era, perhaps in the Deep South in the late 1800s or in Revolutionary America, when skirts and dresses were long and full and crinolines were a daily wardrobe requirement.

And I loved almost as much as my dresses the accessories that went with them: the patent leather shoes, the underwear with the frilly bottoms, the tights that I would carefully pull on.

My mother was at once impressed and confounded by my ultra-feminine tastes, which, she convinced herself for years, must be some sort of passing phase. She loved dressing me up on Sundays for our weekly trip to Mass. She helped me transform into fairy princesses and brides for episodes of Make Believe in my bedroom. But wearing Polly Flanders dresses in the sandbox, or up in the treehouse, or while engaging in a game of tug-of-war with the neighborhood boys, she would tell me, didn't make sense.

"Mary Elizabeth, you'll ruin your dress if you keep playing like that," she used to say. "Come and put on a t-shirt and shorts. You'll be more comfortable."

But I refused. Even then, I was a girl willing to sacrifice comfort for the sake of fashion.

For these girly-girl reasons, it came as a surprise to no one that I spent the first half of 1980 counting down the days to my First Communion, a day I could wear not just a dress, but a Really Great Dress. And not just for an hour or two, but for an entire day. For months, I had scoped out would-be dresses in Lads and Lassies, the finest children's clothing store in Beaver Dam. My mother took me once a week to the store so that she could peruse the sale racks that featured Garanimal sets and out-of-season dresses that might fit me the next year. I spent my time during those visits in the back of the store at the two racks laden with First Communion dresses.

Unlike the other clothing in Lads and Lassies, the First Communion dresses were covered with clear plastic garment bags, undoubtedly to ward off little girls like me, desperate to fondle the taffeta and lace. I must have spent hours looking at the dresses, studying their differences. There were long-sleeved dresses and short-sleeved dresses. Some had great big bows at the back. Some had lacy ribbons that tied at the collarbone. All were lovely.

Atop the racks of First Communion dresses was a series of boxes filled with First Communion crowns and veils. The boxes were sealed but had cellophane tops that allowed me to get an idea of the magic that lay within. At age seven I didn't know much about happiness, but I knew enough to know that its key must somehow lie within those boxes. How could anyone who wore a plastic crown upon her head, rimmed with artificial flowers, be anything other than euphoric?

My mother, serious Catholic though she remained, seemed oddly unenthusiastic about the notion of purchasing for me—her only daughter—a First Communion dress. Not once, not twice, but at least three times that I recall, a store clerk at Lads and Lassies approached my mother.

"Would your daughter like to try on some dresses today?" she'd ask my mother brightly, preparing to take me by the hand and show me to a dressing room.

But each time, my mother refused. "No, thank you."

Then she pried my little hands from the rack and announced it was time to go.

At the time, I thought her behavior mean. But now, of course, I know she wasn't being mean at all. She was trying to survive. Looking back, I realize if it had been up to her, she would have bought me the whole rack of dresses. If, that is, we could have afforded them.

While Aurelia Diener was often overwhelmed as a mother and emotionally unavailable, my mother was unfailingly warm and generous. It's as if, when Anne Diener became a mother, she took all the love and attention she had dreamed of receiving as a child—but never managed to get—and thrust it upon her own children. For as long as I can remember, she began and ended each day with hugs, kisses, and declarations of "I love you." She religiously took us on adventures: to the library, to the Dairy Queen, to community theaters, to the local parks. Her favorite was the city's oldest park, Swan Park. After taking me for a swim in the park's public pool, she'd walk me to the big band shell, where I would mount the stairs to perform a song or dance for her while she sat in the front row and clapped.

"Encore!" she'd cry as she rose to her feet, still clapping. "Encore!"

The magic would continue in the fall, her favorite season. After taking us to a local orchard for a round of caramel apples, she'd drive us to Swan Park in search of autumn leaves. When she found an open area sufficiently covered with red and yellow and brown leaves, she'd clap in delight. "It's time to kick some leaves!" she'd declare, then take us by the hands. Together, we'd kick the piles of leaves high into the air and watch them fall down again.

Anne Diener Pflum wanted desperately to be just as generous with money as she was with her spirit. Little things—like matinees at the local movie theater and Golden Books from the local bookstore—she could afford. But the bigger-ticket items—like dance classes or vacations or new furniture or those fancy First Communion dresses I dreamed about—were out of the question. The fact of the matter was that we were on an extremely tight budget and had been ever since my father left.

Dale Pflum had moved most of his things out of the house in Beaver Dam by the fall of 1979. He'd been steadily moving toward that point for some time. Even when my parents were still together, it seemed he was on the road more than he was home. Always, he would tell us, it was because of a sales meeting or a convention. Or because of a luncheon or a dinner speech he had to give. Sometimes it was because he had to entertain a group of farmers—would-be customers—at a Brewers or Packers game.

We saw him in between his sales trips, often in the home office he kept in the basement, just off the area where my brother and I used to play school, using a large chalkboard mounted to the wall and a pair of old desks my mother had procured at a rummage sale. Between our rounds of reading and writing, we would stop in to see him and watch him at work, huddled over his type-writer or green-and-yellow adding machine. Often, he smoked in his home office. Sometimes he ate. He had gained a consider-able amount of weight at this point in the marriage. His once-wiry frame had expanded so that he sported a potbelly. He'd also grown a mustache. We didn't care what he looked like. We were glad to have him home.

"Daddy, how long will you be here this time?" we used to ask as we begged him to come outside with us.

"For a while," he'd say.

And he would be. He'd stay long enough to toss a baseball around with my brother, put training wheels on my bike, build a campfire so that we could roast marshmallows in the backyard beside the swing set he'd erected.

We'd almost gotten accustomed to the pattern of business trips and homecomings when the hospitalizations started.

My father's hospitalizations began in the late 1970s, in the wake of a pair of suicide attempts. The first time my father tried to kill himself, he chose the winding roads that surrounded Lake Geneva, Wisconsin, home to one of the nation's longest-running Playboy Clubs, as a backdrop. He'd gotten to know the area during the business meetings he'd hosted at the club, meetings

in which he'd had to pretend to be interested in the buxom waitresses his colleagues ogled.

On the day of his would-be suicide, my father told me, he filled
a number of jugs and glass jars with gasoline and placed them in
the front and backseats of the car. Then he went for what he hoped
would be his final drive, hitting the gas pedal hard through some
of the area's sharpest turns.

"It was the perfect plan," he told me years later. "I thought I
was sure to crash on one of the turns. The force of the impact
would cause a spark and ignite the jugs of fuel and cause the car to
burst into flames. I would die in an instant."

But in the end, the plan failed. My father accelerated into a
number of sharp turns, in and around the dramatic hills. But the
car didn't spin out of control as he'd hoped, and ultimately never
crashed. Sometimes, he explained, it was because the car handled
better than he'd thought it would. Other times, it was because another car was coming and he didn't want to take out an additional
life in his bid to end his own.

Months later, he tried again with a different plan, this time on
a plot of land he'd bought outside of Beaver Dam shortly after I
was born. At the time of the purchase, my father had a fleeting
dream about moving all of us out to the land to start a working
farm. He would be Farmer, my mother would be the designated
Farmer's Wife, and my brother and I would be Dutiful and Happy
4-H Kids, in a slightly revamped and, he hoped, improved version
of his own childhood.

The property was picture-perfect. Situated high on a hill, it
boasted an apple orchard, a pair of old barns, and stunning views
of some of the most beautiful farmland in Dodge County. His
instinct was right. The setting would have made an idyllic home.
But we never moved to that land. Instead, as my father's inner
demons caught up with him, the property became a painful re-

minder of the man my father thought he was supposed to be but would never actually become.

"That farm became a symbol of my life at that time," my father said. "It was one unfulfilled dream after another."

After the Minneapolis visit and his foray into the world of bathhouses, my father had been unable to stay away from the gay lifestyle that now not only called to him, but, in fact, screamed his name. He increasingly sought out during business trips to Chicago and Minneapolis and Milwaukee the sorts of gay bars, bathhouses, roadside rest stops that gay men in situations like his—married and feeling trapped—used to gather in during the 1970s. When he frequented these venues, he did not introduce himself as Dale Pflum, husband of Anne, from Beaver Dam. Instead, he created for himself a whole new identity.

"I gave myself an entirely different name," my father explained. "I told everyone in those bars that I was Steve from Waupun, Wisconsin."

Dale's dalliances as Steve the Gay Man were temporary, he told himself, and meant nothing. They fulfilled a passing need, provided him with quick-fix Band-Aids to get him through the long days of his real life as Dale, the dutiful husband who still accompanied his wife and children to Mass and went door-to-door on weekends, selling oranges for the Lions Club.

At first, my father was all right with his dual life and got into a certain rhythm of denial then dalliance, denial then dalliance.

"Then," he told me, "I met someone."

That someone was a truck driver who had once been married and had a family. By the time my father met him, he was out and leading the gay lifestyle my father could only dream about.

"He was handsome," my father says. "He was sexy and charming. He seemed confident and daring. And I fell in love."

This was more than a dalliance, my father would later tell me. This was the partner with whom Dale wanted to share his life.

When Dale came home after a business trip to Anne, who was anxious to hug and kiss him and snuggle up to him in the comfort of their king-sized bed, his stomach turned. When he saw his new love, his heart skipped a beat.

The affair quickly became all-consuming, Dale working to get away from Beaver Dam as often as he could.

"Dale, what's wrong?" my mother asked, her voice increasingly high and pleading, when he came home late or shied away from even a peck on the cheek.

"Nothing," my father would snap.

"But there must be something. You're never home and we never . . ."

At this, her voice would trail off. She was trying to remind him that after I'd been born, they'd had sex only once. She'd begged, she'd pleaded, she'd attempted various ploys of seduction. But— nothing. No perfumes, no rounds of raw oysters, not even trips to Las Vegas, in the privacy of swanky hotel rooms, worked.

For more than three years, she went without sex. The strain took a toll on her physical appearance. Just as my father gained weight, so, too, did she, climbing from a size 10 to a 12 to a 14/16. If she couldn't take comfort in her husband's arms, then she'd take comfort in the cream-based soups and chowders and icing-laden sweet rolls she'd been deprived of for long stretches at a time at Oldenburg.

"I repeat, Anne," barked my father. "Nothing. Is. Wrong!"

And at this, he would reach to throw something—a plate, a jar, an ashtray filled with the ashes of the now nearly three packs of cigarettes he smoked a day. Sometimes he reached for larger things. Once, he threw a fire extinguisher. Another time, it was a clothes hamper. Sometimes the banging of his fists knocked a framed picture from the wall.

When my father lashed out, my brother and I retreated to an-other room. Sometimes we tried to focus on an evening episode of *The Electric Company* in the living room, turning up the volume so that it helped to drown out the yelling. Other times, we hid around the corner from the action, standing so that we could see the throwing without actually getting hit. We were both fascinated by and afraid of the rage in my father's face.

After each outburst, my mother would recoil, retreating to a bathroom or the laundry room, where she would cry. Sometimes my father would storm out and get into his company car and drive away. Other times, he would take a breath and carry on, as if life with a wife and children in Beaver Dam, Wisconsin, was swimming along in a normal fashion.

But caught up in his affair, Dale knew nothing in Beaver Dam would ever feel "normal" again. Now he was no longer content to live a lie.

"Let's run away together," Dale told his new love. They could be a couple, Dale told him. He'd figure out what to do about his marriage later.

To Dale's surprise, his new partner was resistant.

"Dale, you don't know what you're saying," he said. "Trust me. You're better off not being with me. If you stay with me, I promise you that you'll get hurt."

"It's okay," Dale said, half begging, half demanding. "I can handle it!"

For Dale, this was new, to be the one in the relationship pleading, instead of the one who was doing the pushing away.

"No," his love said with certainty, a shadow passing over his face. "No, I'm telling you, you can't. We can't. I'm nothing but trouble."

What my father didn't know at the time was that the man with whom he'd fallen in love had an affinity not only for rough sex, but also for violence. In later years, he would be arrested and sent to jail for severely hurting at least one sexual partner in an S and M stunt gone terribly wrong. He was pushing Dale away in a bid to save the father of two from his clutches. But at the time of their quasi-breakup, all Dale knew was that he'd seen a life he wanted more than his current life in Beaver Dam. More, for that matter, than life itself.

"If I couldn't have a life with him, I didn't want any life at all," he told me later.

And so one evening my father drove his Oldsmobile station wagon to that abandoned property that he'd bought south of Beaver Dam in the hopes of building a dream farm with my mother and raising a dream farm family, sad and desperate and resigned to end it all. With a heavy sigh, he turned on the ignition, made certain all the windows and the exhaust pipe were tightly sealed, and prepared to die.

"I had it so carefully planned," my father said. "I thought carbon monoxide poisoning was the way to go. I just couldn't live with myself anymore."

In the dark of his car, Dale clung to that steering wheel, said a prayer, and waited. The carbon monoxide slowly seeped into the body of the car. Initially, it did the trick. Within minutes, Dale lost consciousness, amidst thoughts and visions, he would later tell me, of his dead brother, Richard.

But then, unexpectedly, came what he has since called a miracle.

When he awoke, he wasn't dead. Instead, he was lying on the ground beside his still-running car, looking up at the sky.

"I don't know what happened," he told me later. "Everything was planned out."

Whether he awoke half conscious and instinctively worked to save himself—or whether he accidentally slumped onto the door handle in his state of unconsciousness and fell out of the car by chance—he doesn't know.

"I remember lying on that ground, on that gravel driveway. I was crying and angry and I said, 'Oh shit—I can't even manage to kill myself right,'" my father told me. "I felt like such a failure at everything. I lay there for the longest time."

Badly shaken, he eventually made his way home to my mother, pale, incoherent, and in tears. Slumped down in a chair in the kitchen, he haltingly told her enough to let her know she needed to get him to a hospital. Fast. Within minutes, she found a baby-sitter for me, then gathered up my brother for moral support.

My father lay in the backseat of the car, sobbing. My frightened brother sat in the front passenger seat. My mother took her place behind the wheel, entirely numb. Together, the three of them drove toward Madison.

"Mommy, what's wrong with Daddy?" my brother asked re-peatedly.

"Daddy's sad," my mother told him, her voice breaking. "We're taking Daddy someplace that will make him better."

The first time my father was committed to St. Mary's Hospital in Madison, it was for four weeks. The second time, it was for even longer. In between those stays came a hospitalization in Fond du Lac where my father grew so enraged with the hospital staff, he told me, that he broke entire pieces of furniture, including chairs.

Each time, my mother handled the hospitalizations flawlessly.

"Daddy's going to be in the hospital for a while," she explained to my brother and me, as if it were a common occurrence to have a father confined to a mental ward where nurses worked side by side with big, burly orderlies who doubled as bodyguards.

"Daddy's not feeling well," she'd continue. "We need to make him feel better."

Each day, for weeks at a time, my mother would wait until we were done with school and swim lessons, then load us into the back of our old beige VW with its rust streaks on the sides. As a threesome, we would make the hour-long trek to whatever hospital he was confined in at the time.

I remember parking the car, riding in the elevator, making our way down the hallway to the mental-health wing, where we would settle into the recreation room. My brother and I especially liked the waiting room in Madison. It featured a foosball table and an old-fashioned exercise bike that my brother and I would spend hours fighting over. My mother, unable to afford a babysitter, would disappear for an hour when we arrived, leaving my brother and me alone. Sometimes during our visits, my father would come out to join us. When he did, he often cried. The tears frightened us. "Why is Daddy crying?" I'd ask.

"He's crying because he loves you so much," my mother told me the first time.

"He crying because he's tired," she told me the second time.

"He's crying because his medicine makes him feel funny," she told me on a third occasion.

None of the answers, I knew, seemed right. I was relieved when we were in the car, heading home.

On the way back to Beaver Dam, my mother would work to make up for the strangeness of the visits by doing something decidedly normal. Sometimes, she took us to a shopping mall. Other times, we stopped at McDonald's for hamburgers or at local diners for milkshakes or tall glasses of chocolate milk. Oftentimes, we talked.

On one of those trips home from St. Mary's, we discussed at length *Little Women,* which I had read during all of that time spent in the hospital waiting room and had promptly fallen in love with. "Jo should have married Laurie and not the professor!" I cried, real tears rolling down my cheeks.

My mother smiled at the seriousness with which I had taken Louisa May Alcott's characters. "But she loved the professor," my mother protested.

"Who cares?" I cried. "Laurie loved Jo more!"

On another drive home, she told me about the many different colleges to which I could one day apply.

"But, Mommy," I protested, concerned. "I'm too little to go to college!"

"It's never too early to start thinking about the places you'll go," my mother said.

If Anne Diener Pflum had failed to see the world when she was young and had the chance, then she was determined to make certain that her daughter didn't make the same mistake.

Without question, a sexless, virtually husbandless marriage in Beaver Dam, Wisconsin, was not the life she had bargained for when she agreed to marry Dale Pflum. She wasn't angry. She wasn't bitter. She was sad. Horribly sad. And she was in need of answers.

Chief among them: Who was her husband seeing?

If Dale wasn't having sex with her, Anne reasoned, he must be having it with another woman. But who? she wondered. Was it an old flame from his undergraduate days at Purdue? Maybe someone from Beaver Dam they'd met in the Newcomer's Club? Perhaps it was one of the bunnies who'd waited on him at one of his meetings at the Playboy Club?

The not knowing was exhausting. Worse, it was lonely. Anne wanted to turn to someone during these emotionally draining times. The trouble was, in her new home of Wisconsin, she had few, if any, options.

Her parents remained at the Pine Patch, eight hours away by car. Even if they had lived closer, it would have been difficult for them to be of much help to Anne physically, owing to Aurelia's deteriorating heart and worsening arthritis. And even if her parents could have been there for her physically, Anne knew it would be next to impossible for Aurelia, in particular, to be there for her emotionally. Aurelia Diener had overcome tragedy in her life: a deaf father, a poverty-stricken childhood, multiple miscarriages, the death of a child. But she'd never had marital difficulties. Not like Anne's, anyway. Aurelia had never had a problem getting her husband to have sex with her. If anything, her six children and her dozen-plus pregnancies were evidence that Aurelia had difficulty keeping her husband away from her. Anne would have killed for such a problem.

"There are things your grandmother just was never able to understand," my mother told me years later. "It's not that she didn't want to. It's just that she wasn't able to."

Anne was able to count on her sister Kathy for some moral support. During Dale's hospitalizations, the sisters regularly chatted by phone. But with Kathy living in Colorado, there was only so much she could do.

And while my mother longed to confide in a girlfriend, her Wisconsin pickings were extraordinarily slim. The women she'd met at church and in the Newcomer's Club all seemed and acted so happily married. She didn't know who, if anyone, would understand her sexless marriage or Dale's multiple suicide attempts— and, moreover, who would honor a request to keep anything she confided a secret. It hadn't taken Anne long to discover that in Beaver Dam, as in so many small towns, women loved to gossip. She needed a sympathetic ear, but she most certainly did not need the details of Dale's hospitalizations to fall into the wrong hands.

No, Anne came to realize, it wouldn't be her parents or siblings or new friends who would sustain her during this crisis. Instead, it would be the loves of her life: her two small children.

She couldn't confide in my brother and me, of course, couldn't ask us for advice, the way she could a trusted adult. But she could hug us to her and know we'd hug her back. She could greet me with a warm declaration of "I love you" and know, with certainty, that I'd return her greeting with an "I love you more!"

As her dreams of a happy marriage imploded, she drew strength from the very act of caring for my brother and me: making our peanut butter and jelly sandwiches, snuggling with us as we watched an episode of *Sesame Street*. She fed off our love—our need—of her. To us, she more than mattered. To us, she was the whole world. And at a time when she questioned when, or if, her husband had ever really wanted her, that did more to bolster her mood and sense of purpose in the world than any medicine or self-help book possibly could have.

It's at this time that our family unit of three was cemented. Together, without my father, my mother, brother, and I learned to care for our great big yard. My mother mowed the lawn and over-saw her beloved flower beds, just as her mother and Trudy had taught her to do so many years before. My brother raked. I helped with the trim work. Together, snuggled on her lap, we read bed-time stories as a unit every night: three books for Anthony, three books for me. And together, as a threesome, we went to church.

Every Sunday, without fail, my mother took my brother and me to the ten fifteen Mass at St. Peter's. Week after week, we sat in the front pew, my mother hunched over the kneeler, pray-ing mightily for an explanation as to what was wrong—really wrong—with her husband.

Eventually, after more than a year of hospitalizations, the truth came out at a joint session between both of my parents and a pre-siding psychiatrist at St. Mary's Hospital.

In a cramped doctor's office—in which, my mother would later recall, there was a brown and nearly dead spider plant that with-ered depressingly in an old green pot—my father came clean.

"Anne," he said, sobbing and looking to his nodding psychia-trist for reassurance. "Anne, I'm gay."

My mother sat stunned for a moment, then surprised him with an audible gasp of relief.

"Thank God," she said, her voice barely above a whisper.

"What?" Dale asked, incredulous.

"All I've been praying for all this time is an explanation. Now at last we know what we're dealing with."

The sessions continued, now with greater progress. My mother was devastated, but resigned and, increasingly, supportive. She drew strength from her belief in God and the teachings of St. Francis to be accepting of others for who they are, not for who she wanted them to be.

Still, Anne didn't know what any of this meant for her or her marriage. One psychiatrist talked to her about the possibility of sending Dale to Canada to take part in a program that claimed to "cure" gay husbands. But my mother wouldn't hear of it.

"I didn't like that your father was gay," she told me years later. "But I knew it wasn't his fault. How could I hate him for something he was born with?"

"Besides," she added, "how could I hate him when he already hated himself so much?"

My mother's compassion surprised Dale's lead psychiatrist in Madison, who was accustomed to wives reacting with a mixture of anger and bitterness when their husbands came out. My mother didn't have it in her to be bitter. If anything, she blamed herself.

My mother's compassion undid my father, who had expected—perhaps even secretly hoped for—a demand for a divorce. But no such demand came. At least not from Anne.

"Dale, what are you going to do?" the psychiatrist asked at one joint meeting not long after my father had come out. "Seems to me Anne is putting the ball in your court."

"I can't—I can't accept who I am," Dale said, beginning to cry.

At this, my mother shook her head and looked my father squarely in the eyes.

"If I can accept it, why can't you?"

My father, surprised, looked from the psychiatrist to my mother, then back again.

"Anne," said the psychiatrist, "why don't you repeat that in case Dale didn't hear it the first time?"

She licked her lips, then took a breath. "If I can accept who you are, then why can't you?"

"I'll never forget those words as long as I live," my father told me more than thirty years after the session.

Crying, he said, "It's the kindest thing anyone has ever said to me, the nicest thing anyone will ever say to me."

Several months after the breakthrough session, after my father had been discharged from St. Mary's for a second time, he made the decision to move out of the house.

I remember the truck pulling up in the driveway and several men, all of whom introduced themselves to my brother and me as "friends" of my father, getting out and proceeding to remove my father's belongings from the house. My brother and I gathered in the front yard with our best childhood friends, Kim and Kevin Swanberg, who lived next door. We crouched behind my mother's VW in the driveway and watched the strange men with their strange tank tops and mustaches load up the truck. The men, including my father, seemed happy and convivial, as if a party, or at least a round of beers, awaited.

My mother made herself scarce, still torn between being the supportive, Christlike creature she felt like she was morally obligated to be and playing the part of a normal woman, angry at the mess her husband had made of all of our lives. When she was around, she looked terribly sad, her face a sickly white.

Watching two of the men struggle to put my father's desk into the truck, Kim turned to me and asked, "Isn't your father going to live with you anymore?"

I shrugged my shoulders. The truth of the matter was, after all of those hospitalizations and business trips, I didn't know if my father was coming or going. I only knew that I didn't like the strange men or how they made my mother feel. When they eventually pulled out of the driveway, smiling, laughing, and waving, I was filled with the strange mixture of sadness and relief that I would feel for years at the close of visits with my father.

When my father left, he took his closet full of clothes, the old adding machine, and a smattering of records and pictures and rocking chairs and books. He also took with him a source of steady income for the family. He sent money each month, but much of his paycheck was now eaten up by his new expenses: his new apartment, new furniture, new bedding, and his growing interest in antiques. My mother, who had stopped working after my brother was born nearly a decade before, tried to make ends meet by reentering the workforce as a teacher's aide at a local public elementary school.

Her meager paychecks helped, but our bills were significant. She couldn't afford, for example, a babysitter. My brother and I would get off the school bus, armed with a house key with which to unlock the door to our empty house. Usually, we were left to fend for ourselves for only two hours. But on nights when she went to night school, we were alone until as late as ten o'clock and were charged with making our own meals and putting ourselves to bed.

Childcare was just one expense we couldn't afford. Our new family unit of three started cutting back on all kinds of things: birthday parties, swim lessons, even the heat.

"Do you see this circle on the wall, Mary?" my mother asked me one day after she got home from work. She was pointing at the house thermostat, which was located in our dining room.

"Yes," I said, nodding.

"This is never to be touched. This little pointer is never to be turned to anything higher than fifty-eight."

I was in the second grade. I had no concept of how heat bills worked. I barely understood the concept of degrees.

"Fifty-eight," she repeated. "Understand?"

I nodded. I knew she meant business. And our heat remained fixed at an often uncomfortably cold fifty-eight for years.

For me, the lack of heat was nothing compared to my mother's unwillingness to invest in items I deemed second-grade luxuries: tickets to Holiday on Ice, boxes of Frosted Flakes instead of the generic flakes that came housed in those awful black-and-white packages, and, of course, coveted First Communion dresses.

"Don't worry," my mother told me reassuringly in mid-April 1980, "we'll get you a dress."

"When?" I demanded.

"Soon."

"How soon?"

In the end, it was my father who bought me my First Communion dress.

He came into the house one day without calling my mother in advance—which he often did in that period of time after he had moved out, but before my parents were formally divorced—with a bag containing three different First Communion dresses: two short-sleeved and one long-sleeved.

It was ten days before the big event. I don't know where the dresses had been purchased, but I do know that they didn't come from Lads and Lassies. They were housed in a bag that bore an unfamiliar logo, likely from a store in Appleton, where my father had moved to begin his life in earnest with his growing circle of new friends.

"Here. Go try these on," he said.

Eyeing the contents of the bag, I was too stunned to speak. I opened my mouth to cry out, but no sound emerged.

Every little girl has her day. And at last mine had come. My mother hadn't been able to afford to take me to the store. Instead, she'd called my father. And he and his credit cards had brought the store to me.

Wordlessly, I ran upstairs with the dresses. I tried on the two short-sleeved dresses first, little frothy confections that poofed at the sleeve and flounced in the skirts. As soon as each dress was on, I flew back down to the kitchen, where my parents waited.

My father sat at the table. My mother alternated between standing in the kitchen doorway and over by the stove, uncomfortable in her own home, as she often was in my father's presence after his departure. My father smiled as I spun around for him on the linoleum floor, pleased to be Daddy Warbucks for the day. My mother was far more somber. She eyed each dress carefully, looking me up, then down, then up again, before instructing me to turn around so that she could repeat the process. She felt the fabric of each dress, examined the hems.

With shakes of the head, my mother ruled out the first two dresses.

"No, not these."

"But why?" I asked, in search of an explanation after she'd vetoed the second dress. The truth of the matter was I didn't like the first two dresses that much either. But there was only one dress left to try on, and I was starting to panic that my mother was going to say no to all the dresses.

"Mary, you have to understand," my mother said, moving from her position near the stove and sitting down at last at the table. She pulled me to her.

"This is not going to be just any dress. This is going to be your First Communion dress. It needs to be . . ."

"Perfect?" I asked.

"No," said my mother. "Special. It's a very special occasion so it's got to be a very special dress. White dresses are always special."

I turned my head sideways, the way I did when I was pleasantly confused.

"White dresses are often what we wear for special ceremonies," my mother explained.

"Or to look pretty," I added.

"Yes, to look pretty," my mother agreed, and laughed. "Or to start over. For the church, white is great for beginnings. The beginning of your life as a Christian."

"Or as a wife," I said.

"Yes," my mother said. She looked both sad and surprised, as if someone had pelted her in the face with an icy snowball she hadn't seen coming. She exchanged a quick glance with my father before continuing.

"Sometimes," my mother went on, "I think of white dresses as a way of starting over. They're sort of a way of wiping the whole slate clean. Just like what happens in the wintertime when the snow comes. It wipes away everything in preparation for a new year, a new spring.

"So for your First Communion, we want the right dress as a way of helping you make the right start. It should be simple. It should be elegant. It should be a dress that you wear—not a dress that wears you."

She looked at me. I looked at her. When I really looked at her, I was often torn between looking into her deep brown eyes, or at her teeth, which I'd always found fascinating. My mother had a slight underbite, which her orthodontist in Dunkirk had never managed to fix, so her bottom teeth, packed tightly together in a haphazard fashion, jutted out slightly past her upper teeth.

"Okay?" my mother asked.

"Okay," I said, still staring at her crooked teeth. I ran back upstairs to try on Dress Number Three.

After sliding the dress over my head and reaching behind me to zip up the back, I studied myself in the mirror. I liked what I saw. It featured long semitransparent sleeves that puffed only slightly before narrowing with a trio of buttons at each wrist. The neckline was high. The bodice was all lace. At the waist, there was a long satin sash that tied in the back. It was more conservative than I would have liked—certainly more conservative than most of the dresses that I'd been eyeing in Lads and Lassies. But it was a fairy princess dress all right. And when I saw my mother give me a small smile and a nod of approval from her post back at the stove, I knew it was something even better: it was mine.

"Oh, thank you, Mom. Thank you!"

My father had made the purchase, but it was my mother I hugged.

I hugged her because I wanted her to smile. I squeezed her tight because I wanted her to share in the moment.

"Oh, Mom," I said, stepping back from her and spinning around in my dress on one tiptoe, "it's going to be the best day ever!"

And it was. The weekend of my First Communion was breathtakingly beautiful. After a long Wisconsin winter, replete with ten-foot snowdrifts and subzero conditions, spring had finally come. So warm was the weekend that the red and yellow tulips my mother had carefully planted the previous fall in front of the house had burst into bloom for the first time. More than the weather, however, what I remember most about that First Communion weekend was the joy of having a relatively clean house full of people and full of laughter. After my father's departure, the four-bedroom home had felt big and empty and increasingly messy. My mother had done what she could to hold things together. But her work schedule, combined with her growing depression, prevented her from being able to expend much energy on making our house a home. The vacuum was put away and stayed away. The bottles of Windex, the cans of Pledge, all of those cleaning supplies that she'd used when my father was home on a weekly basis disappeared. In their place came piles of clutter, dust, hair balls from Blackie, the stray cat we'd adopted when my father left. And the clutter wasn't temporary. It sat untouched for days, often weeks.

But now, just in time for my First Communion weekend, the

clutter was gone. In honor of the houseful of visiting relatives—
and my father's homecoming—my mother had cleaned. The
house shone as it hadn't in months, smelling of Windex and Fan-
tastik and Pledge once more. My father's parents had made the
drive up from Indiana, as had both of his sisters; my mother's baby
brother, Mike; and a pack of cousins. Also present was my beloved Great-Aunt Sis, my father's aunt. She wore nice lipstick and
sweet-smelling perfume and she always came armed with that
most magical of instruments: a Polaroid camera. When my cousins and I were good, she used to allow us to help aim the camera
at one another and then sit for what felt like hours, watching the
magic unfold as the piece of film that was spit from the camera
turned from cloudy to a clear picture of delight.

Sis spent the weekend allowing me to help her make a photo
essay of my moment in the First Communion sun. There was a
photo of me in my white dress standing in front of the tulips.
There was a pair of photos of me attempting to vamp for the
camera, my hair tossed behind my shoulder, my eyes trying to
channel the dramatic looks I'd seen the *Charlie's Angels* actresses
sport on *People* magazine covers. And there was a photo of me
with my hair neatly pulled back into a pair of pigtails, made possible by my mother's limited but sufficient hairstyling skills.

There were nearly fifty of us making our First Communion
that day. We were to be presented to the parish as a group. And
as the tallest girl in the class, I was given the honor of being the
last to enter St. Peter's. Some seven-year-olds would have viewed
this as unfair. I had a flair for drama even then and reasoned that
walking in last would enable me to make the grandest entrance
of all. Perhaps, I thought, they were saving the best First Communion dress for last.

I don't remember much about receiving that First Communion
wafer that day. What I remember most is how proud I was to have

two and a half entire pews of family there to see me accept that wafer.

At home after Mass, I kept my First Communion dress on as we tucked into a family luncheon in the formal dining room that hadn't been used since my brother's First Communion the year before.

I sat proudly at the head of the dining room table, chatting with relatives, admiring the big sheet cake that featured a cross and the lettering HAPPY FIRST COMMUNION MARY! and eyeing the small mountain of First Communion presents that my mother had spread out on the buffet.

I received several stuffed animals, including a koala; a little set of Hello Kitty colored pencils that had a snap clasp and a carry strap; and some new stationery.

"Open this one next," said Great-Grandma Daniels, my father's grandmother. She pushed in my direction a large lavender envelope.

Inside was a yellowing lace-trimmed handkerchief that bore an intricate embroidered pattern. I fingered it gently.

"This handkerchief was made and carried by my mother, your great-great-grandmother," my great-grandmother explained, referring to the Irish woman I'd only seen photos of, a sweet-faced, white-haired creature with an apron forever tied around her waist. "It's one of only a few things that we have of hers. I want you to have it."

The sight of the handkerchief prompted an audible gasp from my father.

"That's very special, Mary. Someday you can pass it on to your own daughter."

He reached to gently stroke the handkerchief.

"You know, Mary, it's so special that if you'd like I can look after it for you—maybe take it with me—"

"That won't be necessary," interrupted my mother.

She'd been watching the scene unfold from the door of the dining room and narrowed her eyes as she flashed an indignant look at my father.

My mother had a cordial relationship with my father's family, but since news of my father's sexuality had spread, several relatives, notably members of the older generation, had come to believe Dale wouldn't be gay, or at least as gay, if it weren't for Anne. If Anne had been different, they theorized, my father would be happy, my father wouldn't be trying to kill himself at every turn. If Anne were different, they speculated, my father would almost certainly be straight. Several stopped speaking to my mother. All but two stopped giving her Christmas presents. It was made clear to her that, in the eyes of many, she was no longer an accepted member of the family.

The idea now that my father was suggesting to his relatives that she couldn't so much as keep track of a handkerchief rankled my mother.

"The handkerchief was given to Mary and it will stay here in the house with Mary," my mother said, locking eyes with my father.

I shifted uncomfortably in my chair, then nodded awkwardly. I would keep it safe.

As it turned out, the handkerchief did not remain safe. Those moments of gift opening were the last time any of us ever saw it. My mother would later explain to my irate father that the handkerchief must have inadvertently gotten caught up in the debris of ripped gift wrap and dirty paper napkins that littered the table and mistakenly made its way into a Hefty trash bag.

He didn't buy it.

"Did you throw the thing out on purpose?" my father screamed when he found out, his face turning red as it did when he was at his most infuriated. "Or did you lose it under one of your piles, one of your mountains, of shit, Anne?!

"You can't keep track of anything in this mess of a house!" he yelled. "This wouldn't happen if you knew how to clean!"

The explosive fight—my mother's pleading and crying—would come later. But on that First Communion Sunday, my mind was not on my parents or even on that handkerchief. It was on my dress. My perfect white dress. I wore that dress from dawn to dusk, even went for a bike ride in it in the late afternoon to show it to Kim, who was Lutheran and intrigued by the pomp and circumstance of the Catholic tradition. It must have been a vision, that white, white dress and that white, white veil, making their way down the street atop a banana-yellow Huffy bicycle my father had bought at the local Shopko and assembled for me two summers before.

I was princess for a day. I had the dress to prove it. It was the last truly happy day of my childhood.

Chapter 8

Daisy Buchanan Graduates

Taking a deep breath, I removed the white dress from the hanger. Then, taking a seat on my bed, still covered with the pink ruffled bedspread that had adorned it since I was four, I began the task of unfastening the buttons that lined the back of the garment—all eight of them.

"Mary!" called a voice from the foot of the stairs. "Mary Elizabeth, are you ready? We're late!"

I didn't know which to do first: sigh or roll my eyes. So I did my best to do both simultaneously. Of all the things Mom had to worry about, why oh why did she fixate on what she liked to call my "perpetual tardiness"? There were a million more important things she could be doing right now: straightening her own hair, straightening her own dress, straightening her whole damn house, but no, these days my mother was exclusively obsessed with how long it took me to get ready. She'd been this way for years, but especially since Anthony left for college.

In some ways, Mom and I, living as just a party of two, were tighter than ever. We dined together every night, sometimes hunkering down to watch China Beach *and* Cheers *and reruns of* Family Ties *when my homework load wasn't too overwhelming. On weekends, we'd go to the library or a movie together—when, that is, I wasn't busy with some school activity. But all that together time wasn't necessarily a good thing. Often we were at odds. Now my every move—how long I took to shower, how much time I took* to curl my hair, how many minutes passed while I dressed for Sunday Mass—was the object of never-ending scrutiny and criticism.

"Mary!" she called again, louder this time.

"I'm. Coming!" I yelled in a halting response. "It's my graduation, remember?"

I rolled my eyes again. It would be great if my mother would remember, for just a moment, that I was not only graduating from high school, but also graduating number one in my class. For most parents, the feat would be cause for celebration. For Anne Diener Pflum, it was not. It was cause, instead, for a lecture:

"Just remember, Mary, life is not about grades. It's about how kind you are to others. It's about how good and generous you can be. It's about being humble. Humility is what would make me proud right now. Can you show me your humility?"

Sometimes it was hard to believe that Mom used to be a nun. Like when she mowed the lawn all by herself in that old pair of blue jeans and sat down afterward beneath the honey locust tree to knock back a can of beer. Or when she talked about the big crushes she had on Hollywood actors, Paul Newman chief among them.

But other times, like now, when she was freaking out about being late and when she was making a big deal about me just wanting to look nice, Mom's former life as a sister became glaringly obvious. She may have left the convent years before, but the convent had never fully left her. Who, other than a recovering nun, would value humility more than her daughter's perfect 4.0 grade point average, and punctuality more than the ability to make a fashion statement? Other mothers would have been bragging about a valedictorian daughter who neither smoked nor drank. Not my mom. She believed boasting about me would only make others feel bad. And always always always we had to put the feelings of others ahead of our own. We had to be humble. If it was Christ's way, or St. Francis's way, then—according to my mother—it had to be our way, too.

Stepping into the dress now, first with my left foot, then with my

right, I returned to my happy place. My "Woo-hoo! I'm about to graduate from high school!!" place. The stiff white frock was just as pretty as
I remembered. In fact, it was even prettier than when I'd first seen it,
back in April. Short-sleeved, it featured a square neckline and a bodice
of rich Belgian lace that swirled in a pretty pattern that resembled a
snowflake. My favorite part about the dress was its lower half, specifically the cut of the pencil skirt. It came down just past my knees and
featured a series of long white starchy pleats.

I loved the dress. It screamed Gatsby to me—as in The Great
Gatsby. I'd read and reread the book throughout high school, longing
for the book to swallow me whole into its pages so that I could become
Gatsby's neighbor or, better yet, his muse. In my mind, the dress was
something Daisy Buchanan might wear, sprawled out on an enormous
white couch, recovering from one party the night before, preparing for
another one later in the day.

Looking at my reflection in the full-length mirror on the back of my
bedroom door, I was reminded of the power of a perfect white dress:
its ability to wipe a slate clean. In this case, the dress almost—yes,
almost—managed to erase from my mind all those yucky memories from
the weekend. Of the huge mess that spanned all three floors of the house.

The dress was so pure. If only life could be as unblemished. How
delicious that would be—to feel as perfect on the inside as this dress appeared on the outside.

Today, hopefully, the dress would do the trick and no one would remember the imperfection that was Sunday. With any luck, they'd only
focus upon the dress that was as picture-perfect as that 4.0 grade point
average that had earned me the valedictorian title.

"For the last time, Mary Elizabeth!" Mom cried. "Are you coming
or not?"

I didn't answer her. Instead, I opened the door, reached for the
manila folder that held the remarks I'd written in preparation for my
role as tonight's mistress of ceremonies, and exited the bedroom. For
Daisy Buchanan, it was showtime.

The dress I wore the day I graduated from high school was purchased from the nicest department store within an hour's drive of Beaver Dam: the Boston Store in Madison's East Towne Mall. I found it in the junior department where I had made some of the more important purchases of my young life, including my prized collection of Esprit and Guess sweatshirts and the skirt and blouse I'd worn for my senior class portrait.

When I saw the starchy white dress with that slim pleated skirt, it was love at first sight. And I knew, as I stepped out of the dressing room, that my mother approved of the look as well.

Seated on a stool in front of a three-way mirror, she motioned for me to turn. She felt the fabric. And she nodded, just the way she had ten years before when I'd tried on my First Communion dress.

"Do you like it?" she asked.

"I love it!"

"Are you going to promise me you'll wear it?"

"What else am I going to wear for graduation?" I laughed.

"Then it's yours," she said, digging into her wallet for the fading Boston Store credit card that saw more action than any of her other plastic.

Money was still tight in our house in 1990. But my mother's teaching position at the Slinger-Allenton School District—a fifty-mile drive from Beaver Dam—had established a source of financial stability for my brother and me. The ramp up had been long. For a time after my father left, our household income was so low we were eating government-subsidized food. But bit by bit my mother climbed out of the financial pit, far enough, anyway, to allow for the occasional splurge like a glamorous white dress. It was the perfect piece of apparel for my big night. I wasn't just graduating from high school. I was graduating number one in my class of more than two hundred—and was charged with sitting on the stage and making a speech.

For my entire high school career, my eyes had been firmly fixed upon commencement. I wanted to get to college just as fast as I could. College, I told myself, was where I would read all of those deep and complicated books and take all of those amazing writing classes I had long fantasized about. College was where I would find those sophisticated friends who liked to sit up late at night in dorm lounges and dimly lit cafés, discussing life, death, hopes, and the sort of weighty dreams that involved international travel and world peace. And college was where I was certain I would find that first boyfriend—maybe even a future husband.

I had accomplished many things in high school. I was the editor of the school newspaper and a science fair champion. I was an accomplished first-chair clarinetist in both the band and the full orchestra. And like my mother and grandmother before me, I was fast becoming an accomplished writer. I wrote plays that were performed for the school and the community. I won writing contests and received scholarships to a host of colleges. I excelled at almost everything I set my sights upon. Except boys.

"I am never going to have a boyfriend," I fretted to my mother one night as I sat writing copy for a press release for the junior prom I wasn't going to attend. My classmates didn't care that I didn't have a date to the dance. They knew I could write and had tapped me to serve on the prom committee's PR team.

Frustrated, I threw down my pen and paper. "I might as well go and join the convent now."

My mother's time in the convent, unearthed when Kim and I found those old photos when I was still in elementary school, had slowly but surely evolved into a topic of conversation, sometimes even into a lighthearted joke, between my mother and me.

"I wouldn't recommend that," my mother said, putting down the newspaper that she'd been buried in a moment before.

"Why not?"

"Because you like clothes too much."

I had to laugh. It was true. But a moment after the laughter began, it was done and I was back on point.

"I'm serious, Mom. I'm going to die alone."

She grew serious then, too.

"First of all, Mary, you are never alone. Secondly, consider who you'd be dating if you were dating someone seriously at Beaver Dam High School. Most of those boys you know don't want what you want. Why are you interested at the age of seventeen in trying to be with someone for the sole sake of being with someone?

"Go out into the world and pursue your passion and he'll be there. Somewhere along the road to your dreams, you'll cross paths. I promise."

I thought about the wisdom of her words for a minute. But just a minute. And then I went back to wanting a boyfriend.

At the time, I blamed the problem on being so tall (I had grown to five foot eleven) and on my very bad hair (I tried again and again throughout high school to get the "perfect perm"—as if there is such a thing—but my dirty-blond hair was a mess with a capital *M*). I realize now that as bad as my mullet-like "hairdo" was, my single status had just as much to do with how serious I was. I wasn't that bubbly young teenager who bounded through the halls of the high school, her mind on the next football game or on whom to spend study hall sessions writing notes to. Instead, I was that girl who looked like she carried the weight of the world upon her shoulders because, in so many ways, I did.

The years after my father left to pursue his gay lifestyle had been an exercise in survival for all members of the household, most of all my mother. Two years, almost to the day, after my First Communion, my father sought and was granted first a divorce and then an annulment. The divorce meant my parents were no longer legally bound. The annulment meant that, in the eyes of the church, the marriage had never existed. With the annulment, my parents could continue to go to Mass and receive Communion. It also meant my brother and I were illegitimate, at least according to the Vatican.

My father celebrated the transition to official singlehood with a vacation in Florida. Anne Diener Pflum, by contrast, stayed home and embarked on a different kind of journey. She was on her way to another nervous breakdown.

The summer after the divorce was finalized, the depression that had long plagued my mother became so great that she checked herself into the mental-health wing of the University of Wisconsin Hospital in Madison.

I watched her pack the night before her departure, placing a robe and some curlers and a smattering of clothes into the same old olive-green pleather suitcase she'd been using since her wedding.

"I don't want you to go," I said, starting to cry. The weather was warm. The windows were open and I could hear crickets.

"It's summer vacation. This is supposed to be the fun time of year. But this isn't fun. This is so—so—"

I started to cry harder.

"So stupid."

"I agree," my mother said, her voice wooden. I would later learn that the woodenness had much to do with the arsenal of antidepressants she was taking that often rendered her numb. She dropped the pair of navy canvas sneakers she'd been holding into the suitcase and walked to me, pulling me into her arms.

"Sometimes we all have to do things we don't want to do," she said, stroking my hair. "And this is one of them."

The stay was a long one—for her and for my brother and me. Since my mother had been our sole caregiver for the better part of three years, her departure left us feeling like unwanted orphans. My father rearranged his business schedule and came to stay with us for ten days in Beaver Dam. For several more days, we were separated and sent to stay with friends. I stayed with my classmate Jenny's family. My brother stayed with his friend Jeff. Then we were shipped off to Indiana for a pair of weeks to stay with my father's parents on their farm.

The term "nervous breakdown" was never used when my relatives discussed my mother in front of me, nor was "severe depression." My father explained away my mother's disappearance as an ordinary blip on the radar of our lives.

"Your mother isn't feeling well," he said nonchalantly, describing her symptoms as if they were akin to a cold. He was trying to serve us a dinner of scrambled eggs at the time. "She needs to rest."

"When is she coming home?" I asked.

"Your mother will get home when she gets home."

That was the answer he would continue to give me during my mother's absence. But it wasn't good enough for me. I missed my mom, needed my mom, cried for her at night. Unsure what was happening, or if anything would ever feel normal again, I started wetting the bed at the ancient age of nine. Worse than the bed-wetting episodes were the recurring nightmares. Again and again I dreamed I was falling down several flights of stairs. In all the dreams, I was stuck in a terrifying free fall, looking back up at my childhood house, or at St. Peter's Church, while my parents watched and did nothing to catch me.

I went to see my mother in the hospital several times that summer before my brother and I were shipped off to Indiana. I remember making my way up to the hospital wing and eyeing curiously the scary pair of electric doors that buzzed open only after a guard signed us in and pushed a button.

"Is Mom in jail?" I asked my father, as we passed through the doors and walked past a sign that commanded STOP! NO PATIENTS ALLOWED BEYOND THIS POINT WITHOUT AUTHORIZATION.

"No, they just don't want patients to go out by themselves," he explained, not looking at me. "It's for their own good."

The patients with whom my mother shared her new quarters

were a curious crew. Some talked to themselves as they shuffled along the floor in slippers. A number of the women—who, my mother explained, suffered from severe cases of anorexia and bulimia—were so gaunt they reminded me of the photos I'd seen of Holocaust survivors in the collection of World War II books my brother kept in his bedroom. They had daily weigh-ins. One dark-haired woman was so determined to keep up her starvation plans that she tried to sneak a full bottle of Pert shampoo into her panties during one of the weigh-ins, so that she'd appear to be gaining weight when, in fact, she wasn't. She was caught one day, just before my brother and I arrived for a visit. We looked on in horror as orderlies strapped her, cursing loudly, down in her bed to prepare her for a mandatory tube feeding. Just as memorable was a large male patient who didn't know whether he wanted to be a man or a woman. The strange combination of his breasts and his facial hair left my brother and me as confused as he apparently was.

My mother was almost always glad to see us. She'd light up when we entered her room, hug us to her, ask us about our summer routine: swimming with Kim and Kevin, t-ball games. But she was in a fragile place. Little things set her off. One day shortly before our visit, my father, not sure what to do with my long and tangled hair, had taken me to a hairdresser in Beaver Dam, who spent the better part of a half hour beautifully braiding my tresses into a look Princess Leia might have sported. I was ecstatic. I'd never felt so beautiful in my life. I thought my mother would be pleased. Instead, upon seeing me, she started to sob.

"Look at you," she cried, touching my braided hair. "I can't do that. I could never do that. You're already better off without me."

When my mother eventually came home to us, she was better for a while. But the next summer, she was back in the hospital.

The little self-confidence she had managed to retain in the wake of her breakup with the convent had been irrevocably knocked from her when my father left. Twice divorced, once from Christ and once from my father, her spirit had been badly shaken.

The broken spirit didn't make her a bad mother. Quite the contrary. Even in the darkest of times, she was warm and affectionate, forever hugging us and snuggling with us as she tucked us in at night or helped us with school projects. No, the problem was that the only energy reserves she had managed to retain during the divorce, which were minimal, were poured into that mothering. Not just into clothing and feeding us, but also into all the other aspects of parenting: attending our band concerts and basketball games and committing to memory our favorite *Strawberry Short-cake* and *Star Wars* action figures and putting them on layaway at the local Shopko, where she dutifully made weekly deposits until the toys were ours.

She worked long hours teaching. She trekked back and forth to Madison and to Oshkosh to take courses and earn credits that would keep her critical teaching accreditation intact. Taking a page from Trudy's book, she pinched pennies so that she could take us to the movies on weekends or to the opera in Madison at Christmastime. And each night, she dutifully stayed up late, packing school lunches for us for the next day, filling out permission slips, looking over our homework.

"Aren't you coming to bed?" I'd ask, finding her still up on those nights when I arose after midnight in search of a cup of water or an extra blanket for my bed.

"Don't worry about me," she'd always answer. "I'll sleep later."

In taking on that beast otherwise known as single motherhood, she left nothing on the table for herself. I often think of my mother when they make the announcement at the beginning of a flight that, in the event of an unexpected loss in cabin pressure, parents should secure their own oxygen masks before securing the masks of their children. My mother never would have abided by that. She would have been one to smile politely before ignoring the rule—reaching first to save my brother and me and then, even after our masks were secure, only taking a sip of oxygen here and there from her own mask, worrying that by taking even a bit for herself, she might be taking something important away from her children. At every turn, our needs and wants trumped hers, even if it meant growing blue in the face.

When a pair of once-close childhood friends turned mean in seventh grade, ostracizing me from certain parties and conversations, she was there for me at every turn, doling out post-dinner pieces of apple pie and sage words of wisdom: "Why would you want to be friends with people who don't want to be friends with you? The problem, sweetheart, is that they see the world in different colors than you do."

"Different colors?" I asked.

"Different colors. This family setup of ours has made you learn to see the world in shades of gray. Those so-called friends you're missing see it only in black and white. Things are good or things are bad. Someone's cool or someone's not. For them, there's no in-between right now because the in-between suggests life is more complicated than they may want to deal with right now. Trust me on this one, sweetheart: stick with those who understand life is all gray and that most of us are, too. The people who see the gray are more fun anyway."

When I told her about ideas I had for short stories and plays, she was encouraging.

"Don't just talk about your ideas!" she enthused. "Make them happen!"

When I won my first citywide writing contest—earning first place for a short story I wrote in the seventh grade—there was no one who seemed less surprised than my mother.

"I told you that was a good story," my mother said when the local paper published it. "You have a real gift with words. Don't waste it."

Anne Diener Pflum was not her mother's idea of a mother. She was the mother she'd always wanted for herself: encouraging, supportive, warm. Just like her beloved Marmie in *Little Women*.

At no time was her support more evident than when, at the age of thirteen, I underwent spinal surgery to address a severe case of scoliosis. During my two-week hospital stay, my mother was my constant companion. She talked to me and sang me lullabies in the dark of night, the ones Trudy had once sung to her and that she in turn had sung to me when I was a baby. Along with the team of physical therapists, she helped me learn to walk again. And she listened—really listened—when I cried.

"Why does it have to hurt so much?" I asked one miserable night midway through my stay. The doctors had moved me from the ICU to a regular room and were trying to transition me to a less-potent level of pain medication. I couldn't sleep. I couldn't eat. I couldn't even breathe without recoiling in excruciating pain.

"That's the age-old question," my mother said. She said it in a tone that suggested she was thinking—really thinking—about my query.

"Many writers and theologians believe great pain is God's way of helping us to appreciate great joy," she said. "That moments like these will open you up to ever greater happiness down the road."

I thought about her words for a minute, then wrinkled my nose. At thirteen, I didn't care what theologians thought.

"What do you think?" I asked.

"I think it's a bunch of hooey," she said, flashing a weary smile. "I've always thought that whole business of 'that which doesn't kill you makes you stronger' stuff is a cop-out that people who have nothing better to say or have never had anything really terrible happen whip out to make themselves feel better. The fact is there's too much suffering in the world—but—"

"But?"

"But then I look at you and your brother. My path to both of you was paved with suffering. And since you two are the greatest source of happiness for me, maybe there's some truth to the theory after all."

My mother best summed up her philosophy of parenthood the fall I was assigned to read *The Scarlet Letter* in a high school literature class. I adored the book and hung on Hawthorne's every sentence. But I was caught off guard by the ending.

"It just wasn't fair," I said to my mother one night over dinner.

"Which part?" my mother asked.

"All of it," I said. "But especially the end."

"How so?" my mother asked, intrigued. "The ending was my favorite part."

"But it ends with Hester Prynne all alone," I said of the lead character, one of literature's original single mothers. "Pearl leaves her."

"No," said my mother, shaking her head. "Don't you remember? It's made clear Pearl married well and had gone on to have a family of her own."

"But Pearl moved far away from her mother," I said, pained at the thought that the woman who had been so publicly shunned for an illicit love affair would go on to be left alone by her only child.

"Don't you see?" asked my mother. "The greatest sadness for Hester Prynne or for any good mother would be to know her child was leading an unhappy life, even if that unhappy life meant Hester Prynne wouldn't have had to live alone. And the greatest happiness for any mother is to know her children are happy and fulfilling their dreams. And maybe even fulfilling a few of their mother's dreams, too, along the way.

"Pearl was living the life Hester had always dreamed of for Pearl and had once dreamed of for herself. She found a good husband and made a life for herself. Hester was thrilled with that."

I shook my head, disagreeing.

"But she was alone."

"She was happy in Pearl's happiness," my mother countered. "You don't have to agree with me now. But someday, maybe when you're a mother, you'll understand."

For my mother, doling out wisdom at critical times was not the problem. The problem was those other moments—the quiet times after dinner, the long drives to and from work. Those were the moments when she was at her loneliest. And those moments are what ultimately undid her. She felt as if she had no one. No grown-ups, anyway. Divorce in Beaver Dam in the early 1980s was very much taboo. The friends she'd made upon moving to Beaver Dam, the ones with whom she and my father double-dated, stopped calling after my parents split up. Neighbors—all couples—didn't include her in their progressive dinners. They skipped our house entirely. Worst of all, even Father Vincent turned his back on her. When he learned that my mother had been accepting of my father's request for a divorce—instead of being more steadfast in insisting upon remaining married, as per the mandates of the Catholic Church—he wrote her a stern letter, lecturing her on the sanctity of marriage and expressing his disappointment in her. My mother was devastated.

Upon learning of the letter, my father asked, "So do you plan to write him back?"

My mother shook her head sadly. "I don't think I'll be hearing from him again."

At her lowest points, my mother cried, sometimes unable to stop the sobs in the hours that stretched between dinner and bedtime. My brother and I would look at each other helplessly. Bouts of insomnia took hold. Soon after the divorce, my mother moved out of the master bedroom that she had shared with my father and began to bed down in various places throughout the house during the few hours in which she slept. For a while, she slept in the living room, falling asleep in an old recliner or on the couch while watching late-night TV. Sometimes she slept on a tired old couch in the basement after staying up late to do her favorite chore—ironing. After she put my brother and me to bed, she spent hours making smooth the wrinkles on our shirts and dresses. "Don't you wish life were as easy as a wrinkled shirt? That you could just smooth out all of the problems with an electric iron?" she used to ask before laughing at the thought.

When she was done with her stack of wrinkled shirts, she'd retreat to the three-seater couch whose fluorescent cushions were so worn and tattered that the stuffing was falling out.

Eventually, after two years of bedding down in the basement, my mother set up shop in the guest room—a bright-green-hued room kitty-corner from my room that housed a pair of twin beds. My brother and I often asked her when she would return to the master bedroom.

"This isn't your bedroom," I gently reminded her one day as she exited the guest room she'd overtaken. "Your room is down the hall."

"I'm staying here for now," my mother said.

"But what about your room?" I protested.

"This is my room now," she said of the guest room.

"But what about your other room?" I said pointing in the direction of the master bedroom. "Your real room?"

"That room needs some work. Let's give it a break for a while. Don't worry about me."

But I did worry, watching as her weight fluctuated—dropping back down to her wedding-day weight in the months surrounding the divorce, then ballooning way up to the plus sizes—18, 20, 22—she would wear for the remainder of her life. Her once-brown hair began to turn silver under the stress. Sometimes, when she had the money or the energy, she bought Nice 'n Easy to cover the gray. But when she was down, she let her hair go.

And just as she began to let her physical appearance go, she also increasingly let the house go. Our house had two phases that I can recall. There was phase one, when my father was home and the house was almost always neat and clean. In hopes of keeping my father happy—or at least to keep him coming home—the windows gleamed. Floors were spotless. Countertops were clear. And mail was opened regularly.

Then came phase two. After my father left, the countertops became littered with debris—school projects, leftover paper plates, a spare set of gloves, a discarded pet leash. Then a little became a lot. The living room became a glorified playroom in one section, with my sticker collections and my brother's Legos and our various books and bags and school projects that had come home to die. In another corner of the living room stood the mountain of newspapers my mother loved to read at night but hesitated to throw away. Like her mother, Anne Diener Pflum read three, even four newspapers a day: the local paper, the *Wisconsin State Journal,* the *Milwaukee Journal,* and *USA Today.* The papers were forever littered around her favorite recliner, never making their way to the garbage can. Sometimes, she explained, the stack grew so high because she wanted to save a coupon from this paper, an article from that. Other times, it was because she hadn't seemed to find the energy to straighten up.

By the time I was ten and it became obvious that things weren't going to change, I tried to wage my own war on the mess. After getting off the school bus, in the two hours before my mother arrived home from work, I used my time in the empty house to try to straighten up. I folded comforters that had been left out in the living room by my mother, who used the large blankets to combat the freezing-cold conditions of the house. I put all the newspapers and magazines I could find into one stack and threw away the oldest ones, which I prayed my mother wouldn't miss. I washed dishes piled in the sink and around the counter. I used the hand vacuum to suck up the fuzzies I found on the stairs.

I mopped up the remnants of Blackie's hair balls my mother seemed to have overlooked. I applied Windex to the windows and Pledge to the end tables until the cleaning supplies ran out. But the mess was overwhelming. And by the next afternoon, it was back—oftentimes greater than the one I'd come home to the day before.

Contributing mightily to the mess: the mail. It was curiously piled up in stacks around the house, generally unopened. I grew used to my mother's moving the stacks from place to place before eventually putting a few piles into a big brown paper grocery bag that would sit untouched until tax time or until she realized she desperately needed an envelope from her father—who, I would later discover, was sending us monthly checks to help pay the bills.

Al and Aurelia Diener knew little of how bad things were getting in Beaver Dam. With Aurelia's health continuing to deteriorate, my grandparents were less and less able to travel great distances. Visits to Wisconsin stopped. They instead relied on my mother to make the drive to see them at the Pine Patch two or three times a year. During our visits, they learned only the specifics of my mother's life that she chose to share. They knew, of course, of her hospitalizations. They knew about her ongoing visits to a local psychiatrist. But my mother filled most of the conversations with her parents with news of what my brother and I were doing in school, how we were growing, what had struck her about the priest's sermon at Mass. There was no need, my mother believed, to worry her parents with tales of our freezing house or her growing inability to find things in the mountains of junk. As far as they were concerned, she had things under relative control.

Her siblings remained similarly in the dark. With Patty and Mimi and Kathy and Mike and Al spread out all over the nation, it was easy for my mother to lead them to believe all was well in Beaver Dam. Only my aunt Kathy, who flew out to visit my mother in the summer of 1986, had any idea how messy the house was becoming. For several days during her visit, she worked to help my mother clean out the master bedroom. But in the heat of summer in our un-air-conditioned house, the mountains of junk became too much.

"Kathy, sweetheart, you're sweet to want to help," I remember my mother telling my aunt the second-to-last afternoon of the visit. "But I'd rather spend this time just visiting with you, instead of cleaning. I'll clean up another day, after you leave. I promise."

That day never came.

Just as mail sometimes went untouched for weeks on end, so too did broken appliances. The big avocado-colored dishwasher that my father had given to my mother on Mother's Day when I was five broke sometime before my eleventh birthday. But it didn't just break for a brief spell before being repaired. Instead, it remained broken and unused for the rest of my childhood. Later, the oven would break, then not one, but two televisions, then the massive Lipton microwave. Each time, the items would sit unused, unfixed, unmoved. My brother and I would ask about replacing the items, and in the case of at least one of the televisions, we eventually did. But the dishwasher and microwave remained broken fixtures, and the kitchen began to take on the feel of a used-appliance museum.

Increasingly, we dined out. Since money was tight, the options were few: fast-food restaurants that featured "specials" and inexpensive family restaurants, notably a local coffee shop called Walker's, which seemed to run a mysterious tab for my mother. We often had sporting events or music practice or play rehearsals after school. Eating out, my mother reasoned, enabled us to visit with one another without having to worry about any dishes or cleanup or the stress of executing an actual meal.

My mother's culinary skills were extremely limited. She had five meals in her arsenal: pork chops, spaghetti with meat sauce, hamburgers, grilled cheese sandwiches, and my favorite—a hot dog casserole that consisted of hot dogs, bread crumbs, green beans, and copious amounts of Worcestershire sauce. But after the divorce and the hospitalizations, the idea of cooking became too much for her most nights. Maybe she had finally caved under the pressure of knowing she would never measure up to the home-making skills of my father's mother, who was known around the county for her to-die-for fried chicken, which she could effort-lessly whip up at a moment's notice.

As a child, I knew the piles that littered our home weren't the norm. I would go to friends' houses and see how everything had a place. My friend Kim's house was one of those houses. In addi-tion to a super-neat family room and an ultra-spotless kitchen, her house had an extraordinarily formal living room that went weeks without being used and looked like something out of a museum. After a playdate with Kim, I would return to our messy house, stunned by the contrast. The funny thing was that my mother didn't seem to really notice the mess. Instead of being bothered by the heaps, she would gamely step around them, as if they were invisible.

"Mom, why can't we have a house where we can walk through the living room?" I asked one evening on our drive home after a dinner out at McDonald's.

"What do you mean?" she said, her grip tightening around the steering wheel.

"Our living room—it's a mess," I said. "We never even vacuum."

"Our vacuum cleaner is broken," she said defensively. "You know that."

"Then why don't we get a new one?"

"Because we don't have the money."

I paused.

"Okay—maybe we could borrow one?"

I watched her face for a reaction. There was none.

"I guess I'm saying it would be nice to have a living room like other people do, where we could have people over to visit us. You know, a living room like Kim's."

"Other people have living rooms that they don't actually live in," my mother said, pursing her lips. "They're just there for show. We actually live in our living room. Consider that."

In spite of the mess, my mother encouraged us to have friends over. For a time, we did—hosting slumber parties and even magic shows for friends and neighbors in our basement. The preparation for the events was always frenzied, my mother working for a pair of late nights on throwing mountains of debris into what had once been my father's home office.

But as the years passed and we became teenagers, we were less than enthusiastic about having anyone other than the closest of our friends enter the premises. My mother was fine with this until my high school graduation. That's when she popped the big question that caused my heart to stop, my eyes to widen, my lower lip to tremble.

"Why don't we have a party?" she asked me one day in early May.

"A what?!" I asked, choking on the Diet Coke I had been sipping at the time.

"A graduation party," she said cheerily, offering me a paper napkin to mop up the soda on my chin. "We can invite all of your friends and neighbors and people who have been important to you."

I looked around the kitchen—at the floor littered with brown grocery bags that had not been entirely emptied after a recent trip to the store, at the countertops covered with unopened cans of cat food and two-year-old calendars—and, to my surprise, she seemed to know what I was thinking.

"Gail Fakes gave me a name of a cleaning service I can call. They're called the Merry Maids. They'll help straighten things out."

This sounded promising. In fact, my mother's desire to hire a cleaning crew was the best news I'd heard in quite some time. Maybe this would be just what the doctor ordered to get our house back on track.

I nodded my head slowly and smiled. "It could be fun. Thanks, Mom."

The last few weeks of high school were a blur to me. There was a final band concert, a final orchestra concert, a final edition of the school newspaper. There was a class picnic. My graduation party was scheduled on the Sunday prior to graduation. As the days wound down to the big party, my mother got things ready: She sent out invitations and encouraged me to do the same. She ordered food. And we oohed and aahed over the commencement dress. That sophisticated white dress. But the house remained a mess. By the Friday morning before the big day, my worry had escalated to a full-throttle panic.

"What happened to the Merry Maids?" I asked my mother in a tone that verged on shrieking. The party was to be spread between two floors of the house—the kitchen, dining room, and living room on the main floor, and the finished basement on the bottom floor that consisted of a big open family den. Both floors remained piled high with clutter. The formal dining room hadn't been used in at least five years, and that many years' worth of papers and discarded mail and shopping bags containing Christmas gifts and baby gifts that were never given were piled high on the dining room table and buffet. The other rooms were no better.

"I left a message for the Merry Maids," my mother said, her eyes not meeting mine. I wasn't sure if she was telling the truth or putting me off. "They never called me back."

My heart raced. My head spun. "What are we going to do?!" I cried.

"I called your father," my mother said lightly. "He wants to have you and Anthony over to his house in Appleton tomorrow for a pre-graduation gathering. Your grandparents will be there. Why don't you and Jamie Fakes go up to see him together?"

My brother was completing his freshman year at Lawrence University, which was located in Appleton, where my father continued to live. Jamie was an old neighbor friend who had known my family for years.

"But what about the house?" I asked, definitely shrieking this time.

"I just need a little time and space and I'll have everything together," my mother said. "You know me—I work better on my own."

I looked at her, wanting desperately to believe her.

"Really," my mother said. "You'll be amazed at how much I can get done in just a few hours."

She had occasionally surprised me in years gone by with her ability to tidy up the house in a matter of hours. One time when I was in the sixth grade I was astonished to wake up to a living room sans debris in honor of a party I was hosting that night. In that case, too, she'd put the cleanup off to the very last minute. Maybe she could work her magic this time as well. But what if she couldn't?

"Maybe we should cancel the party," I said, wondering how, in that long-ago age before e-mail and cell phones, I could reach all of my friends in time.

"No way," said my mother. "The food is all set, and everyone can't wait to see you."

I was looking forward to seeing my classmates, too. And several family friends had called to say they'd be there. But could I trust her to clean the place? And could I stomach seeing my father?

My father's bouts of depression had gotten no better over the years. He was way up for periods—then way down. It all depended on what medication he was on and how much of it he had taken and how well his personal life was going at the time. His temper when he was down or felt betrayed knew no bounds. More often than not, he and I were at odds, especially when he insulted my mother.

"How dare you treat her like this!" I cried the time when, during a particularly bad episode, he had snuck into the house when none of us were home and moved the entire contents of our kitchen—table, chairs, dishes, glasses, even boxes of cereal—into our already-cluttered living room, in a bid to express his anger at my mother over a phone spat. It took us weeks to get everything back in place and his actions made our already messy house even more difficult to navigate.

"She's not married to you anymore!" I cried.

"How dare you for being an ungrateful little bitch!" he screamed in return before storming out of the house.

I was only eleven at the time, but already I couldn't wait for college to provide me the opportunity to get away from him and his episodes.

Nor could I wait to get away from his new life.

My father had finally come out to me when I was fifteen. His timing couldn't have been worse. I had been gunning to earn a coveted National Merit Scholarship. The honors were doled out based on scores earned on the PSAT, a standardized test consisting of an endless series of multiple-choice questions. The test was scheduled for a Monday in February. My father, aware of the test but oblivious to how much the results meant to me, decided to share the news with me on the Saturday prior, in the front seat of his company car. The timing was inexplicable—as was his choice of location. It was dark and cold and, for some reason, we were in the parking lot of the Piggly Wiggly grocery store in the moments before he was supposed to drop me off back with my mother. Without much fanfare, he leaned over to inform me, almost whispering, that there was something he'd been meaning to tell me: "I'm gay."

I had suspected the news for some time. The nude male statues that dotted my father's apartment had long seemed strange, as had his love of needlepoint and his adoration of Broadway show tunes. But suspecting your father might be gay is one thing. Knowing it, and knowing it with absolute certainty, is another. Especially in Beaver Dam, Wisconsin.

The reality was too much. And the morning of that damned PSAT exam my father and my shattered family were all I could think about. Try as I might, I couldn't get any of it out of my mind—my father and his "friends." My poor mother's shame. And what it would mean if any of this got out to the student body. I ran from the classroom mid-test—something I had never done in my history of test-taking—and retreated to a school bathroom where I sat, at first gasping for breath, then crying in silence, my head pressed up against the cool metal of the stall door. My dreams of winning a National Merit Scholarship were ruined. But that wasn't the worst part. The worst thing about my father's admission was that there was no one, absolutely no one, whom I could tell. My best friend in the world during those years was my next-door neighbor, Kim. We had done everything together for the better part of ten years. But telling a best friend in a conservative small town that your father is gay? At the time, I worried that it would be the equivalent of social suicide. Word would travel fast, and I would no longer be known as Mary Pflum: She's So Smart. I would be known as Mary Pflum: Her Father Is Gay.

Looking back, I'm guessing that many already did say that about me when I walked down the hall, since my father had taken to all but flaunting his sexuality by the time he'd come out to me. Beginning in 1985, he refused to go anywhere without Franz, a bearded Austrian man my father always introduced as his "friend." He came everywhere—even to my school band concerts and my brother's football games. My mother would be at those same games. To her credit, she never let on how uncomfortable she must have felt. She grinned and bore my father's new boyfriend in the manner of the former grin-and-bear-it nun who had long been taught that suffering was somehow good for the soul. My brother and I were less understanding. We'd already felt uncomfortable around Franz before my father came out. We felt even more so afterward. Especially when we watched our mother shift uncomfortably in her seat.

So, no, I didn't want to see my father for a graduation gathering that would inevitably include his friends. At this very special time of year I wanted to be around people who knew me, or who were at least sincerely interested in getting to know me. More often than not, my father's friends—some of whom he counted as good friends even though he'd only known them for a couple of months—weren't particularly interested in his teenaged children. They were interested in my father. And when they were around, my father was often more interested in them than in being a father. The same, of course, would have likely been true had he been straight. It was a common problem for children of divorce

Still, as little as I relished time with my father's friends, I didn't want to run the risk of my mother not making good on her promise of at last straightening up our messy, messy house. So, in the end, I agreed to go to my father's gathering. Jamie and I left on our drive at nine o'clock that Saturday morning. We returned around seven o'clock. Ten hours was more than sufficient time for my mother to clean the house, I told myself. It had to be.

I knew as Jamie pulled into the driveway that the house might not be spotless upon my return. But I was unprepared for what I found. After saying good night to Jamie, I walked in the door, and the look in my mother's soft brown eyes told me all I needed to know: they were filled with fear.

Virtually nothing in the house had been touched. Yes, there were flowers in vases where there had been none before I left. But the flowers—beautiful lilacs and lilies of the valley and peonies plucked from the yard—did little to mask the mess that was our house.

"You said you'd take care of it," I said, my voice this time not a shriek, but a whisper. "You said to leave you alone and it would get done."

"Mary, it will get done," my mother told me, her voice pleading.

"When?" I asked, collapsing on the front stairs that, unvacuumed, remained littered with cat hair and fuzzies. "How? The party is tomorrow."

I put my head in my hands and started to cry. I was graduating. From high school. I had a beautiful dress to wear. I had written a fine address for my valedictory role. I was to sit on the stage with the principal. I had envelopes containing acceptance letters from nine reputable colleges, three of which had offered me full academic scholarships. The world, it would seem, was at my feet. But my feet couldn't make their way through my own house.

"We still have tonight," my mother said. "Just wait and see what I can get done while you're sleeping."

I shook my head. I wanted so badly to believe her—but I knew better. I wanted so much to help—but I didn't know where to begin. My things I could take care of. But most of the things that were piled and strewn about were household items or stuff only she could decide what to do with: boxes of Kleenex, grocery bags filled with file folders pertaining to her students, unopened packages of cookies, legal pads, manila envelopes with important documents, pictures that had been developed but never found their way into photo albums because my mother hadn't kept photo albums since my father left. I had learned a long time ago that to meddle with things my mother deemed her personal property was a bad idea, punishable by a harsh tongue-lashing or, worse, grounding.

I went to bed that night with a feeling of dread in the pit of my stomach. How could I get out of this party? How could I find a means of skipping over Sunday and going straight to Monday?

When I awoke the next morning, my mother began barking orders at me to get dressed for church.

"Mary, hurry up!" my mother cried. "You know we can't be late!"

It was baccalaureate. I needed to be at St. Peter's early since the graduating Catholic seniors were being honored at that morning's Mass.

"But what about the house?" I asked weakly.

My mother stomped off in silence. Her mood suggested that she was grumpy either from staying up all night cleaning or because nothing had been done and she didn't want to deal with my shrieks.

Upon entering the kitchen, I saw that it was the latter. I ran down to the basement. Nothing had been touched.

"We'll handle it after Mass," my mother said calmly.

But there would be no time to right the wrong. I hung my head. I had yelled. I had protested. I had cried. There was nothing more I could do.

At Mass that morning, I prayed for the usual things: world peace, another report card of straight A's, a future boyfriend. And I prayed for something more: a clean house. A blessedly, fantastically clean house.

Following Mass, my mother and I came home to find my father and his side of the family waiting for us. More than a decade after he'd moved out, Dale Pflum still had a house key and had let all of his relatives in without waiting for my mother.

On hand to greet us were my grandparents, my dad's sister Mary Jo, and some cousins who had made the drive from southern Indiana in honor of my graduation. My mother sighed, as she increasingly did in the presence of my father's family members, whom she believed still held her responsible for somehow turning my father gay.

I shuddered as I watched them look over our house, their arms crossed, their lips pursed, staring in that awful judgmental way that screamed in silence, "Can you believe this house?!"

"There's no way you're going to have a party here this afternoon," my aunt Mary Jo, the older of my father's two sisters, said, breaking the silence.

I'd always been afraid of Mary Jo. She had never been especially warm to my brother and me, especially since the divorce. But on that Sunday, I had to give her credit for speaking the truth. I wondered if she thought the mess that was our house was somehow my fault. I hung my head in shame. I wanted to tell her how it really was: That I was seventeen. That I was a child who had been living in this filth for ten years. A full decade! I wanted to tell her that I wanted nothing more than a clean house, but that there is only so much a child of a well-meaning but severely depressed mother can do. Especially when there was no extended family around who ever seemed to care. I wanted to tell her all of that. But I didn't have the strength.

Instead, I started to cry.

"Everybody's house looks like this," my mother said lightly. She looked at me, but her words were meant for everyone in the room.

"Nobody's house looks like this!" I yelled, unable to keep my frustration bottled up any longer. "Only our house looks like this. Only our house is this kind of a mess!"

My mother recoiled.

Mary Jo looked at me, then at my mother.

"Where do you want us to put everything?" she demanded.

With a wave of her hands, my mother pointed to two rooms: the upstairs guest room, and a room in the basement, my father's old office.

"What do you want us to do?" asked Mary Jo, incredulous at the lack of specific direction, never mind the lack of cleaning supplies. "Just throw things in there?"

My mother nodded weakly.

My aunt turned to me as if to ask whether my mother was mad. I shrugged my shoulders. What else was there to do? This was the modus operandi for the family. If someone was coming over, this was what my mother had instructed us to do for years at eleventh hours like this one: throw everything into a room, shut the door, say a prayer, and hope for the best.

I helplessly joined in the frenzied pickup process that followed. We created a quasi assembly line—me, my aunt, my father, my mother—hurling newspapers and magazines and paper bags into the rooms.

The frenzied process was still in high gear when the doorbell rang, and the first of my guests, some friends from my graduating class, arrived. I remember greeting them at the door with a mixture of relief at being given an excuse to leave the assembly line and dread at the idea that this secret home life I'd carefully guarded for years might be unveiled at just the moment when I could have made a clean getaway.

I led the trio of friends down to the basement, where the door to the mountains of unloaded debris had been closed and an old toy chest had been not-so-discreetly placed in front of it. I would later nonchalantly tell my friends that the chest was in front of the door as a means to provide more places for people to sit. Little did they know of the heaps of junk that lay beyond.

For the next three hours, the house was filled with the sort of chatter and laughter it hadn't seen since my First Communion. There were neighbors in the kitchen. There were relatives and friends in the basement. There were my colleagues from the school newspaper staff and fellow members of the community orchestra scattered throughout. Also on hand were the families whose young children I babysat for. I flitted around, greeting well-wishers, graciously accepting cards and flowers and hugs and pecks on the cheek, cuddling my young babysitting charges on my lap. One high school classmate gave me a beautifully inscribed leather-bound copy of *The Hitchhiker's Guide to the Galaxy*. Another presented me with a homemade trophy, lauding me for what he called my acts of heroism in guiding the school newspaper. A dear family friend had lovingly handstitched a quilt, made to match my bedroom. Was I excited? they asked. Was I nervous about being up on that stage graduation night?

I smiled at all the right times, laughed when appropriate, posed for photos. But my heart never got over the near attack it had been subjected to in the moments before that first ring of the doorbell. It continued to pound in my chest as if it had been forced to run a marathon when it was only in good enough shape to run a mile. At every moment, I was worried—were the last of the piles safely stuffed away? Would someone open the door to the mountains of debris when I was out of their sight?

The photos snapped of me with guests on that Sunday afternoon show that yes, my relatives and parents and I did manage to clear the house of the heaps of debris and mail and papers in the moments before guests arrived. But those same photos show something else: our efforts could do little to hide the badly scuffed coffee tables, the sagging couch, and the broken chairs that inhabited the home. The carpet had noticeable stains on it; the wallpaper, a paisley pattern that announced itself as a relic of the 1970s, was faded; and two of the lampshades were ripped. There were so many signs of disrepair in the house—too many to count. No amount of fresh lilacs could possibly have masked the fact that our home, with its twenty-year-old furniture and broken appliances, was in a state of decline.

For seventeen years, my mother had been my everything: my North Star, my confidante, my nurturer, my comforter, and my biggest defender. She'd nursed me through countless crushes gone wrong. She'd stayed up late helping me type up the college admissions essays I'd initially written by hand in spiral-bound notebooks. She was the true definition of selfless, unconditional love, always putting her children above all else, always there to offer words of wisdom. And yet on this most fundamental of levels, when it came to keeping house, she had failed me miserably. And she had not only failed me in private. Now she had failed me in public. The image I had worked so hard to cultivate—learned, cultured—had been irrevocably compromised. And so had my impression of my mother.

Every child reaches that point when he or she realizes the parent is fallible. I had seen glimpses of the fallibility before, certainly during her hospitalizations. But for the first time I had come to realize that not only was my mother human—sometimes it was she who was the helpless child in our relationship. It was deeply unsettling.

And as much as I adored my mother, was grateful for all the love and support she had given me, I longed, more than ever, to break free.

When I put on that starchy white Daisy Buchanan dress on graduation night and marched into Beaver Dam High School for the final time as a student, it was with a renewed sense of purpose.

My valedictorian remarks compared life to a road. "How fast can we go?" I asked my fellow classmates. "Where are we headed?" I didn't know the answer to either question. I just knew I wanted to take a route that would get me as far away from the situation that I was in as quickly and safely as humanly possible.

I collected a myriad of awards: two more four-year scholarships, the top English department award, the John Philip Sousa Award. The list went on. By evening's end, my arms were overflowing with checks and certificates and trophies and flowers and diplomas.

And as the applause faded and the gymnasium emptied and the lights of the school were extinguished, my heart burst with pride, my mind clouded with confusion. Daisy Buchanan had left the building—and was going home to one big mess.

Chapter 9

LWS (Little White Suit)

I stood in the Benetton boutique in Atlanta's Lenox Mall, perplexed. I needed one more suit for my upcoming trip to California. Problem was, after spending the better part of the day at the mall, I couldn't seem to find It.

When I accepted the position as a rookie reporter for CNN Newsroom, *a program designed with the intent of enabling young recruits like me to cut their TV journalist teeth, I was told investing in a few good suits was part of the job. And not just any suits. They had to be suits that looked good on camera. I had a red suit. And a black one. And a black suit with red stripes. But I required one more—something for my upcoming shoot on the set of the hit teen soap* Beverly Hills, 90210. *I needed something that, in the words of one of my favorite cameramen, would "pop."*

I was twenty-three and still getting used to the world of TV news. I'd dreamed of becoming a journalist since I was a little girl. And now that the dream was becoming a reality—real assignments! hair and makeup! nights at the anchor desk!—it all felt surreal. I had my own car. A boyfriend. I even had my own checking and savings accounts. Best of all, I had my own space. My own space in a historic old duplex in downtown Atlanta. Even my own walk-in closet. It was so different from Beaver Dam. For the first time in my life, I could move the thermostat as I pleased. I had heat! There were no stacks of unopened mail, no plastic bags full of junk, no broken appliances. For the first time in my life, I was in control.

And this, I hoped, was just the beginning. I didn't want Atlanta to be my last stop. If things went well, CNN Center would be a stepping-stone to more exotic locations, to ever-bigger adventures. I worked for CNN. CNN! It was the world's news leader. I worked for the same organization that employed Christiane Amanpour, the bravest of female war correspondents. My next stop, I hoped, would be the far reaches of Europe. Maybe even the Middle East.

But to conquer those places I had to first conquer the fictitious Brandon and Kelly and the set of Beverly Hills, 90210. *And to conquer Brandon and Kelly, I needed one more suit.*

Walking past a collection of floral sundresses, I ran my hand across the fabric of a powder-blue suit on one rack then a gray suit on another. Those were all right, but they wouldn't jump through the screen the way I wanted them to, or the way others would expect them to. The camera, I was quickly learning, loved certain colors and certain fabrics more than others.

"If you're looking for a suit, we also have something in white," said a voice from behind me.

I turned to meet the eyes of an attractive blond saleswoman. She was a few years older than me and wore a floral shift.

"White?" I was intrigued.

"Yes, white," said the saleswoman, disappearing through a doorway behind the cash register. Moments later, she reappeared, carrying It.

The suit that hung in the saleswoman's hand was a bright white cotton-polyester blend. It featured two pieces: a sleeveless white shift dress that zipped down the back and hit three inches above the knees, and a sleek white blazer that closed at the front with three white buttons. I smiled. It reminded me of the white ensemble Sharon Stone sported in Basic Instinct: *clean, simple, sexy.*

"Would you like to try it on?" asked the saleswoman.

I looked the suit up and down approvingly, using the same eye and head motion men increasingly used when they looked at me as they prepared to ask for my number. It happened everywhere now: bars, restaurants. Once, a pilot even asked me out on the airplane during a flight from Atlanta to New York. It still came as such a surprise to me, to think that after all these years, men found me attractive. Often, I'd look behind me when the especially handsome men smiled in my direction, certain they couldn't be looking at me. In Beaver Dam, I'd been invisible to men. Here in Atlanta, things had definitely changed.

Looking at the suit, I liked what I saw. This Little White Suit would have made Beaver Dam Mary blush. But for bona fide Adult Mary? It was perfect.

"I'd love to try it on," I told the saleswoman. "And I can already promise you I'm wearing it home."

You're going to wear *that*?" my mother asked me.

It was June 1999, and I stood in a hotel room in Muncie, Indiana, wearing the white suit I'd bought three summers before for my CNN trip to California. My mother was clearly unhappy with my fashion choice, but that was only one of my worries.

My thoughts were in Berlin, where I was currently living. I'd flown to Indiana from Germany the day before and was still jet-lagged.

My thoughts were in Turkey, where CNN now wanted me to move. They were launching a twenty-four-hour Turkish network, based in Istanbul, and since I'd recently covered the Turkish general elections, they wanted to know if I was interested in moving there. I didn't have long to decide.

And above all, my thoughts were on my late grandmother. In an hour, Aurelia Arvin Diener's memorial service would be under way.

My mother's mother had died some six months before, on December 26, 1998. But because of an especially harsh winter, my mother and her siblings had decided that they would wait to celebrate her life until warmer weather set in.

Aurelia's passing marked the end of an era. Al Diener had died two years before after a battle with leukemia. Now Aurelia would join him in Oddfellows Cemetery in Dunkirk—and, presumably, in heaven. The dual passing of Al and Aurelia was particularly hard on my mother. Difficult though her childhood had been, she had held tight to her parents and to her visits to Indiana as a source of stability, especially after the divorce.

"I'm not sure who I am without my parents," she'd told me, weeping, in the moments after she learned of her mother's death.

"Sure you do," I'd told her at the time.

"I do?" she'd asked.

"You're a mom. My mom."

"Yes," she said, the smile returning to her voice. "That's absolutely right."

On that day in June, everyone had gathered for Aurelia's service. In addition to my mother, there were her siblings. Mimi had made the drive from her home in Rochester, New York, where she continued to reside with a longtime friend and fellow former nun, Jody, who had become an unofficial member of our extended Diener family. I had come to consider Jody my honorary godmother. Patty had flown in from her home in Beverly Hills with her husband, Marv. Kathy and Mike had flown in from Denver with their respective families. And Al Joe had made the drive down from Illinois.

Besides Aurelia's six children, there were cousins and former neighbors. And there was even my father, who still considered himself a member of the Diener family. After initially being angry at my father after he left my mother, Al Diener had forgiven Dale. The rest of the Diener family had, for the most part, followed suit. So my father had invited himself to the fete. They were all there when I flew in from Berlin. I had to make the trip. For my mother—and for my grandmother.

The tenth of Aurelia's thirteen grandchildren, I had inherited my grandmother's love of writing and had been asked to present a eulogy at the service. I was proud to do so. As a child, I had been oblivious to my mother's rocky relationship with her mother. The memories I had of Aurelia were positive ones. I saw her, along with my grandfather, three or four times a year: once in the summer, once at Christmas, and typically over Thanksgiving and Easter breaks. My grandfather was the more gregarious of the two, frequently helping my brother and me with our chemistry and math assignments and talking to us about his beloved Republican Party. My grandmother was, by far, the quieter of the two, often retreating to a back bedroom to nap or read in silence. Still, I found her to be warm, funny, even generous during our visits. On one occasion, when I was twelve, she gave me her collection of beautiful hats, housed in a series of fancy hat boxes from LS Ayres. I loved all of them—the floral creations and the pillbox hats alike. On another occasion, she asked me to take a seat beside her and together we talked about her quest to write the perfect valedictorian address during her senior year of high school.

"I compared life to a river, Mary Elizabeth," she'd told me, laughing. "It was the most ridiculous thing I'd ever written. I called it long and winding. Can you imagine?"

Sitting in the living room at the Pine Patch, in front of that same fireplace where my mother had posed for the newspaper photographer with her Girls Nation trophy all those years before, we'd compared notes about favorite poems, beloved authors. At the age of nine, I told her about my love of Nancy Drew. She, in turn, introduced me to Agatha Christie.

"If you love mysteries, no one compares to Agatha Christie," she said, plucking one of her many Christie works from her crowded bookshelf and pressing it into my lap.

My mother would often gaze at the two of us during these conversations. She'd stand in the doorway that connected the Pine Patch's living room to the dining room—one foot in the living room, one foot out—looking both pleased and confused by our bonding sessions.

"I wish my mother had talked to me the way she talks with you," my mother told me one night during a visit to the Pine Patch, as she prepared to climb into the double bed in the guest room I already occupied.

"Don't feel bad, Mom," I said, shrugging. "She's probably trying to share things with me she always meant to share with you. Don't you think?"

She nodded then and smiled.

Toward the end of her life, Aurelia Diener attempted to soften her relationship with my mother. She may never have fully understood the dark days my mother experienced in Oldenburg or in the aftermath of her divorce from my father. But Aurelia Diener loved my mother.

In her final years, she rewarded my mother with glimpses of that love. After Al Diener died, my grandmother took my mother's hand. "Of the six children, Anne, you were the most like him," she confided.

My mother repeated the story to me often, relishing not only the words, but the fact that the words had been uttered by the woman who knew and loved Al Diener best.

Aurelia gave my mother further encouragement in letters. Years after my grandmother died, I found in my mother's purse a well-worn letter from Aurelia, penned in the early nineties.

"Do you know how pretty you are?" the handwritten letter asked. *"Perhaps I've never told you so I'll tell you now: you are as pretty on the outside as you are on the inside."*

Aurelia may not have known how to express warmth in those early years of motherhood. But she'd worked to make at least some amends before her death.

Because of Aurelia Arvin Diener's love of the written word, I worked to carefully craft a well-written eulogy that would have

made her smile. And because of my growing love of clothing—
and her old love of accessories like those hats she'd given me—I
selected an outfit for the occasion that would command attention.
That's why on the morning of the memorial service I plucked from
my suitcase not a black suit—but that Little White Suit I'd originally purchased from the Benetton in Atlanta.

"You're going to wear *that*?" my mother repeated as she stood
to glare at the outfit.

I shrugged, half disappointed and half amused by her reaction.
I was twenty-six but suddenly felt as if I were twelve.

"You said it's a memorial service, not a funeral, right?" I asked
my mother. I watched as she continued to scrutinize my attire.

"Right," said my mother hesitantly.

"A memorial is a celebration of life," I responded. "And white,
you always said, is the embodiment of celebrating life. Especially
in the church. It marks the transition from one point to another."

My mother mulled over my words for a minute and slowly
nodded. "Good point," she said at last.

"You argue like a Jesuit." She sighed. "But can't you do anything about the length? You're going to be standing in front of a
church full of people."

I smiled. The white suit featured one of the shortest hemlines
of any skirt I'd ever owned. It barely reached the middle of my
thighs, even when I was standing perfectly straight. When I
paired the ensemble with white three-inch heels, I looked like a
sea of legs capped off by a hint of white. Bending down was not an
option. But it didn't matter. I loved the look. I loved looking stat-
uesque. Most of all, I loved the attention that the white seemed to
command. And commanding attention was what working in TV
was all about.

My TV journalist career was something I'd worked toward
for years. I'd first gotten the bug in the second grade, when my
teacher, Mrs. Laatsch, assigned me the task of serving as anchor-

woman for a class project aimed at exploring the news. I went home that night and started studying the television newscasts, looking for sources of inspiration. There were relatively few women on the airwaves back then, but the one I saw, Jessica Savitch, left quite the impression. As a correspondent and cut-in anchor at NBC, she was a pioneer; a beautiful young woman amidst a sea of graying men. With golden hair and a presence that walked the fine line between glamorous and authoritative, Jessica was who—and what—I wanted to be when I grew up. So when we recorded our first elementary school newscast, and I sat down at my little anchor desk in front of the camera, I announced with great confidence: "Good evening, I'm Jessica Savitch."

My mother was instrumental in facilitating my love of Jessica—and of the news in general. Like her mother, she loved reading newspapers and magazines cover to cover and appreciated good writing. Often, she'd read favorite passages of an article aloud to me, noting their construction. When it came to television, she was equally intrigued. Long before the days of the Internet, she would photograph famous news events, fixing her camera—so old it had one of those little flashcubes on top of it that rotated each time it snapped a shot—on the television screen during moments she deemed noteworthy. She did that when Richard Nixon resigned, again when Ronald Reagan defeated Jimmy Carter.

For years, my mother kept hidden from me the fact that she had been the editor of her school newspaper and that she was a prize-winning debater and orator. But looking at her life, it's clear that she would have been a wicked good journalist. She was a superb writer, a lightning-fast typist, and, most importantly, she had an insatiable sense of curiosity. She not only asked Who, What, Where, When, Why, and How—but also How Come, How Many, Since When, and Is That Really Possible?

And she knew what made for a good interview and what made for a bad one.

"Never ever ever ask anyone how they feel about something," my mother lectured me, disgusted by a local television interview with a then Wisconsin governor. "The news isn't about feelings. The news is about facts."

Perhaps she reasoned that if she couldn't become a journalist, her daughter could.

So when I came home to tell my mother about that second-grade class news project, she was just as excited about it as I was. And she was grateful to have found for me a role model.

Jessica, in part, prompted me to seek out every school newspaper job I could find in elementary school and high school. And Jessica inspired me to head to New York City's Columbia University after high school. Jessica had spent time in Manhattan. I would, too.

Immediately, I threw myself headfirst into all the usual young journalist pursuits. I wrote and later served as an associate editor of the *Columbia Daily Spectator.* I spent summers interning for publications both big (a national magazine, *Soap Opera Digest*) and small (Beaver Dam's daily newspaper, the *Daily Citizen*). By my junior year at Columbia, I scored my big break: a coveted internship at the CNN New York Bureau. In between classes, for three days a week, I worked at the bureau, logging tapes, answering phones, assisting correspondents, and going out on shoots. I loved every facet of it: the fast pace, the energy, the people, and, above all, the excitement. In 1993, in the wake of the Gulf War, CNN was still the only kid on the twenty-four-hour-news-channel block. It was young, it was new, it was exciting—and best of all, for someone as eager as me, it was full of opportunity.

Within a month of starting the internship, I was covering global hijackings and the first World Trade Center bombing. Within three, I was offered a job as a desk assistant at the bureau, working the coveted Monday-through-Friday six A.M. to two P.M. shift. Just twenty years old, I had managed to suitably impress CNN's management team. And so they'd offered me the position, provided I could schedule a full load of senior-year classes around my forty-hour workweek.

I did so enthusiastically, writing term papers and studying for exams while hunched over teleprompters and in the back of satellite trucks. Miraculously, in spite of the demanding work schedule, I still managed to graduate summa cum laude without ever getting anything less than an A in any of my classes.

But dream job though it was, it should be noted that my position at CNN was much more than a career stepping-stone. My job at CNN was also a means of survival. Without it, there was no way I could have kept my head above water financially during those final critical years of college.

Columbia University had offered me a good financial aid package that enabled me to afford my education. My tuition and room and board were covered thanks to a series of grants and loans. But what the school's financial aid package didn't cover were all the little—and not so little—expenses of living in New York: off-campus meals, taxi rides, subway fares, cleaning supplies for my dorm suite, and, of course, clothes. My mother would have loved to send me money. But on her fixed income she had nothing to send.

To make ends meet, I did work-study jobs. I made some additional money babysitting and writing and selling freelance articles. But, for the most part, I was broke. So when CNN hired me, it fast became my financial savior, enabling me to purchase textbooks and toiletries. I could retire the embarrassment of shoes that had holes in their soles and buy a good winter coat. I was also able to invest in the occasional luxury, notably the black sleeveless cocktail dress from Bloomingdale's that I wore to my senior formal.

The one thing I never managed to afford throughout college, with or without a CNN paycheck: plane tickets. And my mother couldn't afford them either. That made for a particularly lonely existence when it came to Thanksgiving.

"It doesn't make sense for you to come home at Thanksgiving when you're just going to need to turn around and do it again for Christmas," my mother told me each of my four years of college.

"But everyone else is going home for Thanksgiving," I would cry, so homesick for my childhood cat, Blackie, and that pink ruffled bedspread of my childhood bedroom that I was sure I was going to die.

At this, my mother would sigh. A long, deep sigh.

"You of all people should know by now, Mary Elizabeth," she would say at last, "that our family is not like everyone else's. There will be other Thanksgivings."

"But I'm sad, Mom," I sniffled.

"I'm sad, too."

Looking back, I realize her inability to somehow come up with the funding to fly me home for Thanksgiving had just as much to do with her growing depression as with her finances.

When I left for college in the fall of 1990, my mother was left with an empty nest, and something more: a feeling of abandonment.

It's not that she wasn't glad to see me reach for my dreams. She'd long been priming me for college, not-so-subtly warning me since childhood of what would happen if I didn't go. But the realization of my dreams coincided with the death of some of hers. My father had left her. And now her children had, too. The house she'd once dreamed of filling with happy memories was now empty, and demons she'd been pushing to the side while I was growing up were now increasingly difficult to ignore.

I glimpsed her fear of the future the morning I left for college in August 1990. My father insisted that he drop me off at college alone, arguing that the drive with my things was going to be long and stressful enough without having the added stress of butting heads with my mother. Since my mother loathed driving and didn't have a car big or reliable enough to haul my things cross-country, she reluctantly agreed.

I thought she was at peace with my decision until moments before I walked out of the house. That's when, in the doorway that connected our dining room to our kitchen, she pulled me into her arms, sobbing.

"You're my best friend, Mary," she cried. "You may not have realized it all this time, dear daughter. But you're my best friend. And I'm going to miss you more than you'll ever know."

I hugged her back, feeling her body shake in mine, hearing her cry into my ear. I cried alongside her. Never had I felt so much sadness and so much guilt as in those moments before I left. I had sometimes wondered if she would feel as if I were leaving her when I departed for school. And now I had my answer.

In those early months of college, my mother and I worked to bridge our new geographical gap with daily phone calls. Sometimes I called her multiple times a day. I told her everything: about my first college dates, about my first college roommates, about my fixation on writing the perfect college term papers. She was supportive for the most part. But sometimes mixed in with our conversations was a sense of growing distance—even a hint of childlike coldness.

That came out the time she called to tell me she'd gone on a trip to my favorite Wisconsin apple orchard.

I was green with envy. "You went to Tom Dooley's without me?! Mom, I miss home so much!"

Her response was uncharacteristically frosty. "If you had chosen a school closer to home, you could join me on these outings. If you'd accepted that full scholarship to the University of Wisconsin, you'd be eating caramel apples with me right now. If you hadn't wanted to go clear across the nation—"

"Mom, I got it," I interrupted. "I got it!"

Her remarks made me second-guess my decision, just as I think she wanted me to. It was her way of saying, "You made your bed when you chose a far-flung university over staying close to me. Now lie in that bed."

And so it felt to me, when she wouldn't find a way to fly me home for Thanksgiving, that she was making a similar point. Mixed in with her very legitimate cash-strapped excuse seemed to lurk the message, "You sealed your Thanksgiving fate when you chose to go to Columbia. Now deal with it."

The inability to go home for Thanksgiving proved particularly devastating my freshman year of college. I distinctly remember sitting in calculus class the morning after my mother broke the news, a morose expression fixed upon my face. My calculus professor, a kind man, called me up to his desk as he dismissed the other students at the end of class.

"What's wrong?" he asked after everyone had left.

My heart raced.

"Did I do something wrong?" I asked. As a scholarship student, I was forever worried about my grades.

"No—not the homework," he quickly reassured me. "You. You look sad."

Not sure what to say, I looked at my calculus book—a big thick green thing that, brand new, had cost me more than $100 at the bookstore. "My parents told me I can't come home for Thanksgiving this year," I confessed at last. "They say it's too expensive."

My professor looked at me with such a sweet expression upon his face. So sweet I was torn between wanting to die of embarrassment and wanting to fling my arms around him out of gratitude. "That's very sad," he said after a beat.

"It's no big deal," I said quickly, working to sound as nonchalant as possible.

He shook his head. "That's where you're wrong. It *is* a big deal."

With time, I learned to accept my Thanksgiving fate. The holiday became an exercise in improvisation. By my senior year, I was rolling with the punches, working the entire holiday at the CNN New York Bureau. I was happy to have a job, grateful to stay busy. Over a can of Diet Coke, I chatted with a pair of CNN staffers also working that day, lying through my teeth when they asked what I'd be doing with my family later. Then I headed home to an empty college dorm to call my mother, have a good cry, and order Chinese food.

My father's reaction to my burgeoning career at CNN was relief. He was glad that I had found a calling—and, more importantly, that I seemed to have found an ongoing source of financial independence. My older brother, an anthropology major, had a less certain future. He had a longtime girlfriend, a young woman named Elise whom he'd met when he was a football player and she was a cheerleader at Lawrence University. But beyond Elise, my brother seemed uncertain as to what he wanted for his future, which worried my father—and his wallet—tremendously. In CNN, Dale Pflum saw an end to any financial obligation when it came to at least one of his children. It also gave him something more to talk about when he joined his growing circle of gay friends. By my college years, that circle stretched into Manhattan.

For my father and me, New York was something upon which we could agree. We both loved the city. And in the city, we managed to bond in a way we hadn't been able to do since he lived at the house in Beaver Dam. It's as if New York hit a sort of *reset* button in our relationship.

In New York, we dined out, frequently in the Village. Some nights we ate Chinese, other nights Indian. My father, more than my mother, enjoyed exploring all kinds of ethnic cuisine. In New York, we attended scores of Broadway and off-Broadway shows. One night it would be a musical like *The Goodbye Girl*, and the next it would be a play like *The Night Larry Kramer*

Kissed Me. And in New York, I increasingly accompanied him to gay bars.

Sometimes we went to a piano bar down in the West Village like Marie's Crisis, where the men took turns belting out Broadway show tunes. Other times, we went to more refined bars on the Upper East Side, where most of the men wore blazers. The men he introduced me to at the bars seemed at once amused and intrigued to meet Dale's college-age daughter. I was simply glad to be off campus for a spell, away from the pressure of the books and term papers.

Our relationship still had its ups and downs. But as my expectations of my father lowered—as I looked to him less for support and more for familiar company—we fell into a somewhat agreeable pattern of being able to sit through shows and bar outings together. More often than not, it was he who was confiding his hopes and dreams in me, instead of the other way around. And more often than not, I was listening to him prattle on about his love life, instead of the other way around.

Now broken up with Franz, he was single and looking again. Sometimes this resulted in funny episodes, like the time both of us insisted that a handsome Italian man strolling through the park had been checking each of us out.

"He was interested in me," my father insisted. "Did you see him looking me over?"

"Dad, really, you need your eyes checked. He was looking at *me!*"

My mother's reaction to my father's love life remained what it had long been—resigned. While he continued to date and frequent clubs and bars, she hunkered down, concentrating on her young students, finding new graduate classes in which to enroll. In addition to helping the children with speech and language issues, she was now increasingly serving children on the autism spectrum. Some teachers were daunted, or saddened, by the autistic students, and shirked away from them. Not Anne Diener

Pflum. She viewed autism as a challenge that she was determined to overcome.

"There's just got to be a way of reaching these kids," she would say determinedly. "I just know there is. And I'm going to find it."

The key, of course, was love. She was known for giving to her young charges, and to their worried mothers, big, reassuring hugs and literature on the latest studies. She worked to find what made each of the children tick. Hot Wheels cars for one child, Ninja Turtles for another, sports stickers and baseball cards for a third. Then she used her own paychecks to buy the children special posters and items to reward them for mastering a particular concept, whether it was uttering a sound, making eye contact, or shaking a hand.

"Those kids need to feel safe somewhere," she would tell me. "And if they're not going to feel safe anyplace else, they're going to feel safe with me in my classroom."

With my brother and me gone, my mother's young students had become the center of her universe. I admired her dedication, but worried she was lonely.

"Don't you ever think about dating again?" I asked her one day.

My mother always told me when Anthony and I were young that she didn't want to take any time away from our years at home by dating.

"I only have you two for a few precious years," she'd say. "Dating can wait."

I'd hoped that when I left for college, she'd try her hand at romance.

"I think about dating," my mother said. "And then I think about how scary it is. I don't know that I'm brave enough just yet. Give me time."

There were small signs of hope. One afternoon during my senior year of college, she called to tell me she'd met an older gentleman at a Country Kitchen, enjoying his breakfast at a table adjacent to hers.

"He was so nice. So interesting. So smart!" she enthused, detailing their hour-long talk that included everything from Shakespeare to the Packers to their favorite philosophers.

"He gave me his card and told me to call him," she said.

"And?" I asked, more excited for her than I think I'd been for my own recent dates.

"What do you think I should do?" she asked timidly.

"I think you should call him!" I cried. "Mom, what would you tell me to do?"

"I'd tell you to call him," she acknowledged. "But I'm not you." Her tone was sad now.

"You're doing things now that I'll never do. You're going places I'll never go."

There was no question that Anne Diener Pflum viewed my growing love of CNN with mixed feelings. During our nightly telephone conversations, she listened to my tales of bureau-related exploits with a combination of pride, awe, and envy. She hung on my every word when I told her about trips to the courthouses of lower Manhattan and stakeouts in the cold. She was fascinated when I explained to her how I was now required to carry a beeper. She couldn't believe the bureau sent a town car to pick me up in the morning—and that when there were no town cars available, they sent me a limousine.

"What's it like to be taken to work in a stretch limo?" she asked, her voice full of wonder.

She also memorized with relish all the names and faces and voices of the correspondents I worked with, watching them with growing interest from her post in front of the television in the cluttered living room in Beaver Dam, Wisconsin.

Jeanne Moos and Richard Roth were far and away my mother's

favorite CNN correspondents—Jeanne for her smart and obser-
vant scripts, which tickled the funny bone; and Richard, because,
well, he was Richard. Tall and wiry with a big booming voice
and just-starting-to-turn-gray hair, Richard was CNN's onetime
Rome bureau chief who'd done a tour of war correspondent duty
in the Middle East during the Gulf War before being "crowned"
CNN's UN correspondent.

Richard had a keen sense of humor. And he was fiercely intelligent. Almost immediately, he took me under his wing, patiently
teaching me how to crash a breaking news package, how to write
a script laced with both intelligence and humor, and how being
smart and being kind in the world of broadcast television don't
have to be mutually exclusive.

Richard was the one to convince my bosses at the bureau to
hire me in the first place. And Richard was the one to inform me
that if I really wanted to jump-start my career, I needed to leave
New York and try my hand at the CNN Center in Atlanta. When
I eventually introduced my mother to Richard during one of her
rare visits to New York my senior year of college, you would have
thought she had met the pope.

"Richard, it is such an honor, such a pleasure," my mother said,
shaking his hand.

Richard was appropriately charming and kind. He was one
thing that my mother and I most certainly agreed upon: he was a
great guy. And not just a great guy, but a Great Guy.

The Great Guy's advice for me to head to Atlanta to pursue
my broadcast dreams was, like most things Richard did, solid.
Within two years of starting work in the CNN Center's illustri-
ous veejay program, I was reporting on air.

My mother watched my move to the front of the camera with
skepticism. I'm not sure why, but she always seemed to be more
comfortable with my CNN career when I wasn't actually on the
airwaves. When I was behind the scenes, tailing House Speaker

Newt Gingrich—with whom I was on a first-name basis for a pair of years—she was delighted. She loved tuning in to a CNN broadcast to hear the words he'd uttered when I'd asked a question of him from behind the camera.

But when I stepped in front of the camera, something changed. Instead of tuning in, she tuned out. I was given my first on-camera break in the summer of 1996, when Bob Furnad, a vice president of CNN, selected my audition tape from a stack of would-be reporter audition tapes and told me I was ready to go on air.

I began my on-camera career with a show called *CNN Newsroom*. The downside was that it aired in the middle of the night: four thirty A.M. The upside was that because the show was geared toward high school students, whose teachers would tape the show and later air it in homerooms and current events classes, it enabled me to gain access to all kinds of fun, kid-friendly story subjects. Once, I was invited with my crew to climb up into the Statue of Liberty in the dark of night. Since we were the only ones in Lady Liberty's crown, we had the fun of playing an impromptu game of hide-and-seek within the empty statue while a driving rain poured outside. I'll never forget taking those narrow steps two at a time to get away from my soundman, who had been deemed "it," giggling as I looked out the little windows in Lady Liberty's headpiece at a dark and stormy New York Harbor.

I filed some sixty stories for Newsroom over the course of two years and additionally anchored the show at least a dozen times, taking my place behind *the* big news desk in the middle of the CNN Center newsroom. But, to my knowledge, neither of my parents ever watched or even recorded me a single one of those times.

There was always an excuse. My father was often on the road, or busy fixing up another investment property. He'd grown fond of buying houses in and around the Appleton area and renting them out as duplexes in the years since he'd left my mother.

My mother blamed her failure to watch on her discomfort with technology. "Honey, you know I don't know how to work the VCR," she would say. "I'll watch you when you're not on so late," she'd add with a laugh.

Other times, she blamed her job. "What am I supposed to do? If I watch you, I won't be able to wake up to go to work in the morning."

I was crushed. I wanted her to see my interview with Ron Howard. I wanted her to watch me take a ride on a grand old riverboat as it made its way down the Mississippi River. I craved her feedback—and, more importantly, I longed for her approval.

I tried to fix the situation by sending her tapes of my shows. But when I would ask about them in subsequent weeks and months, she would grow testy, reminding me that work kept her busy. On a trip home one weekend in the summer of 1998, I found an envelope containing one of my tapes, unopened. It was in a laundry basket in a messy dining room, amidst a mishmash of bills and unused winter scarves that still bore Shopko price tags. I'm not sure if she got so overwhelmed by the mess of the house that she honestly forgot to open the envelope and watch. Or maybe the VCR had broken and she hadn't managed to get it fixed. Perhaps she thought I wasn't good enough—and feared she wouldn't like what she saw. My broadcasts were transmitted to the masses in over one hundred countries. I even got fan mail. But for whatever reason, my broadcasts weren't seen by the one person I wanted to see them the most: my mom.

If my mother wasn't watching my every on-camera move, I could take some comfort knowing others increasingly were: men. After a seeming eternity of being ignored by the male gender, my fortunes changed considerably when I went to work for CNN. Some of this may have had to do with my slow but steady change in appearance. During college, I'd taken a roommate's advice and lightened my hair. What had been dirty blond was now blond.

I had lost weight, too. I was no longer a size 8 or size 10. Now I was a size 6. And my clothing had changed for the better. I had swapped out the big sweaters and baggy jeans that had been trends in the late 1980s and early 1990s. Now I wore clothes that were sleeker and, in the case of skirts, shorter.

Whatever the reason, men, it seemed, were everywhere now. And many of them were interested in getting to know me. There were the video journalists I worked with. All were in their early twenties and all, with virtually no exceptions, were funny and sweet. We went out drinking and dancing on our days off and enjoyed more than a few fierce make-out sessions.

There was the meteorologist fifteen years my senior who watched my every move and took me out on my first grown-up dates. There was the airline pilot I met on a flight from Atlanta to New York who subsequently squired me about to Atlanta's hot spots and CNN parties when he passed through town on his non-stop travels. There was the chef who came over after his shifts at an Atlanta restaurant and picked through the measly contents of my bachelorette cabinets to make me savory late-night dishes. And then there was Steve, the tall, dark, southern audio director who would become my first real boyfriend.

I met Steve not long after moving to Atlanta. He patiently and doggedly courted me for months before I agreed to go out with him. Four years older than me, he hailed from Columbia, South Carolina, and introduced me to a family that was as solid as mine was fractured. While my childhood home was cold, drafty, and piled high with debris and grime, his was a pristine southern gem on a refined street that positively shone. Its beauty was a result of the exceptional homemaking efforts of his mother, Ruth, a wonderful woman as kind and generous as she was dignified and ladylike. She whipped up homemade southern sweets with ease and was an expert at making all of her guests feel at home, including northerners the likes of me.

"Oh, Mary," she was forever asking. "What can I get for you?"

When Steve took me home to Ruth's house, I wanted to stay forever.

I loved the attention of the men in my life and the stereo-typical gifts of flowers and chocolates that they bought for me. Steve wrote me heartfelt poems, mooning over what he called my "spun-gold hair." Another suitor, in a fit of fixation that bordered on obsession, once followed me when I flew back to Wisconsin—driving through the night, all the way from Atlanta, to see me. A sweet young associate producer constructed for me handmade cards.

But while I was showered with gifts by the men in my life, it wasn't because of any sexual favors I was granting them. On the contrary. I was a chaste girl, seldom granting any man, even those who begged loudest and longest or who spent the most money on me, much more than flirtatious smiles, good-night kisses, and, on occasion, some fiercely fun dry humping. To be crystal clear: I was a virgin. And I wanted to remain a virgin.

The men in my life liked to playfully call me a tease. But more than a tease, I was a good Catholic girl who was still trying to live by my mother the former nun's rules, even when I lived a thou-sand miles from that mother. From the time I turned thirteen, my mother had begged me—commanded me!—to wait to give it all up physically to any man until I was a bona fide adult.

"Giving yourself away too soon will only create problems," my mother insisted. "You have enough to worry about as a teenager without worrying about that."

I don't know why I listened as carefully as I did—or for as long as I did—but I did. It's not that I wasn't curious. I most cer-tainly was. But my mother seemed to have a point. Her advice had always been solid, and it seemed to be in this case as well.

My career was going well. I was having fun. And I wasn't ready to settle down. Why complicate things, potentially irrevocably?

So after long good-night kisses, lengthy petting sessions, I politely asked the men in my life to leave. Many were incredulous at my strict rules of conduct. A few were left near tears as they told me about a horribly painful physical condition called "blue balls" that my kisses coupled with my refusal to sleep with them had driven them to.

"Can't you—just this once?" they would ask. But I was fortunate. Almost without exception, the men I dated were gentlemen who seemed to accept that putting out—at least putting all the way out—was not something I was ready or willing to do. My burgeoning career and my mother's approval meant too much to me.

In the end, I lost my virginity to Steve at the ripe old age of twenty-three. But only after two years of begging. I did it more as a means of putting an end to the constant badgering, I think, than anything else. There was only so much begging a girl could take. It was a relief in many ways. My mother's insistence upon saving herself for marriage certainly hadn't worked out for her. Unlike my mother, I knew at least the first man I'd slept with was straight and wanted me. That meant more to me than anything.

I said goodbye to Steve, and to Atlanta, in the summer of 1998, when I was reposted to Germany. The move came thanks to the Robert Bosch Fellowship program. Designed to advance the careers of young American leaders abroad while simultaneously enhancing the relationship between Germany and the U.S., the program offered to pay for me to live in Germany for a year. It was a win-win situation. I could continue to file reports for CNN, this time from European locations.

My mother was gobsmacked when I told her of my plan to move overseas.

"Are you sure?" she asked repeatedly.

"Have you thought this through?"

"Is this what you really want?"

Yes, yes, and I think so, I told her. "Mom, everyone who wants to be a serious journalist needs to go overseas. And besides, I should do these things when I'm in my twenties, right?"

"Right," she said sadly. "It's just that—"

"Just that what?" I asked.

"It's just that I wasn't doing anything like this when I was in my twenties."

When she was in her twenties, she was at Oldenburg.

The move to Germany was among the wisest career choices I would make. The Europe-based stories I was able to file were nothing short of magical. For one story, I donned a ball gown to cover Vienna's fairy-tale-like Opera Ball. For other stories, I spent time at the NATO and European Union headquarters. Just as important as the assignments were the new friends I made, the new men I dated. I was swept off my feet by a Royal Navy officer with piercing blue eyes who wrote me multipage love letters I kept beneath my pillow. I was wined and dined by a mysterious German businessman who loved to buy me designer dresses and airplane tickets "just because."

Especially memorable was the time he decided to "cure" me of a case of homesickness by jetting me off to Venice for the weekend. After a series of gondola rides and late-night dinners, he took me to the Piazza San Marco, where he presented me with a bouquet of four dozen multicolored roses and a diamond ring from Cartier, situated in a beautiful red cushioned box.

I was stunned and met his fervent gaze with nervous laughter.

"What's this?" I asked, hoping I'd misunderstood.

"Isn't it obvious? Marry me."

In my state of shock, I dropped the flowers.

"I can't get married now," I said.

"Why not?" he asked, his blue eyes looking both sad and surprised.

"I'm too young," I told him.

What I didn't tell him was that I was still trying to make up for lost time. Out on my own, reporting and producing for CNN, I had at last discovered a world in which plates weren't shattered and mothers weren't spending their summers in mental wards. I was living in residences that weren't cold and drafty and piled high with debris. Life was no longer controlled by a pair of parents fighting all sorts of demons generated by their own childhoods and their own well-intentioned, albeit questionable, choices. For the first time in my life, I was in the driver's seat. And I was relishing every minute of it. I wasn't ready to cede that control to anyone. Not even rose- and Cartier-wielding gentlemen who declared their love in locales as romantic as Venice.

My favorite assignment during that first year in Europe came in the spring of 1999. CNN sent me to Malta, the tiny island country off the coast of Sicily. Malta was like no place I had ever been, a land of castles and ancient temples sprinkled in their own unique brand of fairy dust. The weather was pristine. It's sunny there 360 days a year. The views were stunning: the rich blue of the Mediterranean stands in stark contrast to the bleached white rocks of the old megalithic temples that predate Stonehenge. The food was to die for: fresh octopus, yummy fish seasoned with capers.

But great though the weather and the food were, the highlight of my trip was Malcolm. He was the young movie producer whom I was assigned to interview for a story about Malta's burgeoning film industry. Tall and lanky, Malcolm was a native Maltese with dirty-blond hair and a matching beard. He was also gifted with a keen sense of humor and palpable ambition. Malta had become the hot place in the world to shoot films, owing to its splendid weather and the great old Roman ruins that had gone relatively untouched for centuries, and young film producers like Malcolm were capitalizing upon the newfound attention the nation was attracting. Among the movies being filmed in Malta while I was there: *Gladiator*, the Russell Crowe period piece that would go on to win multiple Oscars.

After our interview, Malcolm invited me to tour the *Gladiator* set and later to join him for dinner and a nighttime yacht ride around Malta.

It turned out to be one of the most magical nights of my life, perfect in every way. I still remember the red sleeveless shift I wore, the strappy black sandals. Armed with a bottle of wine, Malcolm and I talked for hours on the deck of the enormous yacht, about Malta, and career paths, and dreams. And then, from the upper deck, as the yacht cruised around Gozo, we lay back and studied the stars and talked some more: about life and love and faith and the problems with the Catholic Church, of which we were both conflicted members. I told Malcolm about my mother, the former nun. He told me about priests he had known and feared. And together we looked at those constellations and at the lights of that ancient island nation.

"Where was this?" I asked him, giggling.

"Where was what?" he asked, laughing now, too.

"Where was all of this when I was growing up?"

"It was here all along"—he smiled—"waiting for you."

I closed my eyes and breathed deeply then, wanting to savor the moment for as long as I could. How in the world, I wondered, could those wondrous stars above stare down upon two such different worlds: this wonderland of yachts and temples and Malcolms and that horribly sad world of Beaver Dam where my mother remained in a living room stacked high with decaying newspapers and broken appliances?

Repeatedly in my twenties, I tried to break my mother free of that world. Each time I returned home to Beaver Dam, each time she visited me in Atlanta, I encouraged her to move.

"How 'bout Colorado, Mom?" I'd ask. "You always say how

much you love visiting Aunt Kathy. We could look for a cool condo for you there. Maybe right down the street from her."

"What about Madison?" I asked another time. "It's a college town, and you love college towns. You could get an apartment near the lake and take lots of interesting classes."

"What about Indianapolis?" I offered on a third occasion. "You always talk about how much you loved living there. And the city has really grown. We could help you find a cute place, and you could visit your old stomping grounds."

Always, she refused.

"I need to stay put for you and your brother," my mother would say with a shake of her head. "I need to give you a home base to come back to. Just in case."

"But, Mom," I protested, "we're grown now. And I don't know that we're coming back any time soon."

"I said, Mary," she said, narrowing her eyes as she looked at me, "I need to give you a home base. Just in case."

When my mother refused to leave the house in Beaver Dam permanently, I tried to get her to leave temporarily. She had never been to Europe, so I made it my mission during my year in Germany to get her to join me on a European vacation. The mission was easier said than done. My mother's reasoning for refusing to go abroad stemmed, she said, from a love for the United States.

"Why would I want to visit someone else's country when I haven't finished exploring my own?" she asked.

But the real reason behind my mother's refusal to travel, I knew, went beyond patriotism. Age had not treated my mother's body kindly. Increasingly, her knees—significantly damaged by all of those years of kneeling upon those cold, hard kneelers at the convent and cleaning all of those cold marble floors—caused her trouble, making it difficult and painful to walk. It was easier to stay home. But I was undeterred.

For Christmas that year, I took fifty thousand of the frequent-flyer miles I had painstakingly accrued on Delta Airlines and cashed them in for a round-trip ticket for my mother, which would take her from Milwaukee to Berlin. I wrapped the certificate up in a box, then presented it to her during a family gathering we had in Texas, where Anthony and Elise had gone to live as a newly married couple.

"Honey, I can't go to Europe," my mother had argued almost as soon as she opened the box. "I don't have a passport. I don't speak the language."

"I'll help you get the passport. And I'll speak the language for you," I told her. "You have to do this."

Two months later, much to her surprise—and mine—she did. It was a rocky trip from the very beginning. When my mother tried to switch planes in Chicago to board the aircraft that was to take her on to Europe, she inadvertently got in the wrong line—and on the wrong plane. Instead of a Berlin-bound flight, she had stepped onto a Cairo-bound flight and found herself surrounded by excited women in long dresses and headscarves who didn't speak any English. Thankfully, a flight attendant discovered the error in the moments before takeoff, but the experience rattled her.

By the time she arrived in Berlin, she was fatigued and frightened and refused to allow me to take her to Paris for the weekend of shopping and museum hopping I had originally planned. Instead, she begged me to let her hunker down in my Berlin apartment for the week. I had no choice but to acquiesce. I kept telling her about all the wonderful things we could see and do if she would please just allow me to lead the way. But her idea of fun was taking in American movies at Potsdamer Platz or watching reruns of *ER* and *The Mary Tyler Moore Show* on German television networks. My one victory came in the form of a day trip to Dresden. She adored the old East German city—primarily because of its wicked good bratwurst, which she bought on the street for a couple of euros—and because of its stunning artwork.

A second small but significant victory came later that weekend when we were back in Berlin and she allowed me to take her out for a dinner of paella at a Portuguese restaurant. She had never had the rice-and-seafood dish and was delighted by its contents as well as by the pitcher of sangria that accompanied it. She loved most of all the attention of the restaurant's owner, a graying man from Portugal who found my mother delightful. My mother had always liked to laugh. And that night, she laughed a lot. I'm sure much of that laughter stemmed from the sangria. But I think it was something more—a willingness to let go, if only for a couple of hours.

But beyond the trips to Dresden and the Portuguese restaurant, there were problems with our visit. More specifically, there were fights. When I went to live in Germany, I had made the decision to forward all of my U.S. mail to my mother's address in Beaver Dam. I was especially concerned about staying on top of my bills. Among the bills that were being forwarded to my mother's house: my Atlanta phone bills, a monthly storage-unit bill, and a pair of credit card bills. This was in the late 1990s, before bills could easily be paid electronically.

Each month, I dutifully sent from Germany a check with which my mother could cover my bills. And each month, I would ask my mother, during some of our many phone calls, if the money I was sending was sufficient to cover the bills. She always assured me that it was and, since I knew checks were being cashed, I didn't bother to question her further. But on the second night of her visit to Germany, she stunned me with the presentation of a manila envelope full of my mail.

There was a smattering of magazines, a pair of letters from my university alumni office, a heavy cream envelope that appeared to be a wedding invitation of some sort. And there were many, many unopened bills.

"What's this?" I cried as I scanned the collection of envelopes with little cellophane windows.

"It's your mail," my mother said nonchalantly from her post in front of the television in my West Berlin living room. She'd found an old episode of *Magnum PI* dubbed into German and was transfixed. "I thought you'd like the old issues of the *New Yorker* that you missed."

"Not the magazines," I said, scanning the first of the bills that I came to in the pile. It was the last of my Atlanta phone bills—which had been due seven months ago. "The bills. You told me you were paying them."

"I did pay them," said my mother, pointing to an open envelope on which she'd scrawled, *"Paid—November 1998."*

"But that's just one of the bills," I cried. "What about all of these?"

I held up a handful of unopened bills, many marked "Second" or "Final" Notice.

"I've been sending you money every month," I cried.

"And I've been using it to pay for the phone bills to talk to you over here," she retorted.

I sank down in the folds of the couch and buried my head in my hands. All these months I had thought my bills were being paid on time. But they weren't. I had assumed that if there were problems, she would have told me, at least warned me.

I cringed as I dissected the pile. Each envelope revealed contents that seemed worse than the last. One letter informed me that the lock on my storage unit had been cut since my account was more than ninety days past due. My Macy's credit card, which I'd had no opportunity to use in months, had been cut off.

"Mom," I said, crying now, "I counted on you. You told me you would make the payments."

"I'm sorry, Mary," she told me. "I did the best I could."

That I believed. She was forever doing her best. The problem was that her best wasn't good enough when it was pitted against the beast known as chronic depression.

My mother's failure to pay my bills during my time in Germany would come back to haunt me when I bought my first home two years later. Numerous letters and phone calls and a renewed commitment to pay my bills in full every month eventually salvaged my credit. But I would never regain trust in my mother, who, I had at last come to realize at the age of twenty-six, was stuck in her well-meaning yet terribly disorganized ways.

I didn't see my mother again after her visit to Berlin until the eve of her mother's memorial service in June. Some three months had passed. The time had allowed me to take a deep breath.

The afternoon before the memorial, I flew from Berlin to Indiana to surprise my mother. Her brothers and sisters knew I was coming. My mother did not. When I walked into the restaurant in which she and all of her siblings were gathered, she sat stunned, looking past her salad plate to me as if I were a ghost.

"What are you doing here?" she cried.

"I came to see you," I told her.

"But you were in Berlin," she said, still not believing I was there.

"I know, Mom. But there are airplanes."

I threw my arms around her neck. Moments later, I was relieved to feel the familiar warmth of her arms tightening around me.

"Airline tickets cost money," she said into my hair.

"And you're worth more," I whispered.

My mother, and my grandmother, needed me. And I was there. In that white suit I had bought for my CNN shoot in California.

The eulogy I delivered for my grandmother the morning of the memorial was made up of the top ten things my grandmother had taught me during her life. It paid homage to her love of literature, to her appreciation for great hotel bathrooms, and, above all, to her encouraging me to pursue my dreams. "My grandmother taught me, above all," I told the attendees at the memorial service, "to reach, reach, and reach some more."

It was an apt message. Two days prior to the memorial service, when I was preparing to travel from Berlin to Indiana, I had received a call from Steve Cassidy, the head of CNN's international desk, asking me about relocating to Turkey.

I had been to Turkey in April of that year to file a pair of reports about the Turkish federal election. Now they needed an Istanbul-based staff to help launch a new network, CNN Türk.

"It'll be fun, kid," Steve told me. "And you told me you want adventure. Am I right?"

"You're right," I said.

"Then give it some thought and give me a call on Monday."

I was stunned. Even though I'd been to Turkey, I knew almost nothing of the country aside from the fact that it had amazing views and equally amazing food.

Germany was situated in Western Europe. Lots of people spoke English. But Turkey? I wasn't sure whether this Catholic girl was ready to move full-time to a distant land of mosques, minarets, and prayer calls. I had to make my decision soon.

And so, in the moments following Aurelia Diener's memorial service, as I climbed into the passenger seat of my mother's car, Turkey was very much on my mind.

My mother wanted to drive down the street from the church where the memorial service had been held—the same church where she'd made her First Communion all those years ago—to take one last look at the Pine Patch. A new family owned the property now, but they had agreed that my mother and her siblings could come back for a visit.

"You can leave your rental car here in the church parking lot, sweetheart," my mother told me. "Why don't you come and ride with me to the Pine Patch?"

I agreed. I knew she liked having me home. I was glad that she wanted the company.

Pulling open the passenger door to her car, I gasped.

"Oh my God!"

The seats and floors were piled high with school supplies and newspapers and bills and maps; with Jolly Rancher candies and key chains and a pair of empty McDonald's coffee cups. And the whole car smelled of something I couldn't quite put my finger on—a combination of dust and must, like the bottom of an old purse that's been caked with years' worth of crumbs and dirt and debris and then baked in the sun.

"Mom, what the hell is this?"

I regretted my words as soon as I uttered them. My mother shot me a panicked look.

"It's okay, honey," she said, trying to keep her tone even as she climbed into the driver's seat. "Just throw the things from the front seat into the back."

At my mother's urging, I began the process of moving one armful of things from the passenger seat to the backseat, then another, and then another, so that I could eventually sit my white-suit-clad fanny down in the car. The car was in worse shape than I'd ever seen it. I'd seen piles in my childhood. But not like this. Never had I seen mountains this deep.

"Are you okay?" I asked, looking at my mother as she maneuvered the car. She pushed a pile of coupon flyers from last Sunday's edition of the *Milwaukee Journal* off the stick shift so that she could put the car into reverse.

"I'm okay, honey," she said, oblivious to the mess. "I miss your grandmother. But she's with Dad now."

She paused and reached over to move some mail—all unopened—off the top of a tape recorder that she'd wedged between the stick shift console and the left side of my bucket seat. My mother had always insisted that FM radio and air-conditioning were luxuries we couldn't afford in a car. But an old-school tape recorder? That would make up for the dearth of music choices on long drives. She pressed *play* so that we could enjoy one of her favorite albums, *John Denver's Greatest Hits,* together.

I listened as he belted out, "Country roads, take me home."

After a moment, she turned to me. "What are you going to do now? Are you going to come home for a while?"

I detected in her voice a hint of hopefulness. We had been so busy spending the past twelve hours talking about the memorial service that I hadn't gotten a chance to tell her about Turkey. The truth of the matter was that I hadn't known what to tell her.

For more than a year, I'd been a woman without a country, living out of a suitcase in Europe, avoiding questions from family and Atlanta-based friends about when I was coming back.

But at last, at that moment, looking at the dirty cup holders in the car coated in a thick, sticky mess of coffee and Diet Coke stains, then at the floorboards stacked so high with magazines and old Styrofoam cups and cookie wrappers from McDonald's that they hid my white high heels, I knew.

"CNN called," I told her, looking ahead now at the road that stretched in front of us. "They asked me to move to Turkey."

My mother looked from the road to me, stunned. "Turkey? What did you tell them?"

"I'm going to do it," I said. "What do I have to lose?"

I didn't know a soul, didn't speak the language, wasn't sure what I was getting myself into. But sitting in that white suit in that filthy car, all I could think about was all that I had to gain.

Chapter 10

The Bride Wore White

May 28, 2005

"Well, my dear, I think it's time."

The petite brunette stood behind me, gently using her French-manicured nails to poof the white silk veil she'd planted on my head moments before and then nodding approvingly.

"You look exquisite," Marie said in her beautiful Ecuadorean accent. *"Absolutely exquisite."*

"Promise?" I asked.

"Would I lie?"

"I don't know. Would you?"

At this, we both laughed. I'd flown Marie in from New York to Wisconsin the day before. She was the older sister of Nelson D'Leon, a makeup artist who was a leading bridal stylist on both coasts. Like Nelson, Marie had an ability to make a woman look like the most beautiful version of herself on her wedding day. And the fifty-something-year-old immigrant possessed something more: a maternal touch. Today of all days I needed that mother's touch.

For months, I'd painstakingly planned every moment of this day. I'd picked the date—May 28—specifically because of the flowers I knew that would be in bloom at the time: lilies of the valley and peonies. My favorites. And my mother's favorites. And Trudy's favorites before her. Some of the blooms were plucked from the yard in Beaver Dam. I'd carefully selected the priest, Father Ed, the *same wonderful man who had overseen my First Communion all those years ago. I'd found the perfect venues: a cathedral for the ceremony and the Milwaukee Art Museum—the new place in Wisconsin for all things glam—for the reception. And after months of deliberation, I'd picked the gown—the Vera Wang silk sheath I was now about to step into.*

I'd wanted everything to be perfect. Absolutely perfect.

Looking at my reflection in the mirror, I gently placed a hand to my head, stroking first the veil, then the blond locks Marie had lovingly curled. I'd told Marie I wanted to channel Veronica Lake. And she'd listened. Today I was the embodiment of 1930s glam. My hair, held half up and half down with a replica of a 1930s hairpin, had a dramatic cowlick in the front, then fell down past my shoulders in screen-siren waves. My lips shone in a sexy dark pout that stopped shy of being red. And the false lashes that Marie had added to the corners of my eyes were just right. They made my already long lashes appear fuller, sexier. Seductive without being too over-the-top.

Inhaling deeply, Marie patted both of my shoulders and repeated her earlier compliment: "Absolutely exquisite."

Then, nodding, she walked to the bed and picked up the gown that had been lying in wait. Shaking, I stood and removed the white bathrobe that bore the Pfister Hotel's insignia in one corner and stepped into the dress that Marie held gingerly in her hands. One zip later, the dress was on. Marie clapped her hands.

"It's gorgeous, Mary. Really."

"Really?" I asked. I knew from the fittings at the Vera Wang bridal headquarters that the gown fit me like a glove. That the dress, which I'd specially ordered as "long" for my five-foot-eleven frame, and which I'd asked them to custom-make in a bright white—not ivory!—and with an extra-long train, was just right. But of course I still worried. Of course I longed for the reassurance.

"Really," Marie said with certainty.

Then she spun me around so that we faced each other.

"Really," she repeated once more for good measure.

I loved Marie. She was worth every penny her services had cost me. And more.

I'd always thought it would be my mother dressing me in these final moments. Helping me into my gown. I'd wanted so very much for her to be the one with me now. But after those visits to New York this past year, after what had happened at that last fitting I'd taken her to, I'd followed the advice of my girlfriends: I decided to dress without her and share my joy with her when the dress was on. Now, for a split second, I wondered if I'd made a mistake.

As if on cue, I heard the knock on the door.

"Mary? Mary, are you ready?" called my mother's voice from the hotel hallway. I wasn't sure, but I thought I sensed impatience.

"It's okay?" Marie asked. "Are you ready?"

Biting my lower lip, I nodded and made my way over to the door.

Taking a deep breath, I turned the handle and pulled back the heavy door to reveal my mother.

"Mom, you look beautiful!" I cried.

And she did. Her silver hair had been professionally blown out at the hotel's salon. It looked lovely. It was soft and feminine—more so than I'd seen it in years—and set off the blue floor-length dress she wore.

"Thank you," she said appreciatively, entering the room.

"And you, dear daughter," she said, stopping short. She took a step back to look me up and down, then down and up.

I held my breath, waiting for her to finish her thoughts.

"You look like you're still wearing your nightgown."

The white dress I wore on my wedding day on May 28, 2005, made me feel like any great wedding dress is supposed to make a bride feel: glamorous, gorgeous, beautiful. And not just beautiful—but Deliciously Beautiful. The best part? I got to wear it on the happiest day of my life. The worst part? The dress that I adored—and that my bridesmaids swooned over—was the same dress my mother had loathed from the moment I tried it on.

The snow-white dress in question was a sleeveless Vera Wang silk charmeuse slip of a gown. A bias cut, the V-necked gown hugged my every curve before falling down into a train that extended a few feet behind me as I walked. Swarovski crystal-beaded brooches placed on both shoulder straps and a pair of snow-white opera gloves that reached to my elbows heightened the glam look. Pulling it all together: the cathedral-length veil, which gave the entire ensemble a fairy-tale feel.

When I emerged from the fitting room for the first time wearing the dress and took my place atop a raised platform in the middle of the showroom at the Vera Wang flagship store on Madison Avenue, a group of four fifty-something sisters who had flown in from Minnesota to help their niece shop for her wedding dress spontaneously burst into applause. One of them even cried. I watched, half stunned, half flattered, as they momentarily left their poor niece—standing atop her own platform on the other side of the floor—to fend for herself and gathered around me to ooh and aah, as if I were some sort of celebrity.

"Could we take your picture?" they asked, beginning to snap my photo before I'd even said yes.

"Did you always know you wanted to wear something this sexy?" they queried.

"Isn't this just like the dress Carolyn Bessette wore when she got married to John Kennedy Junior?" they asked. "Girl, you're lucky you've got the figure to pull it off!"

Their niece, wearing a lacy ball gown that wasn't particularly flattering on her pear-shaped figure, smiled at me from the other side of the store. The saleswoman nodded approvingly as I turned around to inspect my backside in the three-way mirror. And my mother—who had flown in the night before, and for whom I had

specifically scheduled the dress appointment, weeks in advance—
shook her head.

Her crossed arms spoke volumes, as did her sighs. But even I
was unprepared for what she would say of the dress:

"You look like you're wearing a nightgown."

The women from Minnesota gasped. The saleswoman dropped
her pen.

"A what?" asked the saleswoman.

"A nightgown," my mother repeated, taking me in carefully.
"She looks like she's wearing a nightgown I used to have."

The women from Minnesota protested. "She's beautiful!" they
cried. "She looks fantastic!" A third gently mouthed to me, "Don't
listen to her!" before scurrying off to rejoin her niece.

How could I not listen to her? She was my mother. And I was
the bride. The bride! Wasn't she supposed to be as happy as I was
about shopping for my wedding gown? Wasn't she supposed to be
as crazy about weddings as I'd always been? For as long as I could
remember, I'd longed for this moment. I had been *that* little girl
who grew up cutting images of bridal gowns out of magazines so
that I could hang them over my bed. I'd sketched my own dream
gown dozens of times in notebooks, carefully constructing the
waist that would be just so, the veil that would hang to right about
there.

Becoming a bride was not just a moment for me—it was
The Moment. So hearing from my beloved mother during said
Moment that a four-thousand-dollar gown from a top designer
reminded her of something she'd likely bought on clearance at
some department store and would only wear to bed in the dark of
night stung mightily.

And, strangely, that seemed to be her intent. It must have been,
since it wasn't an isolated incident.

At the Carolina Herrera boutique, she would spend the entire time telling me what was wrong with each dress. Too low in the front. Too low in the back. Too bumpy. Too poofy. Not simple enough.

At the Monique Lhuillier trunk show the following day, it was more of the same. The gowns were too busy or too lacy, too modern, too confusing, or, my favorite, "too look-at-me."

"What does 'too look-at-me' mean?" asked the saleswoman overseeing the trunk show.

"If Mary wears that, it's obvious she just wants everyone to look at her." My mother sighed, eyeing the figure-forming sheath from Monique Lhuillier that was so tight I could scarcely breathe.

"But she's the bride," the exasperated saleswoman said. "Everyone is *supposed* to be looking at her."

A large part of the problem, of course, was that the gowns I loved were light years away from the simple gown my mother had worn for her own wedding. She wanted my wedding dress to have sleeves. And a high neckline. And with nothing that hinted at the figure that lay beneath layers of satin and silk.

In the end, two months after my quest began, I purchased my wedding gown—the Vera Wang "nightgown"—all by myself, trudging back to the boutique with no mother in tow. For the sake of maintaining a good relationship with the sales reps at Vera Wang, my solo mission was for the best. But it was more than a little bit disappointing. I wanted my mother with me.

It's not that my mother didn't like my future husband. No—Dean Peterson was a subject on which the two of us could wholeheartedly agree. Within moments of meeting him, my mother declared, "Mary, he's wonderful!"

And he was. For both of us. Dean had it all: brains, a sense of humor, kindness, and manners galore. Plus, he was a Catholic who'd grown up in the Midwest. A Catholic! The first Catholic man I'd ever seriously dated. Add to that Dean's tremendous patience and his strong physical resemblance to her father—like

Al Diener, Dean has soulful brown eyes and a head full of dark curls—and my mother was over the moon.

"He's wonderful," my mother said again and again.

I met Dean on my birthday, October 25, 2003, at a party given in my honor at a bar on Manhattan's East Side. I've always said Dean is the best birthday present I've ever received. And it's true. When I met Dean, I felt as if I'd found the piece of the puzzle that at last made me whole.

The years leading up to that birthday had been particularly tumultuous. I had been faced with my first serious health crisis. I had lost a job at CNN that I dearly loved and that had come to define me. I had fumbled financially. And, perhaps most significantly, I had broken a heart and had my heart broken.

There was only one man I loved before Dean Peterson. His name was Mesut. He was Turkish. He was Muslim. And he was everything my mother feared when I moved to Istanbul.

On so many levels, Mesut and I were opposites. I was a Westerner who adored short skirts, bright red lipstick, and silly soap operas. He was a proud Turk who counted among his friends Turkish nationalists who despised the U.S. and its foreign policy and questioned its seemingly loose morals. But from the moment we met in July 1999—within a week of my moving to Istanbul to work full-time for the fledgling CNN Türk network—we were drawn to each other.

We were introduced one sunny afternoon in a hallway of the *Hürriyet* newspaper building, me with a notebook in my hand, he with a camera in his. I was twenty-six. I was immediately struck by his prematurely graying hair, his piercing brown eyes, and his muscular physique, honed by years of lugging heavy equipment up mountains, in and out of war zones. Most of all, I was struck by Mesut's wisdom, which was palpable.

I was new to Turkey and its East-meets-West ways. Istanbul was divided between two continents: Europe and Asia. Fittingly,

I lived on the western, European side of the city, while Mesut and his identical twin brother shared an apartment on the Asian side.

In those early weeks, I was still adjusting to my new environment. There was new food—one part Middle Eastern, one part Mediterranean. There were different customs: important decisions weren't made by asking direct questions and taking part in frank discussions, but instead by drinking round upon round of Turkish tea. And there were decidedly conflicting views of Western women. To some Turks, Western women represented a brave new world to be embraced, and to others, we were the embodiment of evil and little better than prostitutes. I found that out the hard way. On more than one occasion in those early months as an American journalist living abroad, authorities pulled me over to question me for having the audacity to take a taxi home from the office by myself after nine P.M.

"What are you?" they queried, shining a flashlight first on my blond hair, then on my reporter's notebooks. "A hooker?"

And so as I worked to navigate my new country of residence, and my place in the fledgling CNN Türk organization, Mesut and I struck up a friendship. We put aside all the glaring differences, focusing instead on what we had in common: We were both children of divorce who adored our mothers. We both had conflicted relationships with our fathers. We both had majored in history in college.

When a 7.8 earthquake struck Istanbul in August—killing nearly twenty thousand people and causing the buildings we lived and worked in to rumble and crack—we stopped the delicate dance of flirtation that we had been engaging in and launched full-throttle into a passionate affair. Lovemaking came easily and frequently after long days of work. It struck us both as funny that some of our most intense limb-locking sessions took place during afternoon prayer calls, when conservative chants were blasted from the spindle-like minarets of nearby mosques.

But while a torrid affair—and an affair with a Muslim, no less—was decidedly un-Catholic, my life in Turkey actually strengthened my Catholicism, thanks in large part to the support of Mesut.

On Sundays, Mesut protectively accompanied me to Mass at the Catholic church in central Istanbul and watched as I hung my head in prayer in the aftermath of the quake. There in a Muslim country, I was forced for the first time to think deeply about the meaning of the words to prayers I'd recited since childhood:

"We believe in one God."

"One baptism for the forgiveness of sins."

"He was born of the Virgin Mary."

"We believe . . . in the life of the world to come."

My deepening faith was further bolstered by the historic environs in which I lived. On long weekends, Mesut and his friends delighted in taking me to Christian sites throughout Turkey: To Haran, where it's believed the Virgin Mary was born. To the Pool of Abraham on the Syrian border. To the ancient home of one of the Three Kings. To the caves and tunnels of Cappadocia, where ancient Christians gathered and painted beautiful frescoes devoted to Christ in the fourth and fifth centuries A.D.

My mother marveled at my stories, which I would share with her during late-night or early-morning phone calls, owing to the eight-hour time difference that separated Istanbul from Beaver Dam.

"How do you know that's where the Virgin Mary lived?" she would ask, half excitedly, half skeptically.

"Mom, it's not just me saying these things. Historians and biblical scholars say it, too. Just because Muslim people live here now doesn't mean Christians didn't live here before. And Christian people live here, too, you know."

Then I would pause and offer the invitation I know she dreaded.

"You should come here to visit me. You would like it."

I knew she would never come. If she hadn't liked Germany—a

Western country with the comforts of America—she would never tolerate Turkey.

"Why don't you take the money you'd spend on a ticket for me to go there and use it to come home and see me instead?" she'd counter.

She wanted to remain at home. And she wanted me home, too. She remained concerned about my safety.

When I got a high fever in the wake of the earthquake—likely as a result of spending so much time in the hardest-hit areas, where the mountains of debris and the dead bodies beneath baked in 90-plus-degree temperatures—she sent me and my colleagues a box filled with latex gloves and masks she'd secured from the local Fleet Farm in Beaver Dam.

"Wear these!" her handwritten note implored. *"Please!"*

And when I wrote to her of my travels with Mesut, my delight in learning more Turkish, she countered with questions about my future.

"When are you coming home?" she would half ask, half demand. "I have your room all ready for you."

My answers were vague. "I don't know. I'm not sure. Maybe in a few months?"

It was the truth. I didn't know where my relationship with Mesut was headed, but I knew I wanted to follow its lead.

Every day was a new adventure.

In addition to the ancient Christian sites, Mesut took me to Aphrodisias, an amazing collection of ancient temples devoted to the goddess of love, located on the western side of Turkey. I'll never forget the sight of pomegranate blossoms billowing in the breeze in the midst of the sun-soaked ruins.

On another vacation, we journeyed to Cesme, a beautiful little town on the Aegean. By day, we swam in water bluer and clearer than any I'd ever seen and fell asleep on white sandy beaches, the taste of the salt water still on our lips. And at night, we feasted on local cuisine. One evening Mesut asked me what my heart desired for dinner. I told him I didn't care so long as we could eat it outdoors and look out onto the water. I watched as Mesut passed my wish along to a balding restaurant owner, who wore a suit and tie. Smiling at me, the owner nodded graciously, then clapped his hands and instructed a team of waiters to lift a white-cloth-covered table from inside the restaurant high into the air and to follow me to any outdoor location of my choosing.

"Anywhere?" I asked, delighted by the display of over-the-top chivalry.

"Anywhere," the restaurant owner told me, bowing.

I laughed as the waiters dutifully followed me for nearly a block before, at the nod of my head, they dramatically set the table down on a patch of land that overlooked a series of little boats that danced in the moonlit water.

Mesut clapped his hands and laughed as he took his seat opposite me. "Tatlim, do you know why I love you?"

"Why?" I asked, placing my napkin in my lap.

"I love you because you are three."

"Three?" I asked, confused.

"Yes, you are three. All of us—we have an internal age, the age we are on the inside. You are three."

The words might have insulted most women, but Mesut's body language and tone were warm.

"The way you smile and laugh, the way you ask all those questions, the way you love with your whole heart—you are three," he said, nodding once more.

Our love was simple and sweet and pure and like none I had ever experienced. Everything, it seemed, was possible with him at my side. Even overcoming those pesky cultural differences. I met Mesut's family—his two brothers and two sisters and mother. His mother spoke no English and wore a veil at all times. I worried what she might think of me, an American girl who wore sleeveless dresses that fell only to my knees. But at the end of our first visit, she embraced me and called me "daughter."

My mother was less certain of our match. From the moment I showed her pictures of Mesut, a year before I brought him home to the U.S. for the first time, she was uneasy.

"Why are you wearing this shirt?" she asked, looking uneasily at a photo of Mesut and me happily fishing on the Bosphorus at sunset. She looked not at the stunning site, the sunbeams dancing on the water's surface, but instead at the man's-style green polo shirt I wore in the photograph. I squirmed uneasily. Did I tell her it was because the sex had been so good the night before that I hadn't bothered to go home to change in the morning and had instead borrowed Mesut's shirt?

"Why are you wearing his hat in this one?" she asked, looking at another photo, this time with the two of us happily posing in front of an old lighthouse in Istanbul that had been converted into a restaurant. Mesut had taken me there one chilly evening and offered me his wool stocking cap when the wind ripped through us as we waited for a boat to take us back to the mainland. It was an odd match for the elegant long black wool Calvin Klein dress coat I wore. But I didn't care. As the photographer snapped the photo, Mesut and I exchanged glances—the ones that said, at that very moment, he and I were the only two people in the world.

I was happy. And my mother knew it. This, I think, made her the most uncomfortable of all—not that I was sharing articles of clothing with a man, but that I was so happy with that man—a Muslim from the other side of the world whom she knew so little about.

Our once-tight mother-daughter bond was still tight, but it was shifting. Phone calls that had formerly occurred once a day now took place just a couple of times a week, owing to the time difference and the expense. And while I had once felt free to tell her everything about my life, now I hesitated.

When my mother eventually met Mesut in the flesh, more than a year after our courtship began, she eyed him skeptically, treating him as if he were some sort of science fair experiment she'd reluctantly agreed to let me bring home to tinker with on the condition that I would ultimately take it back to the laboratory from which it came. The meeting took place not in Wisconsin, where I'd wanted to bring Mesut, but instead in downtown Indianapolis.

"The school year's been so busy," my mother had said, sighing into the phone, when I'd initially called her from Turkey, announcing that Mesut was coming with me to the U.S. for a visit and wanted to see Beaver Dam.

"But, Mom—he wants to see where I grew up," I protested. "Maybe I can make some calls and find a cleaning crew to come in while you're at work. You wouldn't even know they were there."

"Where would he sleep?" she asked.

"Maybe he could stay in the guest room?"

"The guest room isn't in good shape," she said. "And do you know anything about chipmunks?"

"Chipmunks?" I asked.

"Chipmunks," she repeated, as if this were a most natural question to bring up in the middle of a conversation about introducing her to my new boyfriend. "I think they're trying to get into the house from somewhere around where the front garden meets the foundation."

My mother paused, then sighed.

"Mary, you won't be happy. It's not a good time. For me. Or the house."

"Oh," I said, nodding sadly. Of course the house was a problem. Again. When would I learn? "Okay."

My mother had last promised me she would work to clean up the house the previous December, when I'd flown home for what would be my last Christmas in Beaver Dam.

Walking in through the front door, I had been stunned. The debris in the hallway that had once consisted of newspapers and magazines and laundry baskets full of school supplies had multiplied. The kitchen table was piled high with random items from the grocery store—jars of peanut butter and jelly and paper towels that had not managed to make their way into the cabinets, which were now overflowing with cans of soup and boxes of pasta and bags of flour and jars of sauce that had expired one and two years ago. Grocery store bags littered the kitchen floor, full of boxes of cereal and oatmeal and cans of Diet Coke—all untouched. Some bags contained perishable food—bread, hot dog buns—that lay decaying. Peering through the plastic wrap, I saw the mold growing and cried out, looking for a garbage can. But there were only small wastebaskets to be found. And all of these were full.

While the kitchen floor was strewn with food, the refrigerator was oddly barren. I looked in vain for something to eat but found nothing other than a few cartons of yogurt that had long since expired and taken up residence in the small white refrigerator my mother had somehow purchased to replace the big old avocado refrigerator that hadn't worked properly since I was in the sixth or seventh grade.

In the living room sat a television that no longer worked. Beside it sat its smaller replacement. The floor surrounding the televisions was piled high with blankets, towels, plastic bags filled with this and that: boxes of plastic utensils, a scarf with the price tags still on it, a set of discount thank-you notecards still sealed in their plastic wrapper, a packet of pink foam rollers, three sets of clip-on earrings that still bore the bright orange sale stickers from Shopko. The dining room was unrecognizable—a room where half-unpacked suitcases, old record players, a 1980s desktop computer she'd borrowed from school, and a stack of unopened mail had come to die. And the staircase that led to the upstairs was little better. It was riddled with random items—unopened vacuum cleaner bags, boxes of Kleenex, a new game of Boggle still sealed in its wrapper—without rhyme or reason.

But far worse than the sight of the mess was the smell that permeated the place. While our home had long been cluttered, it had not smelled when I was a child. Not reeked, anyway. If anything, my mother had worked to disguise the clutter of my childhood with good smells: fresh flowers, scented candles.

But now it was different. Now the smell on the main floor of the house was wretched. It made me want to vomit. It smelled as if the whole house were a litter box that had not been cleaned for weeks, maybe months, on end. The odor confounded me, as my beloved childhood cat, Blackie, had died two years before, after living to the ripe old age of twenty-one.

"Where's that smell coming from?" I asked my mother, unable to hide the look of disgust on my face. I worried that my clothes—the suits and dresses that I'd brought home in my suitcase, the ones I'd carefully saved to buy in exotic locations like London and Paris, where I'd traveled for stories or on weekend getaways—would pick up the smell the way my clothes picked up the smell of cigarettes when I stayed in smoking rooms in hotels or spent time in my father's home.

"I'll get a maid to come in," my mother said absently before blurting out, "Do you want to call Kim?" She was anxious to change the subject. "I know that she'll want to see you."

I had come home for the holidays, but, of course, there were no Christmas decorations to be found. My mother, the former nun who continued to attend Mass on a near-daily basis, had given up putting up large Christmas decorations in the house, including a tree, when Anthony and I left for college. And this particular Christmas, even the small decorations were absent. There wasn't so much as an artificial wreath or Christmas candle to be found in the house.

"Getting decorations down out of the garage—it's just too much," she said.

"I could hire someone to help you," I offered. "I'm sure there's a kid in the neighborhood who would love to make some money. Or someone from town? From church?" I offered.

"Christmas is in the church," she said firmly. "It doesn't need to be in the house. Besides, I told you, it's too much."

Everything, it turned out, was too much for Anne Diener Pflum, since her beloved parents had died.

When Al and Aurelia Diener were alive, they served as my mother's touchstones, the sun around which she found purpose in revolving. The convent had failed her. My father had failed her. My brother had moved to Texas to marry my new sister-in-law, and I had moved to the other side of the world. So in a way we had left her, too. Her siblings were spread throughout the nation. And those few friends she had in Beaver Dam called less and less and less.

But Al and Aurelia Diener—and her home state of Indiana— had remained her true things. Two or three times a year, she had happily piled into her aging, un-air-conditioned car and made the ten-hour trek to Indiana. At times, the visits lasted little more than a day. But she was thrilled with the contact, happy to throw her arms around her father, whom she still called Daddy, and to talk with her mother, whose approval she still sought even at the age of sixty. And every Sunday, without fail, she looked forward to the weekly phone calls they would place to their Annie, after all parties were home from Mass.

Now, in the wake of their deaths, the phone was largely silent on Sundays. She sometimes talked to her sister Kathy in Colorado. And her sister Mimi sometimes called from Rochester, New York. But it wasn't the same without her parents. And my mother's will to remain in the land of the living—or at least in the land of the Christmas decorations—waned.

"Is this mold?" I had asked her during that last visit, pointing to, but afraid to touch, film on a lampshade in the living room.

"Should we maybe get rid of this?" I pressed, unable to stop my nose from wrinkling. "I bet we could find some new lamps at Shopko or Walmart. They both have decent home goods sections. It could be my Christmas present to you?"

I looked at her hopefully. Shopping for the house, I reasoned, might be fun. It might be cheery. It might make both of us feel better.

"Why don't you call Kim?" my mother asked, repeating her earlier request.

I wanted desperately to wave a magic wand, to call in a cavalry, but there was no one to call. My brother had moved on to his new life in Texas. My father had moved on to a new house and new friends in Florida. And my mother was moving on—internally, anyway—to a place that was harder and harder for me to reach.

She remained in that distant place when I eventually introduced her to Mesut in Indianapolis.

The location was my mother's suggestion.

"Indianapolis is a perfect meeting spot," my mother offered. "I can stop there on my way to visit Mother's and Daddy's graves. It might even give me a chance to visit Trudy's and Dad Diener's graves."

If I couldn't bring him to Beaver Dam, Indianapolis wasn't an entirely bad idea, I conceded. It would enable me to introduce Mesut on that same visit to some of my father's relatives and show him the Pflum family farm in southern Indiana.

"All right," I agreed, "if that's what you want."

"It's for the best right now if you want me to meet Mesut," she said.

"And if," she added, "you're really that serious about him."

I was serious. I knew it was this or nothing.

We ultimately met at a bustling breakfast café on a hot August morning. I sat nervously beside Mesut at the window table my mother requested. My mother sat across from us, wearing a new pink cotton short-sleeved blouse and matching pants she'd purchased from Beaver Dam's Shopko. I knew this because the price tags had still been attached when I hugged her that morning, and I'd had to help her to remove them.

Her hair was now entirely silver. She'd given up on the hair dye. And her face was red from the summer sun. She never could be bothered with sunscreen.

I watched that red face, those deep brown eyes, studying Mesut as he finished off his plate of eggs. Then came the questions, one after the other:

"So, Mesut," my mother asked, "how long do you intend to be a cameraman?"

"Would you say you're very religious?"

"Could you see yourself living here in the U.S.? Someplace like here? Like Indianapolis?"

Mesut answered each question perfectly. He'd be a cameraman as long as he could, but he had other interests: history, tourism, maybe business. He was Muslim, since that's the way he was raised, but he had friends of all religions. He liked what he'd seen of the U.S. as there were so many opportunities.

"And besides, Mary is from the U.S., isn't she?" he said, smiling and taking my hand. "She is wonderful. The States are wonderful."

My mother nodded politely, asked some more questions. About his siblings. About his travels. About the weather. But it was clear that, no matter how well he answered any questions, he was failing her test.

Two hours later, as we said goodbye on the street adjacent to the restaurant—my mother to head to her parents' graves, and Mesut and me to head down to visit my father's relatives—she asked me to walk with her to her car.

When we were almost to her parking space, she pulled me to her in a hug.

"Mary," she whispered into my ear. Her tone was urgent. "What are you doing?"

"What do you mean?" I whispered back.

"You know what I mean," she said, louder now. "What. Are. You. Doing?"

A lump formed in my throat as I pulled away from her grasp and studied her face. Slowly, I shook my head. She thought this was some sort of game I was playing. She thought that because she wasn't taking my relationship seriously, I shouldn't either.

"I'm. Living. My. Life."

I spoke to her through gritted teeth, the way I used to when I was a child.

My mother shook her head right back at me. "Is that what it is? Living your life? You're flitting around. First you're in this country. Then that one. You have this address. Then that one. You never stop."

"What are you trying to say, Mother?" I demanded. My cheeks were flushed now. I could feel them burning, out of both rage and embarrassment.

"Do you know where you're going?" my mother asked. Her tone was low and direct, the way she'd always told me, during my years on the high school forensics team, mine should be when driving home the critical points in a speech. "Are you running away from something? Or to something?"

I took another step back from my mother. "I could ask you the same thing."

My mother nodded, wordlessly hugged me once more, then got into her beat-up old car. I watched her drive away in silence, then returned to my rental car, where Mesut stood waiting for me and wrapped his arm around my waist.

"Your mother," he said. "She is all alone. It makes me sad."

I nodded. "It makes me sad, too."

Much to my mother's chagrin, Mesut and I grew closer. As I transitioned into a position at CNN that allowed me to divide my time between Istanbul and Atlanta and to report for the CNN feature shows *Earth Matters* and *Science and Technology Week,* we increasingly traveled to far-flung areas to cover stories together—he with the trusty camera, me with the notebook. We traveled to cover Europe's worst cyanide spill. We trekked to Transylvania in the midst of a blizzard. He made me feel more protected than any man I had ever known. Never more so than when we journeyed to the Khyber Pass.

It was January 2001, and we were on a harrowing trek through the area connecting Afghanistan to Pakistan, that mountainous region famously inhabited by foot runners bearing arms and electronics, dealers bearing weaponry, and a number of footholds and caves ideal for terrorists in search of places to hide. Osama bin Laden was on the run, and I had hired a driver and a guide and joined forces with Mesut and his mighty camera to bring to the world the story of a suffering population of Afghan refugees looking for peace and stability in an unstable region ruled by the Taliban.

The assignment was an intense one. Western women—particularly blond Western women like me, who wore blue jeans and leather jackets instead of burkas—were not the norm in the region. I sat in the backseat of the car with Mesut. An armed guard and my interpreter sat in the front with our driver. We spent the day in what aid workers call a tent village—a collection of hundreds of tents, inhabited by Afghan families desperate to get their children to safer ground.

In the course of our visit, we'd gotten good pictures and compelling interviews. And I'd gotten the chance to play with many of the children.

Each time I put my notebook or backpack down, the children

ran to follow me, stroking my head as I bent down as if I were a dog.

"Why are they petting me?" I asked my guard, laughing. Their little fingers tickled.

"They touch you because you are like—how do I say this?" He paused. "Like a unicorn. Yellow hair is something they have not seen so they want to touch you to make sure it's real."

I liked this idea of being a unicorn and smiled some more. The children were delighted. But as I laughed, a representative for the villagers, wearing a long robe, shook his head, expressing his discontent.

"You should not let the children touch you," he told me sternly through the interpreter.

"Why?" I asked, exchanging glances with Mesut. "They're just children. I don't mind."

"I'm not worried about them," he said. "It's you. Several of the children have died in recent weeks. They carry much disease."

I looked at the children. There were a dozen of them, a mixture of boys and girls. All were small, ages five to twelve. Their eyes were large and brown and seemed to dance in the light of the sun.

"They don't look sick," I told Mesut. I would know if they were sick, I told myself.

Two hours after we arrived at the tent village, we were back on the road. That's when trouble began. As we wound our way around the hilly terrain, our driver motioned to our guide.

"What is he saying?" Mesut asked the guard, his eyes widening.

"He says there is a checkpoint ahead," answered the guide.

Mesut possessed many gifts—and a sixth sense like none I've ever encountered was chief among them.

"But why?" Mesut asked, seeing the blockade in the road from a distance of a quarter mile. "There was no checkpoint when we came. Why is there a roadblock now? What are they checking?"

The driver shrugged.

Turning to me, Mesut flashed a look of concern. "I don't like this, Tatlim," he said, using his favorite pet name for me, the Turkish equivalent of "my sweet."

"Don't stop," he said to the driver in a tone that bordered on a bark. "Go faster! Hit the gas!"

Nodding in agreement, the interpreter reiterated the orders to the driver, this time in his native tongue.

As the driver sped up, Mesut pushed me down in the backseat so that my head—and my blond hair, the dead giveaway to the locals that I was a Westerner—was out of sight. I felt the car accelerate, then heard the noise—like a car backfiring—as we sped through the checkpoint. It was gunfire.

"Was that what I think it was?" I asked, my head still beneath Mesut.

"Yes, Tatlim," Mesut said.

"How did you know?"

"I just did," Mesut said with a shrug. It wasn't a shrug of arrogance. It was the Mesut shrug—one of a natural, easy confidence.

It would be a few months before *Wall Street Journal* reporter Daniel Pearl would be kidnapped and later beheaded in Pakistan—and before dozens more American and European journalists met with angry, anti-Western kidnappers, often at makeshift checkpoints like the one Mesut had known to blow through. But Mesut was anxious about my fate in Pakistan even then.

It turned out that checkpoints and gunfire weren't the only things I should have been afraid of on my trip to the region.

First came the layoff: When I arrived back in Karachi the next day, I received a call from my then boss at CNN, Peter Dykstra, who informed me on a static-filled cell-phone call that my show and my job had been eliminated sometime when I was in the mountains of Afghanistan. The brand-new merger between AOL and Time Warner had been solidified during my journey to

Pakistan, and as "cost-saving measures," hundreds of positions at CNN were eliminated. Mine was one of them.

"Our shows are canceled," Peter said, referring to *Earth Matters* and *Science and Technology Week*.

"Are you telling me I'm fired?" I asked, straining to hear Peter on the bad phone lines, and to make sense of being cut from a network just a day after having my car shot at.

"I'm afraid so," responded Peter's distorted voice. "If it makes you feel any better, you're in good company. More than four hundred people have been let go.

"I hope you understand why I had to call you now before you returned home. If I'd waited until you got back, it would be a new month and you'd be entitled to another month of benefits. And AOL doesn't like the idea of spending extra money."

At this, Peter laughed nervously. And I hung up.

Then, not long after the phone call, came the fever. A bad one.

By the morning, it had climbed to more than 104 degrees. And by the time I arrived back in Istanbul, my temperature was accompanied by a cough so tight and dry it made me feel as if my entire chest might break apart. Each time I hacked, I was left with a taste of metal in my mouth that I later learned was blood.

Concerned, Mesut took me to Istanbul's International Hospital. The young female doctor who examined me that day had a good grasp of the English language but struggled to explain to me what was wrong.

"You have inhaled something, no?" she asked, looking at me with concerned brown eyes. "You were around sick people on your journey, no?"

Mesut nodded for me. "It must have been the camp," he said, angry not at me, but at the memory of Afghanistan and the tent village we'd visited. "It was those kids."

I nodded weakly. I had thought for sure that I would have

known, would have sensed something, if the children were really sick. Apparently, I was wrong.

After giving me an IV, the doctor at the International Hospital sent me home and instructed me to rest.

Eventually, the fever subsided. But my body was not the same. I lost weight—one entire clothing size in just a week—and my skin grew pale. My hair was in bad shape, but I attributed that to too much hair-dryer and hot-roller use. When it came to my health, I was in denial.

I was in denial about a lot of things—not the least of which was my layoff.

One moment—before that trip to Afghanistan—I was a jet-setting producer and on-camera reporter for an international news network. The next, after that fateful call, I was an unemployed nobody coughing up a lung.

The layoff didn't just strip me of a monthly income or of a job to report to—it also robbed me of my sense of identity.

For eight whole years, CNN had been my one constant in a dramatically changing world. College had ended, my circle of friends and addresses had changed, my father's boyfriends had come and gone—but CNN was my steady ship. The network had allowed me to see the world. It had taken me light-years from the cold, messy house in Beaver Dam. The layoff felt like an epic failure and an epic breakup all at the same time. Without CNN, I didn't know quite who I was. And without CNN, I didn't know how I was going to pay the bills.

A month before the CNN layoff, I had invested in a condominium in downtown Atlanta. I was still dividing my time between Atlanta and Istanbul but was spending ever-greater swaths of time in Atlanta. And since Atlanta was where I thought Mesut and I would ultimately settle, friends had pressured me to take a ride on the real estate bubble that was rocking the city. Colleagues bought properties one year for one price, then flipped them the next for considerable profits.

"Don't rent," lectured my friends. "You're throwing your money away. Turkey or no Turkey, you need a place to crash when you're in Atlanta. It might as well be a place that you own."

What do I have to lose? I reasoned, settling on a one-bedroom place in a 1929 building in the heart of Virginia Highlands. Priced in the low six figures, it was deemed a "bargain" by my enthusiastic and decidedly ambitious real estate agent. I showed up at the closing all by myself, check in hand, and signed my name to the thick stack of forms. I, Mary Pflum, was a property owner at the ripe old age of twenty-eight.

And now, also at age twenty-eight, I, Mary Pflum, was unemployed and saddled with a mortgage for a place I couldn't afford and hadn't even moved into.

I was mortified. About all of it. For weeks, I was too embarrassed to tell my family about the layoff.

"Tatlim, jobs come and go," said Mesut, before heading off to his own job, which remained secure. "This will pass."

He was right, of course, but I felt like the kid who had been thrown from her bike for the first time in her life—now that I was aware of the destructive forces of gravity, the world would never be the same.

Eventually, I broke the news to my mother in a late-night phone call.

"Mom, I lost my job. I really lost my job," I said, my voice cracking. "And I don't know what I'm going to do with the condo. And I don't know where to live. Atlanta. Or Istanbul. Or—

"But the point is I'll be all right," I told my mother, hurrying to convince myself more than her.

"I know you will," she said gently. "But maybe it's time to sell your place in Atlanta and say goodbye to Turkey and come home."

I shook my head into the phone. My stomach churned at the idea of seeking refuge in the house in Beaver Dam with its mold-covered lampshades. I knew what she was getting at: she hoped my unemployment would drive a wedge between Mesut and me. In the end, the layoff didn't tear us apart. Instead, 9/11 did.

When those planes struck the World Trade Center, it was a watershed moment for the world—and for my relationship with Mesut. At first, he and my Turkish friends were sympathetic. "We're so sorry for your and America's loss," many told me. "We are crying, too."

But soon came the conspiracy theories that were anti-U.S. in nature. One night in late fall, after a long day of Ramadan-related fasting, Mesut took me to break fast at a dinner party at the home of an old friend from his university days. I was just one of a couple of women who had been invited, and was seated across from the friend's father, an elderly Turkish man who eyed me suspiciously and pounced upon me between the first and second courses.

"You know the CIA was behind all of it," he said, watching me over the top of his glass filled with raki, a milky-looking concoction that consisted of a potent mix of alcohol and water.

"Behind all of what?" I asked, confused. I shifted uncomfortably in my seat. I felt unexpectedly exposed.

"Behind what?" he asked, smiling. "Behind that World Trade Center attack."

"Osama bin Laden was behind the attack," I said, my stomach turning. I narrowed my eyes as the man stared me down.

"That's what your government wants you to believe. They don't want you to know the truth. That it was Israel who worked with your government to do it. They wanted to make Islam look bad and Israel look good. That's what's behind all of this."

I looked at the man in disbelief. Like so many other Americans, I was in a period of mourning over what had happened to New York and to my homeland. Thousands of innocent people had perished. And now a strange old man was trying to tell me that my country had killed them.

"Osama bin Laden and al Qaeda—they're who killed those people," I said, looking for Mesut, seated to my left, to rescue me from the conversation.

But Mesut and his friend and his friend's brothers sat in silence. And now an entire table of Turks stared at me.

"Tatlim, there is a lot of evidence to suggest the U.S. and its relationship with Israel had a lot to gain by allowing the attacks to happen," Mesut told me with a shrug.

My heart sank. I had come to the dinner thinking we were a team. Now I realized that we were two distinct entities. I was the odd one out. I was the lone American. It was one of the loneliest moments of my life.

In the months that followed, Mesut made his mixed feelings about the U.S. increasingly clear. The U.S.—the land he had once said was the place of opportunity and liberty—was now, according to him, self-serving, freewheeling, and morally loose. And its people, whom he had once described as friendly and tolerant, were increasingly labeled obese, ignorant, and spoiled. Many of the charges had merit. But it was my home he was talking about. And it was a home I increasingly realized I needed to remain in. Full-time.

The situation came to a head in October 2002. After more than a year of working as a freelance journalist in New York and in Istanbul, I at last succeeded in finding a staff position as a producer at a mainstream American news program with a mainstream American network: *Good Morning America*. The idea was that I would move full-time to New York and take the job and that Mesut would follow.

"It will be better for us to live in the U.S.," Mesut reasoned, even after his love affair with the U.S. began to wane. "It will be better for us to marry there. To raise a family there."

Before I left for New York, we decided to go on one more Turkish adventure: I wanted to go to Hissarlik in western Turkey, to see the site of the ancient city of Troy. As both a history major and a fan of Greek mythology, I'd long wanted to see where the epic battle for Helen of Troy had taken place. It would be our farewell tour.

The beginning of the trip was lovely. We hiked. We ate amazing food and watched sunrises and sunsets. But on the day before we were slated to return to Istanbul, our trip—and our relationship—went up in flames.

At a market on the way to Troy, Mesut bought a jar of homemade honey from a local vendor. Without telling me, he placed it in my bag, then put the bag in the backseat of a cab. When the honey jar broke because of a sudden stop and its sticky contents spilled all over my things, including a favorite red dress, I screamed in exasperation.

"That stupid honey!" I yelled, stepping out of the cab moments later. "I knew we shouldn't have bought it!"

Mesut's eyes widened in surprise. So did the eyes of the taxi driver, who had been helping me with my bag at the time. Feeling the eyes of the cabdriver upon him, an embarrassed Mesut yelled back. "Don't be a stupid little girl. Don't be a stupid American!

"That's what you are!" he yelled even louder now, so that people on the street stopped to look. "A stupid, spoiled American!"

I knew then that this was it. This was what our relationship would forever boil down to. When I spoke my mind, the way most American women are raised to do, I wouldn't be just a woman speaking her mind, I would be a stupid American. I would be the loathed American. The traits Mesut and I had once found so adorably enticing in each other—his machismo and national pride, my forthrightness and independence—were now the very things driving us apart.

In the moments after the public scolding, as I worked in vain to wipe the honey from my red dress, my mother's words from that awkward meeting in Indianapolis rang in my ears: "What are you doing? Are you running away from something? Or to something?"

We muddled through the rest of the trip. But Mesut and I knew what was coming. After three years together, our lives were veering in decidedly different directions.

Days later, when Mesut saw me off at the airport in Istanbul, as he had a dozen times before, he bade farewell with a different kind of kiss: warm, sweet—and tentative. This was goodbye.

The week after I arrived in New York, this time to live full-time, a package came in the mail. It was a series of photos from Mesut of our last journey together. Us in Troy. Us at dinner. Us cuddling. With the photos was a note, written in his familiar scrawl: *"Thank you, Mary, for teaching me the meaning of love. I will love you forever."*

Tears pricked at the back of my eyes. I had found a new job—but I was on my own.

Waiting to fill the void: New York City. And my mother.

"You'll get through this, Mary," she barked at me via phone at night, channeling both the gentle early childhood teacher and former nun within. "Remember: put one foot in front of the other."

When I secured my new apartment in midtown Manhattan—a one-bedroom in a walk-up that boasted two big fireplaces and exposed brick walls—she cheered.

When I managed to temporarily rent out my place in Atlanta, which enabled me to pay off some more bills, she celebrated.

And when I tried my hand at dating again, post-Mesut, she applauded, though not without a bit of armchair quarterbacking. "Why not join a singles group at church?" she asked.

For Christmas that first year that I was back in the U.S. full-time, she came to stay with me in New York, never complaining once about her travels. For Easter, she offered to treat me to a weekend in Milwaukee. We stayed at the historic old Pfister Hotel downtown and shared delicious plates of cheese and Caesar salad and a bottle of Chardonnay. We avoided talk of the house in Beaver Dam, concentrating entirely on the lovely weekend at hand.

Anne Diener Pflum had her daughter back, and she was loving every moment of it.

And just when she had me back, just when I was starting to feel settled, those darn lungs reared their ugly heads.

A few months after settling into my position at *Good Morning America,* the coughing and fevers that had plagued me post-Afghanistan began anew. At first, I was able to keep the condition under control, balancing the occasional trip to a hospital emergency room with my growing roster of assignments. I had pneumonia, the emergency room doctors told me—not once, but twice. Rest, they told me. Take some pills. I didn't question the diagnosis, nor did I think much of the increasingly violent hacking attacks that left me breathless and in pain.

It wasn't until a coughing fit took hold of me in the presence of Dr. Tim Johnson—ABC's preeminent medical contributor—that I realized my coughing fits needed more serious medical attention.

"How long have you had that cough?" Dr. Tim asked, putting down the script he and I had been going over before I started hacking.

It was August and I was producing a piece about the flu for *Good Morning America,* to which Dr. Tim was supposed to lend his voice.

"Eighteen months," I said between coughs. I was embarrassed. Dr. Tim was an institution within the hallowed halls of ABC News. This was one of my first times working with him, and I couldn't stop coughing.

"Eighteen months?" Dr. Tim asked in surprise. "What does your doctor say?"

"I don't have a regular doctor," I managed to spit out between coughs. "I keep going to the ER. They've told me every time it's pneumonia."

I cringed at how stupid I sounded. The truth was I worked so much—sixty to eighty hours a week, depending on the assignment—that I didn't feel as if I had time to find a doctor, especially in a city as big as New York.

"You mean to tell me you've been told you've had pneumonia multiple times in a year?" asked Dr. Tim, shaking his head. "You need to see a specialist."

Within a day, at Dr. Tim's behest, I was in a pulmonary special-ist's office. X-rays were ordered. Then a CT scan. Then came the phone call. I was sitting at my *GMA* computer on a Friday morning.

"Miss Pflum, I'm afraid we've found spots all over both of your lungs," the doctor said.

"From the pneumonia, right?" I asked, distracted. I was trying to concentrate on the script I had pulled up on my computer screen at the time.

"No," said the doctor. "Pneumonia doesn't cause that kind of spotting."

"What does?" I asked absently, concentrating more on what possible cuts I could make to the script than on the phone call.

"It's more consistent with cancer. We need to schedule a lung biopsy."

My heart pounded loudly in my chest. A biopsy? Of my lungs? That was bad. Not just bad—but potentially *really* bad.

I hastened to get off the phone with the doctor. *Mom*, I kept thinking, as the doctor talked, *Mom!* I needed my mom. She would know what to say, what to do. She had to.

I saw that it was just ten A.M. in Wisconsin. My mother, I

knew, was at work. Her new school year had just gotten under way. But since she had neither a cell phone nor a phone in her classroom, I called the home phone. The phone rang once, twice, then five times before I finally heard my mother's recorded voice and a beep. Gulping, I blurted out a panicked message. "Call me. As soon as you can. Please?"

The next two weeks were a blur as I prepared for the procedure. There was a PET scan, a series of blood tests.

"Why are you taking so much blood?" I asked the lab technician who filled vial after vial with the blood that flowed from my arm. She was a pretty young woman with dark skin who wore her hair in cornrows; around her neck was a gold necklace that bore the face of the ancient Egyptian queen Nefertiti.

"We're looking for markers," she said, her gaze fixed on the needle in my arm.

"What are markers?"

"Markers," she said, looking from my arm to my eyes, "tell us if there's cancer in other parts of your body. If it's cancer that's in your lungs, it started someplace else."

This was news to me. "Where?" I asked.

"Could be anywhere," she said, giving me a sad smile. "Lung cancer looks like one big mass—one tumor—if that's where it started. You've got spots on your lungs. And lung cancer only looks like spots if it spread from someplace else."

I left the doctor's office feeling as if I needed to flee. Not just from the city—but from my life. I was young, I kept telling myself. Too young to deal with markers and cancer. Too young to think about death. I hadn't gotten married yet, hadn't had children. Those things came before the C word, didn't they? At least that's what I'd always thought.

I repeatedly tried to turn to my mother in my hour of need. But my conversations with her about the biopsy hadn't gone as well as I'd hoped—nor did any subsequent conversations.

"Mom, what am I going to do?" I'd cry, sobbing into the phone.

Usually, even at my lowest, my mother had something to say, some pearls of wisdom to impart. Even when I was at my most serious with Mesut, she still worked to comfort me when I needed her. But now she didn't know what to say. Instead, the phone line was filled with silence. Deafening silence.

"Mom?" I'd cry. "Mom? Please say something. What am I going to do?"

I hadn't counted on how sad my sadness would make her—how helpless my helplessness would render her. The depression that she was still being treated for was something she generally kept carefully hidden in our conversations. And that's the way she liked it. She seemed to understand my mind—that of an often self-absorbed twenty-something—and generally let me blather on about my latest night on the town with my girlfriends or a work assignment that had proved especially stressful. We'd talk about her, too—about her school year, or her teacher friends, or her on-going worries that her car might be on its last legs after racking up more than 125,000 miles. But she always seemed to prefer to talk about me and my life.

When the talk of cancer entered the conversation, that changed. She seemed to not want to talk about anything at all. The fear in my voice—and the sobs—was too much for her. I realize now that her long pauses weren't because she didn't know what to say—but instead because she likely couldn't speak. I know now that she was silently crying alongside me.

"Will you come?" I asked her more than once. I wanted her with me in New York, needed her with me on my doctor's visits.

She paused. I could hear the hesitation. "Honey, I want to be with you. But my job . . ."

Her voice trailed off.

"If I take time off now, I might not be able to get the time off if—well, if the results aren't good and you—"

"And I need more help," I said, finishing her sentence. At this, we both began to cry.

Strangely—surprisingly—it was my father who came to my rescue in my hour of need. Dale Pflum had retired to a gay-friendly retirement community in Boynton Beach, Florida, in 2000 and seldom let anything, he liked to brag, get between him and his happy-hour socials in nearby Fort Lauderdale. New York, and the North in general, he said, was too cold and too expensive, and we saw each other less and less after his move—sometimes little more than once a year. And when we did see each other, the visits were often riddled by fights in which I reminded him how badly he'd hurt my mother.

But when they found those spots on my lungs, it was Dale Pflum who miraculously dropped everything and showed up on my New York City doorstep. He'd moved out of my childhood home and left our family more than two decades before. Now he'd come to assist me in my hour of need. I'm not sure who was more surprised by the turn of events—me or him.

"Now just be calm," he said when he arrived at my apartment, a suitcase in hand and a canary-yellow windbreaker on his back. "We're going to get this all straightened out. Just you wait and see."

His demeanor was calm. He was focused. He seemed to recognize that I needed to be taken care of—and he was there to do it, even if his approach struck some as odd.

Our trips to the various doctors' offices as a father-daughter team were especially comical. Here I was, the patient: pale, thin, scared, and suffering from debilitating coughs that sometimes lasted for minutes at a time. There he was, the father. At six foot six, he was larger than life and, fresh from the beaches of Florida, he also sported a leathery tan that stood in stark contrast to my pasty white skin. My friends liked to joke that he was the eternal bull in a china shop, commanding attention everywhere he went.

He raised more than a few eyebrows with his standard bright pink polo shirt, his extremely loud voice, and his inability to put his cigarettes down for more than ten minutes.

"Mr. Pflum," lectured Dr. Lawrence Scharer, the renowned pulmonary specialist Dr. Tim had helped me find, "you do realize why we're treating your daughter, don't you?"

Dr. Scharer stood in a crisp white lab coat in front of Roosevelt Hospital, where we had gone to find my father after one of my appointments. The decorated doctor, a short man with closely cropped white hair, had wanted to share his latest theories about my lungs with my father and, not finding him in the waiting room where we'd left him during my exam, had joined me in looking for him in front of the hospital.

My father took a long, deep drag on his cigarette as he nodded down at the considerably shorter Dr. Scharer—not realizing for a moment the error of his ways.

"We're concerned she could have lung cancer," Dr. Scharer said, peering up at my father. "*Lung* cancer!"

My father nodded once more, still unwilling—or unable—to put that damned cigarette down.

I stood between the two of them, not sure whether to laugh, cry, or referee.

But in spite of some of his clueless ways—or perhaps because of them—my father was just what the doctor ordered when it came to handling my illness. He placed calls to ABC to help me straighten out my insurance plan and medical leave. He went to the pharmacy to pick up my medication. He prepared meals for me and encouraged me to meet up with friends in an effort to keep my mind off my deathbed.

And on a near-daily basis, he said something so ridiculous that I had no choice other than to burst out laughing.

Arguably the most outrageous comment came one morning over breakfast at my favorite neighborhood diner. Between bites of bagel, I noticed that my father looked particularly preoccupied. "What are you thinking about?" I asked him.

"I was just thinking we don't have a place for you to be buried."

"What?" I asked, spitting out my bagel. Surely I had misheard!

"I bought a plot for me years ago, one for your mother, too. But we don't have one for you. I wonder if I should make some calls."

The comment was insane—something that no father should say to his still-alive daughter when the results of her biopsy were still unknown. If anything, it was something to be thought, not uttered.

But there it was. And I had no other choice than to laugh, shake my head, and reach for my phone so that I could regale a pair of girlfriends with the tale, beginning with, "You will not believe what the *fuck* my father just said to me!!"

A week after the procedure, my father took me to Florida with him for a couple of weeks to rest and wait for my results. A little-known fact is that results for lung biopsies don't take days. Full results take weeks, while cultures grow. It was an agonizing wait. To pass the time, I went to the beach, looked at seagulls, and largely felt sorry for myself. I also agreed during that time to start organizing a small birthday party for myself to be held back in New York at the end of October when I returned to the city.

I didn't feel like celebrating. My future felt less certain than ever. In just two years, I'd moved countries, lost love, changed jobs—and now this. But my father, who never let personal problems stand between him and a potential party—was among those who believed I should.

"Have a party," my father told me between rounds of Bourbon and Seven at Tropics, his gay bar of choice. "It'll be good for you."

His circle of gay friends, the vast majority of whom wore a uniform similar to that of my father—dark tans, bright polo shirts, and gold necklaces that covered their tufts of graying chest hair—nodded good-naturedly as they polished off their own drinks. "A party is always the way to go," they agreed.

So I suppose I have my father's love of social gatherings to thank for meeting the love of my life.

Dean Peterson was a man I had heard great things about prior to our meeting. He was a member of Manhattan's Michigan State University Alumni Association. A male friend of mine—an MSU alum—had befriended Dean at a city alumni event and suggested Dean stop by the party at New York's Bowery Bar, a restaurant and watering hole in Lower Manhattan.

When Dean entered the bar the Saturday night after I returned from Florida, it was one of those moments I thought existed only in my beloved soap operas. The noise around me—the music playing overhead, the loud din of bar conversation—faded away and it was just the two of us. Our eyes locked, and as he made his way toward me, I, the usually confident journalist, felt my face burn unexpectedly red and my always-dry palms grow sweaty. This was my *West Side Story* Tony-meets-Maria moment. Forevermore, there would be two halves of my life: Before Dean and After Dean. I think a part of me somehow knew even then—a split second before we were formally introduced—that life on the After side was one I'd been waiting for all of my life. When I met Dean, I came home.

"Hi, I'm Dean," he said, taking my hand in his. "What kind of drink can I buy the birthday girl?"

My pulse went from a trot to a sprint. Stammering, I spit out a request for my favorite concoction at the time—a pretty pink watermelon martini. And that was it. With drink in hand, I took a seat beside my future husband.

Dean was everything I'd been looking for, everything I'd been waiting for. He was tall, dark, and handsome. He was smart and kind. And without question, he was the funniest man I had ever met—prompting me to burst into schoolgirl giggles at every turn. He regaled me with stories of the two cats he'd rescued and was happily raising in his one-bedroom apartment, told me about his work as an international tax attorney, his upbringing in south-western Michigan with his close-knit family. Then, pointing to his head, he made fun of his recent bad haircut, which had resulted in the unfortunate decimation of his trademark head of thick dark curls. "I fear that barber irrevocably altered my personality," he said, noting that next time he'd fare better if he went to his cats' groomer.

But smitten though I was, the last thing I was looking for the night I met Dean was a new relationship. I had lungs to worry about.

So within a week of our meeting, I tried to set him up with two different girlfriends. If I couldn't have this great guy, then some deserving single woman certainly should.

Dean wasn't into the setups.

"I don't want to date those other girls," he said, his eyes locking with mine as we shared our second round of drinks in a week. "I want to date you."

"I don't have time for dates," I told him. And I meant it. "I only have time for doctor's appointments."

"That's fine," Dean said, his eyes still locked with mine. "Then let me come with you to those appointments. I'm good company in waiting rooms."

"You want to come and hang out in a doctor's office?" I asked disbelievingly. In New York, men acted put-upon if a girl so much as wanted them to pick her up for a date at her apartment—and he wanted to spend his lunch hours taking a girl who wouldn't kiss him to the doctor?

"Why not?" Dean countered. "You'll be there, right?"

And so, within two weeks of our first meeting, Dean Peterson started tagging along when I went in for CT scans, kept me company as I waited for PET scans.

"Are you the husband?" he was asked by nosy receptionists on more than one occasion.

"No," he said. "Not yet."

I would later learn from some of Dean's old law school friends that he was so smitten, in part, because I was his "type."

"Dean likes tall, skinny, brainy women," his friend Eddie would later tell me. "Always has. Always will."

Then Eddie laughed and winked. "You are smart, aren't you?"

Not only was I Dean's type, but I was also from the place that he loved most in the world: his native Midwest. Dean had been in New York for six years before meeting me. He'd dated plenty of women from California, from New York, even from Scotland. But he missed his Michigan roots. And he longed for a woman who appreciated the beauty and simplicity of a small town, knew how to handle herself in a snowstorm, and understood the significance of Sunday-afternoon football, particularly if it involved his Detroit Lions or my Green Bay Packers.

After dating so many serious, career-driven women, some of whom didn't know if they'd ever want children, he also was looking for a woman who appreciated his sense of humor. I was most definitely that woman.

During one appointment, when I was waiting to go in for a scan in a doctor's office that had unexpectedly lost heat, I sat shivering in my winter coat and mittens. Wrapping his arm around my shoulders, Dean cracked joke after joke about the cold. "If this is what this doctor calls a warm-up act when it comes to courting new patients, he'd better rethink his business plan," he deadpanned before chivalrously wrapping his wool dress coat around me.

The joking worked. I burst into laughter.

On a later date, he made light of the story I'd told him about my father's tasteless ruminations about where to bury me. "Tell your dad I saw a sale on pine boxes," he said with a wink, as we strode hand in hand through the East Village. "On second thought, I bet your dad's already all over that one."

On New Year's Eve that year, he arrived at my apartment with a split of champagne, a pair of flutes, and a VHS copy of *The Bionic Woman* pilot episode.

"I thought it fitting to ring in the new year with an incredible woman watching the tales of another incredible woman," he said, remembering my adoration of vintage TV.

I was in love. And, as luck would have it, the feeling was mutual. We said the L word to each other within a matter of weeks. It wasn't planned. Like the rest of our relationship, it just happened with the greatest of ease. Every step felt natural, unforced, drama-free, and, in his words, blissfully "meant to be." There were no issues about conflicting nationalities, religion, and politics. Instead, there was passion and partnership, love and understanding.

In the words of one of my girlfriends, "With Dean, there are no buts." No "He's a great guy BUT he's not sure if he wants to have kids." No "He's a great guy BUT he only wants to marry a Jewish girl." No "He's a great guy BUT he's married." He was a great guy. One who got me. And one who, from the start, set out to prove he loved me for better, for worse, in sickness and in health.

So when the news finally came that the sputum collected during my lung biopsy and related tests had grown in some dish in some lab—and that whatever had grown was inconsistent with the kind of tuberculosis found in the United States, but consistent instead with strains of the disease native to Pakistan and Afghanistan—Dean was my first phone call and the first one there to celebrate with me, another bottle of champagne in hand. I didn't have cancer after all. Mesut had been right from the very beginning.

My trip to that refugee camp—my interaction with all of those beautiful, sickly children in Afghanistan—had been ill-advised. They had left me with scarred lungs, a permanent souvenir from the region.

My body had fought a yucky disease that had left me, Dr. Scharer said, with lungs no stronger than those of a seventy-year-old woman. My lung capacity was nil. I might have recurring fevers for years to come, he warned. But I would live. And with Dean at my side I had a bright future to look forward to.

By Valentine's Day, I had met Dean's parents. By April, we were talking marriage.

Dean knew about my previous boyfriends, the earlier proposals, the paths I'd almost gone down. He didn't care. He had the quiet confidence to know that just as I was the one for him, he was the one for me. There was never any doubt. "I'm not only going to marry you, Mary Pflum," he told me over a late-night dinner. "I'm going to marry the hell out of you."

When he got down on bended knee in front of the Jackson Pollock statue on Central Park's famous Poet's Way on Labor Day 2004, the world that had once seemed so cold and bleak now radiated with a sunshine I had never known before. Where there had once been doubt and sadness, now I saw nothing but endless possibility.

I pinched myself nightly at my great stroke of luck: a relationship that made me feel both safe and drunk with excitement. I'd found a man whose kisses sent electric shockwaves through my nether regions and whose intellect not only matched mine but also kept me guessing.

My mother watched the unfolding of our love story with decidedly mixed feelings. She liked Dean. But beneath her smile lingered an air of hesitation.

"Are you sure you're ready?" my mother asked when I called to tell her of our marriage plans.

"Mom, I'm in love!"

"But you've had so many boyfriends."

"Not like this," I said, shaking my head. "Mom, he's the one."

My mother pressed on. "I love Dean," she said when I called her to discuss the wording of the wedding invitations. "But please understand—no one's pressuring you to do this."

"Lots of wonderful people—famous people—remain single and are perfectly content," she said when I delightedly told her of the *New York Times*'s intention to not only run an announcement of our wedding, but also to include a longer article about our courtship.

"Mom, what are you trying to say?" I asked, exasperated.

"I'm trying to tell you what I wish someone had told me before I got married—that you have options."

"Mom," I said at last. "Dean's not Dad. And I'm not you."

In a bid to get my mother excited about the wedding, Dean and I ultimately decided to get married in Milwaukee. We had it all planned: guests would stay at the Pfister Hotel, which my mother adored; we would marry at the nearby cathedral; and we would have a reception to end all receptions at the world-renowned Milwaukee Art Museum, a stunning Santiago Calatrava display of architectural wonder that had been completed only two years before. Mammoth and white, the museum boasted a pair of humongous wings that opened and closed and fanned out over the blue of Lake Michigan. The Wisconsin wedding plan would enable Dean to get married on his beloved Lake Michigan, on whose eastern beaches he had grown up. And it would allow my mother to invite all of her teacher friends—and her friends from Beaver Dam—to the weekend festivities. Surely that would make her feel more involved, more included. Surely that would win her over to the pro-wedding team, I reasoned. Wouldn't it?

I also thought that maybe, just maybe, having the wedding in Wisconsin would prove a source of inspiration to my mother to at last get her house in order. From the time when I was a boyfriend-less high school student, my mother had talked about the possibility of having a big family gathering at the house—a post-wedding brunch or pre-wedding party—when the time eventually came for me to marry. For years, she'd talk about what trees we'd gather beneath, how nice it would be to have all of her siblings and nieces and nephews assembled alongside me and my brother and my future groom.

But when the possibility of an engagement became a reality, my mother panicked. Instead of encouraging me to come to Beaver Dam for a wedding-related activity—or even for a pre-wedding visit—she did the opposite.

"I don't think any of you will have time to come to Beaver Dam. It's too far from Milwaukee."

"But, Anne," Dean told her one night over drinks in New York, after my mother and I had completed a particularly disastrous day of nightgown/wedding gown shopping, "I love Mary and I'd love to see her hometown. Why don't we visit you in Beaver Dam during our next trip home?"

I watched as my mother nearly dropped the glass of wine in her hand.

"You really want to come to Beaver Dam?"

"Why not?" Dean said, gently pushing. "I want to see where Mary's from."

My mother studied her drink.

"I tell you what. Why don't we do this? Since you're getting married in Milwaukee, let's just keep everything—including our visits—in Milwaukee. You can see Beaver Dam some other time," my mother said. "Maybe next year."

At this, Dean nodded agreeably—confused, but resigned to the fact that he might never see my childhood home.

"All right, Anne," he said to her, looking at me. "If that's what you want."

And I grew resigned to the fact that I might never see my childhood home again. Not for a pre-wedding shower I'd always assumed I'd have there for old friends. (My mother never even offered to organize one.) Not for a post-wedding brunch. Not, it seemed, ever.

Although Dean and I were never formally invited to the house, we were given an inadvertent glimpse of the place and its ongoing state of decay the day Dean insisted upon taking my mother's suitcase to her car following one of our wedding-planning weekends at the Pfister. It was February 2005 and at this point we were flying back every six weeks to take care of final wedding details.

"I can handle my bags, Dean," my mother said, protesting. But Dean was undeterred.

"No, Anne, I'm going to insist on this. If you're not going to let us take you home, at least let me take you to your car."

My mother was nearing seventy. Her arthritic knees were hurting her badly, and Dean was determined to show his future mother-in-law that he was a gentleman.

I pulled my mother into a hug as Dean led the way to my mother's car, located in the dark recesses of the Pfister's parking garage. My mother pulled out of my grasp, trying to catch up to him, to head him off. But she was too slow.

"Dean, no, really!" my mother cried, hobbling to catch him. Her voice grew higher as she called across the garage. "I'd prefer to go to the car by myself!"

It was too late. Dean was upon the car, and as he opened the trunk, a veritable garbage dump was revealed: newspapers, brown paper grocery bags, white plastic bags from Shopko. There were fast-food bags from Hardee's and Culver's and Styrofoam cups and cream packets from McDonald's. I watched as a stunned Dean took a step back from the trunk. There was no room for a suitcase.

The interior of the car was no better. The entire backseat and the passenger seat were piled high with debris: more empty Styrofoam coffee cups, more fast-food bags, canvas bags full of student assessments and school reports, an assortment of Jolly Ranchers and stickers and Hot Wheels intended for her young students. The car was worse than I had ever seen it—even worse than on the day of my grandmother's memorial service. The debris reached up past the windows, as if the junk were vying for positions from which to watch passing traffic.

Looking at all of that stuff, I remembered a conversation I'd shared with my mother the month before when she'd failed to call me back for three entire days.

She didn't answer the home phone. Not even in the middle of the night. Failing to return my call in the course of one day was unusual, but it had happened on occasion. Failing to return the call in three days was cause for alarm. When I finally reached her in the middle of the school day on the fourth day by calling the school's main office, my mother laughed good-naturedly when she heard the concern in my voice.

"Mom, where have you been?" I asked, breathing a heavy sigh of relief.

"I'm afraid I've been phone-less," she said. "I didn't call you back because I didn't know you called. I managed to misplace my phones this week."

"How do you misplace all of your phones?" I asked.

"You know how it goes. Sometimes things go missing in the house," she told me with a laugh.

At first, I thought she was hiding something from me, that the missing phone was just an excuse. But looking at the mess of the car in the Pfister parking garage, I realized my mother had been telling the truth. When I'd called and called and called, the phones had likely been buried beneath piles of trash in the house, the likes of which Dean peered at in my mother's car now.

Watching Dean watch the car, my mother's nervousness turned to testiness. "I told you—I didn't want you to see the car, Dean.

It's been a busy time. I've been moving classrooms. I just didn't get things cleaned before our visit."

I had heard all the lines before. I eyed the car, horrified. There was scarcely room for my mother to sit. I had no idea where she'd manage to fit the suitcase or what she'd do if she had to make any sudden movements with the car on the drive home to Beaver Dam. A sharp left turn would send a mountain of trash into her seat, or worse, onto her foot operating the gas pedal and the brake.

Dean nodded at my mother good-naturedly, keeping to himself any feelings of surprise or disgust.

"You shouldn't be lifting any suitcase," he said reassuringly, looking my mother in the eye. "I'm here to help you now. Understand?"

If I could have hugged my future husband then, thrown my arms around him without embarrassing my mother, I would have. I don't think there's been a moment I've ever loved him more. But I couldn't hug him then without further humiliating my still-proud mother. So I looked away, trying to hide the tears of love, gratitude—and relief.

Moments later, as she drove off with that strange look of pride and shame etched on her face, I began to better understand the source of her ongoing lobs about my wedding dress, her hesitation about the nuptials. I was moving forward to a bright, shining future replete with a gallant knight named Dean. She was stuck where she was, in a decaying house, a foul-smelling car. If anything, she was sinking fast.

Later, back in the safety of our hotel room, Dean would ask me about what he had seen.

"How long has this been going on?" he asked. His tone wasn't angry. It was his lawyer tone. He was seeking facts.

"For years," I said, my voice breaking. "But it was never this bad."

"We need to help her," he said.

"I've tried," I said, the tears starting now.

I felt naked. I'd been sleeping with Dean for months. He'd seen every square inch of my body. And never before had I felt more vulnerable.

"I've tried to clean up," I said, gulping. "I've tried to hire people over the years. She just won't let anyone in to help."

"Well, now I'm here," Dean said. He moved from the doorway of the room in which he'd been standing and came to join me on the bed, folding me into his arms. I buried my face in his cashmere sweater and breathed deeply.

"Maybe," Dean said, kissing my salty cheek, "it's a two-person job."

The last night I spent with my mother as a single woman reaffirmed for me just how bad things were growing, not only when it came to her housekeeping, but also when it came to her mental health. For three decades—through my childhood and then my young womanhood—my mother and I had shared hotel rooms on trips to see her parents, her siblings, my brother. Our late-night routine was always the same: we'd get a hotel room with a pair of queen-sized beds, and bed down in a darkened room to chat about our respective lives and watch what we liked to call "junk TV": late-night talk shows, reruns of *Friends* and *Cheers,* old movies. It was fun, relaxing "girl time."

This was precisely what I had counted on—looked forward to—the night before the wedding when Dean walked me back to the hotel room in the Pfister just before midnight in the wake of our wildly successful rehearsal dinner. We had hosted 150 out-of-town guests in the Pfister's grand Rose Room, presented our parents with beautiful paintings and drawings depicting their parents, including a beautiful sketch of Albert and Aurelia Diener for my mother. We'd wowed our guests with musical entertainment and fine dining, which included a sumptuous croquembouche. But the atmosphere in the hotel room was anything but fun and relaxing moments after Dean kissed me good night.

My mother greeted me at the door, a bundle of nerves. "Where were you?" she asked.

"We had post-party drinks up at Blu," I said, referring to the Pfister's trendy bar, which overlooked the city. More than fifty of our friends had joined us in raising some post-party glasses.

I hurriedly put on my nightshirt in the bathroom and climbed into the bed across from my mother's, anxious to talk about the success of the rehearsal dinner, the excitement of the day to come. I thought we might reminisce about my childhood or I might listen as my mother doled out the sort of sage advice mothers were always giving daughters on soap operas moments before the heroine took a trip down the aisle. I thought, if nothing else, my mother might let me take control of the television in my final hours of singlehood and that we might enjoy a good chick flick, the way we often did in Beaver Dam on Sunday afternoons when I was growing up.

But my mother, gripping the remote control tightly in her right hand, seemed uninterested in doling out advice or reminiscing. And she refused to turn the channel from the *Law and Order* rerun she'd been watching.

"I like this episode. And I was here first," she snapped.

"Can we at least turn off some of these lights?" I asked, reaching to turn off the pair of lights that divided the two beds.

"No!" she snapped, swatting at my arm before I could turn off either lamp.

"But, Mom, it's late. And I'm getting married tomorrow. If I can't watch what I want on TV, at least let me go to sleep."

"This is the way I sleep," she said. "And if you don't like it, you can find your own hotel room."

I raised myself onto one elbow and stared in disbelief. My mother refused to return my gaze, opting instead to raise the volume on the television so that she could drown me out.

"Mom, I need to sleep," I moaned.

"I like the lights on," my mother said, refusing to budge. Lights, she said, were part of her new sleep routine.

I tossed and turned, worried about the dark circles that were bound to form beneath my eyes, wondering if my veil could hide them from the unforgiving lens of the wedding photographer's camera. I watched my mother from my bed in sad silence. She fixated first on Vincent D'Onofrio's detective character, attempting to crack a *Law and Order* case. Later she turned on an old black-and-white movie on AMC. Then came a series of infomercials imploring her to purchase ponytail devices or fountain of youth serums.

When I begged once more at three thirty to please let me turn off the lights, my mother snapped, "Tomorrow night you can turn out whatever lights you'd like."

I turned over and placed a pillow on top of my head. One thing was clear: just as I was gaining a husband, I was losing a mother.

The next morning I awoke tired and achy. But it didn't matter. I was getting married. And I knew as I sat down to breakfast with my beloved childhood friend–turned-bridesmaid, Kim, that was all that mattered.

Four hours before the wedding Mass was slated to begin, Marie, the hair and makeup artist I had flown in from New York for the occasion, lovingly sat me down in the suite Dean and I had rented for our wedding night and meticulously applied concealer and powder to the areas around my eyes.

Moments before I was to walk down the aisle, I stood in the back of the cathedral in my Vera Wang gown, my parents at my sides. I couldn't decide what made more sense—to walk down the aisle alone or with my mom and dad. In the end, I wanted them both there. They had put me on this earth. I wanted them to help bridge the gap between my old life and the new one awaiting me.

I was feeling calm, feeling happy, and then I heard it: the first strains of Pachelbel's Canon in D, the processional I'd selected.

Suddenly, the calmness escaped me and I felt in its place overwhelming emotion. I began to cry.

My mother was at my side in an instant, presenting me with a white handkerchief.

"Mary, it's okay, sweetheart," she said, blotting gently at my eyes.

Her tone was warm, reassuring. Just as it had been when she had held me in her lap as a child. Just as it had been when she nursed me back to health after spinal surgery. This was the mother I had needed last night. She had been so unpleasant then. She was back to her old nurturing form now.

"You have to know, everything is going to be all right."

She was right. As it turns out, the wedding day was all that I dreamed it would be. Dean was handsome, crying as he waited for me at the end of the aisle. My girlfriends looked resplendent in the white satin Vera Wang bridesmaid dresses that I'd carefully selected as part of our all-white wedding. Guests were presented with watermelon martinis as they entered the museum in honor of that first drink Dean bought me the night we met. The flowers—including the white lilies of the valley I'd instructed the florist to pick from around my childhood home—were breathtaking. Trudy Diener would have been proud.

Dean and I danced and marveled at the vision of white we had helped to create. My mother had started that affinity for white. It had blossomed into a night more magical than I could ever have imagined possible. White was the perfect blank palette from which to launch a new life.

Even my mother marveled at the evening as she stood, microphone in hand, to greet our guests midway through our dinner. "Tonight is a night unlike any other," she said. "It is a night unto itself. Never have all of us gathered like this—and never will we gather like this again."

She never acknowledged to me her moodiness from the night

before, never apologized. I didn't expect her to. The mood swings hurt. But I took comfort in seeing the joy on her face as she took in the beauty of the night. All of her siblings except for Patty had flown in to be with her. She delighted in their company, laughed loudly at their jokes, introduced them to the two dozen teacher friends she'd invited.

I saw her cry only once, when I asked an old friend to serenade her with her favorite John Denver tune, "Annie's Song." Listening to the lyrics, "Come let me hold you, let me give my life to you," my mother melted, resting her head on the shoulder of her brother Al.

At the close of the song, I ran to hug her.

"How did you remember that was my favorite song?" my mother asked. "How did you find the sheet music?"

"Because I love you, Mom."

Two mornings after the wedding, after we'd gotten a chance to visit with our out-of-town guests and take in a Brewers game, Dean led me—half awake, half asleep—down through the Pfister's lobby. It was five A.M., and a town car stood waiting to sweep us off to our honeymoon. Yawning, I was preparing to hand my bags to the driver when I spied my mother wobbling toward us on her arthritic knees.

My eyes widened in surprise.

"Mom, it's early," I said. "You should be sleeping."

"I don't sleep so well these days," my mother said. "You know that. Besides, I wanted to see you one more time."

I dropped my bag and hugged her, unexpectedly beginning to cry.

"I love you," I said, hating that my departure meant I was leaving her alone. Again.

"I love you, dear daughter," she said, leading me to Dean, who had begun to work with the bellhop and driver to load the car.

"But no tears," she said. "This is a happy time."

"We'll be back this summer," I said, watching Dean and the driver load my wedding gown into the car. "We'll come for your birthday. And you need to come and see us."

"I know," my mother said, nodding. "I know."

"Take care of this one," my mother said as she hugged Dean.

"You know I will," he said, hugging her back.

Then it was my turn to hug my mother once more.

"It was beautiful, wasn't it?" I asked her, referring not only to the wedding, but to everything.

"More than you'll ever know," she said.

"Even my nightgown?" I asked.

"Even your nightgown."

Then, pushing me gently into the backseat of the car, she looked at me intently and pressed her face up close to mine.

"Be happy," my mother said.

And at that, I cried harder, knowing that she meant it.

Chapter 11
Vera Wang Nightshirt

December 15, 2010

Taking a step back from the full-length mirror that hung on the back of the bathroom door, I studied my reflection and sighed.

On the upside, my blond shoulder-length hair looked good—better, in any case, than it did when I wasn't pregnant: thicker, shinier, healthier. On the downside, I looked like I'd swallowed a basketball, and the bridge of my nose seemed to be widening by the day. The plum-pink nightshirt I'd slipped into moments ago barely covered my growing tummy, which was now seven months pregnant. As recently as a month ago, the garment had hung in pretty folds and pleats that accentuated perky breasts and toned legs. Now it looked like a fashion misfire. That's what the third trimester was like—one day clothes fit, the next day they didn't. I should have been used to all of this by now. This was my third pregnancy. But the absence of a waistline still took me by surprise.

"You okay in there?" called a voice on the other side of the door.

It was Dean. I must have lost track of the time. Again. Between working full-time and caring for the two boys, I never had a moment alone. Except when I closed the door to the bathroom in those few moments after I awoke in the morning and again at moments like this—at night, when I slipped into my nightgown and literally let my hair down.

"I'm okay," I said, still studying my complexion. "It's just . . ."

"Just what?"

"Just," I said, opening the door to meet Dean's big brown eyes. "Just that I look like a beached whale and none of my clothes fit."

Dean laughed and hugged me to him.

"You're hardly a beached whale," he said, squeezing me tighter now. "You're beautiful."

I knew that he meant it. Dean always told me I was beautiful. Especially when I was pregnant. Without question, that's when he was at his most protective and loving.

"I have something that might make you feel better," Dean said.

"Oh yeah?"

He pointed to a box on the couch.

"Just picked this up from the doorman. It's from your mom."

"Uh-oh," I said.

Dean laughed. A box from Anne Diener Pflum typically contained toys for one or more of the boys—three-year-old Roman or one-year-old Creedence. And more often than not, the toys—Hot Wheels, Sesame Street books, Thomas the Train engines—were things that made lots of noise.

Sitting down on the couch, I tore away the packing tape and pulled open the lid to reveal a thick layer of tissue paper and the softest white jersey material.

"What is it?" asked Dean, intrigued. "Something for the baby?"

"No," I squealed. "It's something for me!"

It was a nightshirt. A delicate white cotton nightshirt. Lined with little buttons and a long, luxuriant grosgrain ribbon down the front, it featured an adorably stiff white collar that popped up preppy-style, like something ordinarily reserved for a rugby shirt. On either side of the buttery-soft garment were hidden pockets. Best of all, the shirt fell beautifully, in soft pleats, with a scalloped hemline that would, I knew, show off the one womanly feature that remained unaffected by pregnancy: my legs.

Clutching the shirt to my growing belly, I ran to the desk phone and dialed my mother's cell phone. She'd gotten the mobile phone when I was pregnant with Roman. And, when she remembered to keep it charged, it was a godsend to both of us. She answered on the sixth ring.

"Mom, I love it! I love it! I love it!"

"So you got the nightshirt?" she asked, her tone pleased.

"Yes! Have I mentioned that I love it?"

"Did you see who designed it?"

"No," I said, confused. Since when did my mother send me designer anything?

I looked down at the shirt and gasped. There, on a blue fabric label, was none other than Vera Wang's signature logo.

"You got me a Vera Wang nightshirt?"

"Why not?" My mother laughed. "You told me you needed something to make you feel pretty. And I thought you needed something practical, too. And we both know that Vera Wang is the best when it comes to nightgowns."

At this, we both laughed. Hard.

My mother became my unofficial pajama supplier in 2007 after the birth of my first son, Roman. At the time, the maternity ward nurses strongly encouraged me to invest in a number of nightshirts that buttoned down the front. Easy access to the boobs was key for breast-feeding, they said. They couldn't have been more right. The two or three nightshirts that I had pre-pregnancy barely got me through a day in those early weeks of sleepless nights and lactating angst. And my mother, aware of my determination to breast-feed her grandson, offered to become my pajama point person. Over the course of those first months of motherhood, she sent me a half dozen nightshirts—some cotton, some flannel, all desperately needed.

By the time I became pregnant with my third child in three years, she asked what more she could get me. I told her, without hesitation, that I needed still more nightshirts.

"What kind?" she asked me on the phone. It was January 2010.

"Just the usual. Something that buttons down the front."

"Any particular color?"

"White," I told her. "You know me—I love white."

And that is how my favorite gift from my mother, that white Vera Wang nightshirt, came to rest in my dresser—when, that is, I wasn't wearing it. My mother found it in Beaver Dam, of all places, deeply discounted at the local Kohl's. My hometown, she said, clearly did not share my deep and abiding love for Vera Wang and her new discount collection of clothing.

"Beaver Dam's oversight is your gain, dear daughter!"

She was thrilled with her purchase, pleased that she had managed to surprise her fashion-loving daughter. And I was ecstatic. Baby number three was on its way. And I had the perfect nightshirt with which to welcome him.

Augustine Pfister Peterson entered the world on March 29, 2010. As was the case with my first two sons, Augie was born naturally, with Dean at my side.

Everything seemed perfect. More than perfect. Doctors had told me at my thirty-eight-week appointment that Augie was likely to weigh no more than six pounds, owing in part to a bad stomach virus I'd contracted in my third trimester that had forced me to lose weight when I should have been gaining. But Augie bounded out of the womb at a strapping ten pounds, demonstrating his capacity to surprise and thrive from an early age.

"He's enormous!" the delivering doctor cried.

While Augie got through the delivery unscathed, I did not. I was sent home from the hospital after just two nights, as is typical in the wake of uneventful deliveries. But within a week, I was experiencing sporadic fits of uncontrollable chills that left me temporarily unable to move. At first, the fits passed quickly, often in a matter of a minute or two. I told myself—as did Dean—that I must be having some kind of strange reaction to breast-feeding or perhaps was going through a post-pregnancy hormonal shift. But when the chills grew so bad that I was forced to retreat in my new Vera Wang nightshirt to a fetal position on our living room couch for more than an hour, huddled beneath a pile of blankets, I knew something was wrong.

"Maybe take some Tylenol?" Dean asked helplessly. He looked nervously from me to our two older boys, seated in front of the television, watching an episode of *Sesame Street* we'd recorded the day before. The sun had set on that Sunday, and bedtime was upon us. Augie was just six days old. I'd managed to get him to sleep, and now Dean was waiting for me to assist in putting the bigger boys into their pajamas.

"I already took some medicine," I said, my teeth chattering uncontrollably. "It's not working."

I started to shake harder now. "Dean, I'm scared."

For the nearly five years that we had been married, Dean had been the perfect partner. He patiently got up with me and the babies in the middle of the night, bringing me glasses of water while I nursed. He continued to cheer me on through career developments, applauding loudly when I brought home my first Emmy Awards. It was not unusual for him to arrive home from the office armed with my favorite flowers or a bottle of Chardonnay "just because."

But on this particular night of fever and chills, just one week into Augie's new life, Dean wasn't feeling particularly romantic or heroic. He was tired.

"Let's go to bed," Dean said, yawning. "You can go to the doctor in the morning."

"I think I should go now," I said, shaking my head. "Something doesn't feel right."

He sighed. "But what do we do about the kids?"

Choosing to raise our children in New York had distinct advantages and disadvantages. On the upside: We lived in a bustling, exciting city full of culture and career opportunities. We resided in a beautiful prewar building on Manhattan's Upper West Side. We had a growing family. And we were in love. On the downside:

We had no family in the city. And while we had friends with whom to socialize, and a nanny to help us during the week, we had no one we could call upon in our non-weekday hours of need. That meant that if I took off for the emergency room to address the paralyzing chills, I had to do it alone so that Dean could look after the older boys.

After a beat, I had a solution. "I know what I'll do. I'll call my mom. She'll know what to do."

No matter how old a woman gets, or how complicated her relationship with her family might be, she wants her mother when she's sick. At least I did.

My mother answered the phone on the third ring. At the sound of her voice, I surprised even myself by bursting into tears.

"Honey, what is it?" she cried.

"Mom, I'm sick. I can't stop shaking."

As my teeth chattered, I described my symptoms. Then I told her of Dean's suggestion that I rest at home and go to the doctor in the morning.

My mother sighed. "Dean has a point. You do sound tired. But what does your gut tell you to do?"

"It tells me something's wrong, Mom."

"Then go to the hospital. Now."

A half hour later, I'd mustered the strength to gather up Baby Augie and hail a cab to the emergency room. The plan was for Dean to stay with the older boys while I went to the ER for what we hoped would be a quick exam. Because Augie was a newborn and nursed every two hours, he would come with me. If things went well, I would get some antibiotics for whatever ailed me and be back home in no time.

As the cab made its way across Central Park to New York Presbyterian Hospital, I continued to shake. By the time I arrived at the emergency room entrance, I could barely walk.

Within a minute of my stumbling into the hospital's triage station, the ER's front desk nurse had a thermometer in my mouth. Within two, she had me on a gurney. Things moved so fast, I didn't understand what was happening. I remember being whisked into the deep recesses of New York Presbyterian Hospital at breakneck speed, staring up at the blinding overhead lights that lined the hospital ceiling and crying out to the orderlies pushing me, "My baby has to come with me! Don't leave my baby!"

A half hour later, I was in a hospital gown and had not one, but two IVs in my arms. Augie, in his stroller, reclined by my side. I lay looking up at the ceiling, praying for Augie to sleep. When he let out a wail, I willed myself to prop myself up onto two IV'd arms and reach for him.

That's when I heard the bark.

"Ms. Pflum, lie down!"

The source of the bark was a tall bespectacled man in civilian clothes. He'd entered my little tent of an examining room when I wasn't looking and, judging from his partially untucked shirt, had been roused from his home in the middle of the night to inspect me.

"He's my baby!" I cried, looking from the man back to a crying Augie. "I need to nurse him."

"What you need," barked the man again, "is to lie down and listen to me. You have an infection. A potentially fatal one. In your womb. For centuries, women died from this kind of thing. Don't add your name to that list."

The man who was doing the barking, it turned out, was one of the leaders of obstetrics for the New York Presbyterian Hospital system. He'd been called from his home to the hospital to inspect me when I'd presented signs of a post-delivery infection. The potentially fatal condition was due to what were later called "unsanitary conditions" at the time of childbirth—possibly resulting from something as simple as the delivery room doctor's failure to wash her hands properly. Now Dr. Barking Man was there to try to right the wrong.

"Who's with you?" the doctor asked, still barking.

"N-no one," I stammered. I looked at my arms, covered in tape and IV tubing, and began to cry. "I just came with my baby. My husband is home with our older children."

"Call him. Or call someone. You shouldn't be here alone. We need to keep you here for a few days. And that baby can't stay with you unless someone is here to help you. Getting better—not worrying about a baby—should be your top priority."

I waited for the barking man to examine me and leave, then worked with a kindly nurse to locate the cell phone that was buried at the bottom of my purse. Dean's phone rang once, twice, ten times, then went to voice mail. The home phone did the same. I looked at the clock in my little examining room. It was nearly midnight. He must be asleep. And he was a hard sleeper, especially now, in these sleep-deprived days since Augie's birth. Between the nonstop feeding schedule of a newborn and helping me to care for the older boys, Dean was exhausted. I tried his cell phone again. Then the home phone again. Then his cell phone again. Still there was no answer.

"I need to take you to your room now," said the nurse. "Think your husband will be along soon?"

"Uh-huh," I lied. "I'm sure he'll be here."

"You know the baby can't stay with you unless someone comes," the nurse reminded me. "Maybe your mom can come?"

I smiled ruefully. "Maybe."

If only she could. If only she would. I knew my mother would be waiting for a call from me, anxious to know how the trip to the emergency room had gone. Talking on the phone with me late at night? That wasn't a problem. But flying out to take care of me and the baby? That, I knew, was a tall order.

Becoming a parent had done some wonderful things when it came to my relationship with my mother. We talked frequently now—as much as or more than when I was in college. More, certainly, than when I'd been overseas. More than around the time of my lung problems. Now we chatted like old girlfriends, about balancing work with motherhood, about teething and fevers, and about questionable pediatricians. When I was in labor with each of the boys, she was my first phone call. The same held true when I gave birth. And when Roman was diagnosed at just three months with a heart murmur, which eventually turned out to be nothing, she was the one I tracked down by cell phone, sobbing—knowing she was the only one in the world who could fully understand my fears and calm my nerves.

But while I could talk for hours a day to my mother about ear infection woes and the best means of combating the croup, about Pampers versus Huggies and about when to introduce an infant to solid foods, the chasm that divided us in other areas of our lives grew ever greater.

More than ever, I was losing her to that damned house.

Not only was my mother incapable of cleaning it, but she was increasingly loath to leave it—or to talk to anyone interested in helping her to clean it up.

There were a multitude of red flags. After the wedding, Dean and I tried unsuccessfully to visit. We made it all the way to Beaver Dam one weekend and were making our way from the airport to the house when my cell phone rang.

"Change of plans," my mother said. "I know you talked about staying at the house this weekend, honey. And that would have been great. But I have an even better idea. I made you and Dean a reservation at the Best Western."

"But, Mom, why?" I asked, disappointed. "We were looking forward to seeing you and the house."

"It'll be better this way," she told us. "The Best Western has a pool. And a coffee shop. Won't that be more fun than staying at the house?"

I put my head into my hands. I didn't want to go swimming on my visit back to my hometown. I didn't need a coffee shop. But my mother left us with no choice.

During our visit, my mother worked to entertain us. She took us to a number of local restaurants and gave Dean a grand tour of Beaver Dam's main city parks and St. Peter's. But she refused to let us go anywhere near the house.

"It's just not a good time," she told us, repeating the mantra she'd used for years. "I've been tired. So the house looks tired. It's not up for entertaining. You understand."

Neither Dean nor I understood. But there was nothing we could do. It was her house. Violating her wish for us to remain in the hotel would have done irreparable damage to my relationship with her and undoubtedly resulted in tears and arguing all around.

"Mary, you have to trust me on this one," my mother told me over dinner at the local Applebee's. "And I will not tolerate you failing to respect my personal space. Do you hear me?"

I heard her. Loud and clear. She wanted to keep me as far away from my childhood home as physically possible.

Eventually the oddity of the situation—of my being back in the town I'd grown up in but unable to go to the house I'd called home—became too much. On the final afternoon of our visit, when my mother was out running errands, I took Dean out to my old neighborhood for a drive.

It had been seven years since I'd last seen the outside of the house. The place was largely unchanged. It was still two stories tall, still red with yellow trim. All that was different was the garage door. My mother had gotten a new one to replace the old one, which had broken a couple of years before. All white, and decidedly cheap looking, it stood out like a sore thumb against the red-and-yellow backdrop.

"Should we go in?" asked Dean, slowing the car as we drove by.

"I wish," I said, shaking my head. "But we can't. She'll know. Somehow she'll know. And she'll never forgive us."

The summer after Roman was born brought more red flags. My mother came to stay with Dean and me for two weeks to help me when I returned to work. But while she was supposed to be there to care for her newest grandson, she often seemed more interested in the large television in our living room than our company. She was at her happiest when she sat with the remote control in her hands, scanning channels in search of *Law and Order* and delighting in our other cable offerings.

The situation came to a head on one of the final nights of her visit when I tried to coax her into joining Dean and me at a local Italian restaurant while the baby stayed home with a babysitter.

"Come on, Mom," I said, trying to pull her up from her place on the couch. "It'll be fun. The food is great and so is the wine list."

"But I'm watching *Law and Order*," she said, the remote still in her hand. Her eyes didn't even meet mine. They were focused on the TV.

"You can watch *Law and Order* when you go back home."

At this, her face fell.

"Anne, what's the matter?" Dean asked.

"I can't watch *Law and Order* at home," she said, still not meeting our eyes. "The TV doesn't work."

"Since when?" I asked.

"Since a few months ago."

This was news to me. When I was last in the house, there were two working televisions.

"What about the one in the basement?" I asked.

"That's the one I'm talking about. The one in the living room hasn't worked for years."

I exchanged glances with Dean. My mother looked so heartbreakingly sad—and embarrassed—at the admission.

"Well, we'll fix it," I said. "I'll call the Best Buy in Madison tomorrow. We can have one delivered to you as soon as you get home."

"No!" cried my mother. "Don't do that!"

"Anne," interrupted Dean, as he sat down beside her on the couch and took her hand, "it'll be no trouble. We'll take care of the TV and make the arrangements. It'll be easy."

"But they'll want to come inside," my mother said, panicking. Her voice rose an octave. "They always want to come in. I don't want anyone in the house."

The terror in her voice broke my heart. When I was growing up, Anne Diener Pflum was unfailingly assertive when it came to getting things done. If one of my teachers wasn't performing up to snuff, if the coffee in the restaurant wasn't hot enough, if there was a change in local church policy that seemed discriminatory— she spoke up. Even after her hospitalizations for the deepening depression, she took on school administrators, restaurant managers, and church councils with ease. She had been fearless. But now, when it came to doing something as seemingly simple as allowing a stranger to enter her home to install a television, she was timid as a child, afraid of any shadow that threatened to darken her decaying house's doorstep.

TV was the one link to the outside world that she'd still been able to enjoy in that albatross. The idea of her going without newscasts and old movies and *Law and Order* reruns because of her growing paranoia was just too sad to bear.

"Listen to Dean, Mother," I said, sitting down between her and Dean. "Please? Let us fix this."

It wasn't easy, but after a week of cajoling, Dean and I finally convinced her to allow the Best Buy team to do its magic. Within a week of her return to Beaver Dam, the old TV had been removed and a new television and DVD player were delivered and installed by an electronics expert my mother deemed "unbelievably helpful."

My mother was ecstatic. "I can't believe how good Vincent looks," she gushed the day after the television was installed.

"Vincent?" I asked.

"D'Onofrio," she said, referring to her favorite *Law and Order* actor. "He was so blurred the last time the old TV actually worked. Now I can see him."

But while she could see Vincent now, she still couldn't see the floor of the house on any of its three levels. That's what we learned from her brother Al, the only person I knew, aside from the Best Buy deliveryman and a property tax assessor, who had been allowed to view the interior of the house since 2000.

My uncle Al entered the house in 2009, nearly four years after his quest to help my mother began.

A resident of Decatur, Illinois—he moved there from Chicago after his divorce, when his four children were grown—Al was the only one of Albert and Aurelia's six children besides my mother who had remained in the Midwest. A former IBM executive, Al was the closest sibling my mother had in physical terms and, soon, in emotional terms as well. They hadn't been particularly close as children owing to the age difference. Al was six years younger than my mother and had seen little of her once she left for college and then the convent. But with Al and Aurelia gone, my mother was hungry to fill the void they'd left behind and to reconnect with fellow Dieners. Uncle Al was just what the doctor ordered.

Shortly before Dean and I got married, Al started calling my mother more frequently and driving up to Wisconsin to meet her for a dinner here, a lunch there.

"When we started getting together, just the two of us, after all those years," Al said, "she was a bit like a scared animal. I had to win her trust."

Slowly but surely, both he and the meals broke down my mother's defenses, and Al became a trusted confidant in her life.

"Your mother is an unbelievable woman," Al said, referring to their shared childhood, then life with Dale and beyond. "I have so much respect for all that she's been through."

I was grateful for his newfound friendship with my mother. She was willing to listen to her brother in a way she wouldn't—or couldn't—listen to her children. And just as he represented a source of comfort to my mother, he represented a source of hope for me. Here, at last, was an ally in the battle to save my mother from her depression, and from the house.

What started as long talks between two siblings eventually turned into monthly meetings and in-depth conversations. For years, my mother balked at the idea of allowing Al into her home. She was reluctant to have him so much as drive into the driveway when they met for meals in Beaver Dam. Eventually, however, Uncle Al talked his way into the house. And though I had warned him in telephone conversations about its condition, he was unprepared for what he saw.

"Mary," he said, his voice full of incredulity when he called me a few days after his breakthrough, "you can't open the front door."

"What do you mean?"

"The front door of your mother's house," he repeated. "I couldn't get it open."

"Is it sealed shut?" I imagined my mother accidentally spilling something on the threshold years ago—syrup or paint—and never wiping it up, and the door remaining stuck forevermore. Crazy as it might sound, it wasn't an unrealistic scenario.

"No," he said. "The problem is the *stuff*. There's so much junk in there that you can't physically push the door open wide enough for a human being to enter. I had to go in through the screen door in the garage. And that entrance is almost as bad. I was swimming through stuff."

"Swimming?" I asked, my heart racing. "Was there a flood?"

"No," he said. "At least I don't think so. You wouldn't have been able to tell if there was one. Your mother has so much junk in there that it was like wading through a swamp. My feet never touched the floor the whole time I was in there. It's chest-high in places. Three feet in the shallow areas. And I never made it farther than two rooms—just the living room and the kitchen."

I nodded in silence.

"Mary," my uncle said softly. "It's bad. I think it's probably even worse than you thought."

There was the smell, he said. The whole place reeked. There were the appliances. Uncle Al said nothing in the kitchen worked. Now the stove was broken as well and joined the broken microwave and broken dishwasher in the kitchen that had become a morgue. And then there were his safety concerns.

"Mary Elizabeth, I could hardly walk. Your mother is seventy with arthritis and cataracts. I promise you this: she is going to fall over or into one of those piles of crap. And chances are she's not going to be able to get back up."

In subsequent weeks, Dean and I had long talks with my uncle, trying to cobble together a plan of action. There were no easy answers.

Dean and I talked about moving closer. If we relocated from New York to the Midwest, she would have an incentive to clean up—wouldn't she? Or maybe our presence would serve as an impetus for her to move to a condo—or even to a wing of a house we would buy for our family.

"If she moves in with us, we could help her find new furniture and new clothes," I said hopefully. "Or if we help her to move into a condo of her own, we could hire a maid to help her keep things clean."

"And what about her current house?" my uncle asked. "And all of the stuff in it?"

"We'll get rid of it. All of it. That's the whole point. Without the junk, she can finally start over."

My uncle sighed. "Mary, I think you need to accept the fact that your mother's problems go way beyond an inability to keep a house clean. She has been suffering in silence for years. A new home—even a new home with a maid—that's just window dressing. Her real problems go much deeper than that."

"I know," I said, my voice breaking. "But we can fix this."

"You can hope and you can try," said my uncle. "But sometimes when things have been broken for a long time, they . . ."

He stopped for a moment to collect his thoughts before continuing. "They can't be fixed."

I didn't want to believe that this was the situation for my mother. The house was broken. I could live with that. I didn't care. Let the damned house fall apart. But I couldn't bear the thought that my mother could be so broken that she couldn't be brought back to the land of the living.

So when I lay there in that New York City hospital bed that night, with those IVs in my arms, and that beautiful newborn baby boy by my side, and called my mother in tears to ask, as the nurse suggested, whether she might be able to fly out to see me for two days—to help me with the baby until the infection subsided—I still had a glimmer of hope that she was fixable.

After I cried my way through my recounting of the doctor's orders to get family assistance to the hospital immediately, I paused.

The trouble is she paused, too. That pause, that hesitation, said it all.

"Honey, I'd love to help," she said nervously. "I would. But I have to work. You know how I have all of my students. And the principal doesn't like for me to take time off work."

I nodded, crying. It was just like when I had the lung procedure. She wanted to help. I could feel it in my heart. I could hear it in her voice. But she couldn't.

"And there's the house. I just can't leave the house like that on such short notice."

That damn house.

"What about Dean?" she asked brightly. "He'll be able to help, won't he?"

I silently shook my head, then rested it against the cool of the IV pole.

"Only for a couple of hours a day," I said, my voice barely above a whisper. "He already took time off for Augie. And he has meetings and—never mind."

My womb hurt, my head hurt, and I continued to shiver from the fever. Augie, thankfully, lay contentedly for the moment in the car seat attached to his stroller that they'd rolled into the room and placed beside my hospital bed.

"You understand, honey," said my mother, almost pleading. "You need to get better. And I'd probably just drive you and the hospital staff crazy if I came."

I nodded sadly once more. She couldn't see the nod. She couldn't see the tears. It was just as well.

"But I'll get the house together for you—just the way you've been asking me to do. I have a plan. Just you wait and see what Uncle Al and I are going to do with the place this summer."

"Okay," I said weakly.

"Get some sleep, sweetheart—and call me tomorrow. Infections are very serious business. I'll be saying lots of prayers. And I'll light a candle for you tomorrow after Mass. I love you."

"I love you, too," I said. I listened to her hang up and sat stunned, unable to move. What was I going to do? I wondered. About the infection? About caring for a newborn while my very tired body worked to fight the infection? About my mother?

"What'd your mom say?" the nurse asked me moments later when she popped back into the room to take my temperature again. "Is she coming?"

"She's working on her flight now," I lied, knowing that if I said otherwise, she would take Augie away from me.

"Aren't moms the best?" she asked.

"Totally," I said, fighting back the tears as the nurse jammed the thermometer into my mouth.

When the nurse left, I finally allowed myself to break down. Heaving and sighing, I cried harder than I'd cried in years.

Slamming an IV'd fist into my hospital bed, I let out a strange mix of sobs that was one part anger, one part sadness, one part fear. I cried because my exhausted husband wouldn't answer the phone. I cried because my mother couldn't bring herself to leave that wreck of a house. I cried because I had never felt more sick or weak or helpless in all of my life—and I wanted nothing more than to put my head down, but I couldn't because I had a teeny-tiny little baby who needed me.

I racked my mind, wondering whom else I could call. My father had been of tremendous help to me when I was sick with TB. He could be of help to me now. But I knew from his latest phone calls and e-mails that he was in Texas, helping my sister-in-law watch my brother's kids. He was off the list.

My father's youngest sister—the aunt I was closest to—lived in Indiana. But she was a nurse and would have to work. My girl-friends all had jobs and children of their own. This was that time when a girl needed her mom.

Not surprisingly, my tears roused Augie. What started out as little newborn moans quickly escalated into a full-on wail that told me he was hungry and ready for his food source to come to the rescue. I looked at my IVs. Then I looked nervously at the door, waiting for the nursing staff to swoop down on me and toss Augie out of the room. I had no choice.

I gingerly reached to stroke my tummy, which continued to feel as if it were on fire. This wasn't going to be easy. But he needed me. Drawing in one long breath, I managed to steady myself at the side of the hospital bed and reach for Augie. Gently, I cupped his torso into the palm of one hand and pulled him to my breast with the other. I winced, muttering a few four-letter words owing to the pain. But as Augie's bellowing mouth found the waiting nipple, his cries ceased, and I heaved a sigh of relief.

"Thank you, babe," I whispered to him, the tears still flowing. "At least I've got you."

Three days and several courses of antibiotics later, I was released from the hospital, infection-free. Against the odds, Augie had remained by my bedside during the entire hospital stay. It took some doing. With Dean unable to get the time off work to stay with me and Augie, I'd had to do more than a bit of tap-dancing with a suspicious nursing staff. But by strategically placing Dean's sweater and briefcase on a chair in the hospital room and arranging for Dean to drop in at a few key times—once before work, once at lunchtime, and once in the evening—I'd managed to convince them that Dean was staying with me in the hospital.

Only one of the nurses caught on to my scheme. When she came to check my vitals at midnight on the second night of my stay, she surveyed the room, shook her head, and waved a disapproving finger at me. But since she was a mother herself, she agreed to keep my secret.

By the time I left the hospital, I was physically and emotionally exhausted. I made a solemn vow to Augie: never would I let a house—or anything—prevent me from coming to help him or any of his siblings in their future hours of need.

No sooner had I returned home from the hospital than I started receiving ever-lengthier phone calls from Uncle Al about my mother and the house. She was apparently serious about letting him help her remove some of the bigger piles of debris as she had allowed him to set up a three-ton Dumpster in the driveway. It peeved some of my mother's image-conscious neighbors no end to have the eyesore of the Dumpster so publicly displayed in the neighborhood, but the gigantic trash bin served a vital purpose: it enabled my uncle to painstakingly remove some of those five-foot drifts of debris from the main floor of the house.

"You wouldn't believe how much stuff we threw out!" my uncle said. "That's the good news . . ."

"But the bad news?" I asked, dreading his answer.

My uncle paused.

"Mary Elizabeth," Uncle Al said, then stopped. "I need to ask you some rather personal questions about your mother and the house."

This didn't sound good. I took a seat on the rocking chair in our living room and pulled Augie onto my lap. "Okay," I said hesitantly.

"Did you have much of a problem with vermin when you were growing up?"

"Vermin?" I asked, my stomach clenching. "You mean like mice?"

"I mean vermin," my uncle said.

"Blackie caught a mouse in the garage once," I said.

"Not a mouse in the garage—I mean multiple mice. And bats. And chipmunks. In the house."

I swallowed. Was this why my mother had been asking about chipmunks when I wanted to bring Mesut home from Turkey for a visit?

"Multiple? In the—"

I paused and pulled Augie closer.

"They're in the house?" I asked at last.

"Yes," said my uncle solemnly. "They're everywhere."

"Where are the bats coming from?"

"Best I can tell is from a hole in the roof your mother hasn't had fixed. I don't know if she even knew it was there. She spends most of her time in the basement, as you know.

"But I wanted to know if there's a history of the problem—or if there's an exterminator or someone you or your mother used over the years?"

"No," I said, shaking my head. "Does she know you know about the . . . creatures?"

"That's the thing with your mother these days," my uncle said. "I don't know that she even knows. It's like she's closed her ears and her eyes to them. She lives in her world and they live in theirs."

It made me think of *Grey Gardens*. I'd gone to see the musical about the real-life Long Island mother-and-daughter team, living in modern-day ruins without ever seeming to fully grasp the depth of their living conditions. Was this what my mother had become? A Big or Little Edie, living in denial?

I stroked Augie's hair with one hand while I held the phone with the other. "Uncle Al, let me come out there. If she's let you in the house, maybe she'll finally let me in. Dean and I can come this weekend—"

"With a new baby?" my uncle snapped. "I don't think so. This place is a health hazard for an adult. It's not safe for an infant. Besides, mice and bats aren't the only reason I'm calling. There's more."

More? My heart raced.

"Like what?" I asked. I heard the fear in my voice as I said the words.

"I don't know how to put this," my uncle said hesitantly, "so I'll just ask you straight out. What do you know about where your mother uses the bathroom?"

"The bathroom?" I asked, confused by the question. "The house has two bathrooms. There's one upstairs and one down."

"Have you seen the bathrooms lately?"

"No," I said, growing more confused. "You know that. My mother hasn't let me in the house in years."

"I know." My uncle sighed. "I guess I'm asking—did the bathrooms work when you last saw them?"

"The shower in the upstairs bathroom always was a problem—but—"

"Not the shower," my uncle interrupted. "The toilet."

My heart began to pound loudly in my chest. "Uncle Al, what are you trying to get at? Are you telling me that my mother doesn't have a working toilet?"

My uncle, the usually stately former IBM executive, always calm and serene in the face of pressure, sighed nervously. "Yes. It would appear to be that way."

"That can't be," I said. "I'm sure she just doesn't want you to use it. She's probably just embarrassed by the mess and doesn't want you to see the bathrooms."

"That's what I thought, too. So I've worked out a system of never using her bathroom on my visits. I've always waited and gone back to the hotel or made a trip into town. But then I began to get suspicious and did some investigating. Mary Elizabeth, neither of your mother's bathrooms works."

"They must," I said, stroking Augie's hair. "They have to."

"I'm telling you they don't."

"They must—"

"Mary Elizabeth, listen to me: they don't."

"That's her home," I said, my voice rising. Augie, feeling the tension, began to cry. "Where does she go?"

My uncle was silent for a beat. "I don't know. But that might explain . . ."

An air of awkward tension filled the line.

"The smell," I said softly, finishing his sentence. My uncle had repeatedly noted the smell of the place in his calls to me. It had grown so bad he'd invested in a mask that he wore sometimes when he cleaned. A lack of a toilet—a makeshift chamber pot or outhouse—might explain the horrible smell.

It all made sense. Maybe that's why some of the boxes she'd sent in the mail to us, full of seemingly new baby clothes with the tags still attached, smelled so horrible. One box was beyond the point of repair. Even after multiple washings, the baby clothes still had a bad odor. We'd had to throw out everything in the box.

The lack of working bathrooms, too, might explain some of my mother's strange habits from the past two years. Without notice, she'd go to stay at a hotel near the school where she taught for one, two, even three or four nights in a row.

"It's nice to get away sometimes," she'd say when she called to tell me she was staying at the AmericInn. Again.

Now I knew she likely meant it was nice to be able to have access to indoor plumbing.

I started to cry, holding a fussy Baby Augie to me as I did so.

"How can she live like that?" I asked my uncle. "Uncle Al, she's not an animal. Really she's not."

"I know," my uncle said softly.

"She's a teacher," I said. "She's educated. She brings home a decent paycheck. Her students love her. She puts herself together and goes to work and goes to church and you saw her—she looked beautiful at our wedding. So lovely. So composed. How can she not have a running, flushing toilet?"

"Mary," my uncle said. "You know I know how brilliant your mother is. This toilet thing—you know it's just a symptom of—"

I nodded. "I know. It's just a physical manifestation of what's going on inside her." He'd said this to me before. It was an extension of the depression that was ravaging her.

Her toilets needed fixing. And she did, too.

"Uncle Al, I'll talk to her," I said at last. "I'll handle this. I'll call her tonight."

"No," said my uncle softly. Firmly. "You can't."

"But I can—I want to—I have to—"

"If you do," he interrupted, "it'll kill her. I promise you—the knowledge that you know—that her daughter, whom she adores, knows—that humiliation—it'll kill her. Don't tell her you know.

What I want you to do instead is this: if she asks for your advice about whether you think she ought to get a new bathroom in the next few days, the one that I'm going to pressure her to get, just politely encourage her to go along with my prodding. But don't tell her you know about anything else."

I nodded, the tears streaming down my cheeks.

"But I want to help," I said, my voice breaking. I not only wanted to help—I felt like I should be equipped to help. If only she would let me.

"I *need* to help!" I cried, to further underscore my point. "Why can't I help her?"

"Mary Elizabeth, you are helping. You've told her for years you've stood ready to help. You called me and we're working to help her together," my uncle said. "You are doing something. But her knowing that you know—that will only make matters worse."

"Okay," I said at last, hugging Augie to me. "Okay."

With my uncle's help, my mother agreed to allow a new toilet to be installed on the main floor of the house. It was just one of many small victories my uncle would score.

Another victory came in July 2010 when Dean and I were finally invited to visit my mother at the house. It was Dean's first chance to see where I'd grown up, and my first time home in ten years. The invitation came about as a result of my high school reunion. We were attending and booked a room at a hotel a mile from my mother's house for several nights. I knew staying at the house was out of the question. But I hoped a visit was not.

It wasn't easy to arrange. For the first two days of our stay in Beaver Dam, my mother remained a nervous wreck, insisting upon meeting us at our hotel or the nearby Applebee's. She came armed with toys and books for the boys and with an insistence that we remain away from the house. But on day three, she caved.

"Would you maybe like to come over to the house later on?" she asked timidly on a Sunday morning.

"Absolutely!" Dean and I told her.

"Great," she replied. "Why don't you stop over after Mass?"

It wasn't much of a visit in the traditional sense. When we pulled into the driveway, my mother stood waiting with Uncle Al and made clear that she didn't want Dean or the kids—or even me—to enter the home.

"It's so nice out," she said of the eighty-something-degree day. "I thought it would be fun if we all had a seat outside."

She directed us to a circle of lawn chairs she'd set up in the driveway. They were essentially front-row seats to her pride and joy: her recently overhauled garage. The garage door was open so that we could admire the transformation. Where there had once been mountains of junk five and six feet high, there were now nice, neat rows of shelves lined with equally neat rows of boxes and lawn equipment. Best of all, after all those months of Dumpster dashes, there was actual room in the garage for my mother to park her car—something she had been unable to do for years.

"Isn't it neat?" my mother said, offering us cans of Diet Coke that she'd placed in the garage in advance of our visit. She smiled proudly.

"It's great, Anne," said Dean. "It's really terrific."

Knowing how hard my mother had worked to create an outdoor living room, Dean and I settled into the webbed lawn chairs beneath the hot sun in a way normal visitors to normal homes would plop down onto a comfortable sofa: we worked to make ourselves at home.

But while we worked to mask the awkwardness we felt over our inability to enter the house, our oldest son, Roman—who was three at the time—did not. "When do we go inside Oma's house?" he asked repeatedly when he grew tired of looking at the toys my mother had set out in the garage for him. "Why are we only sitting on the outside of Oma's house?"

Thankfully, Uncle Al ran interference. "Why would you want

to see a house when you can take a walk around the block with me?" he asked, taking Roman by the hand to lead him on a tour of the neighborhood.

But even after a walk around the block, young Roman remained perplexed. "I don't understand, Mama. When can I see your room? Didn't you say you had a room in this house?"

"I used to," I said, looking Roman in the eye. "But my room isn't important now. Visiting with Oma is."

Pulling Roman onto my lap, I encouraged him to tell my mother about preschool, about his favorite things about the hotel room, about anything to make the visit feel more normal—and to make me feel less sad. Dean and I went on to talk with my mother about local politics, the age of different trees in the yard, what I was like as a baby.

For two hours, I managed to keep the tears at bay. But all my efforts came crashing down when I discovered Augie's dirty diaper.

Changing a diaper on the road is ordinarily no big deal: fetch the diaper bag from the car, lay the baby down on a blanket on a clean patch of grass, and presto change-o! Problem was, while I'd come to the house armed with diapers, I'd left the baby wipes back in the hotel room. In any other setting, at any other house, I would have run into the kitchen and wet some paper towels and the problem would have been solved. But this was no ordinary house. I couldn't run inside. Doing so would unnerve my mother. And even if she allowed me to enter the forbidden zone, I knew the odds were great that there would be no paper towels to be found.

"I forgot the wipes," I said to Dean, emptying the contents of the diaper bag for a second time on the front lawn to see if there was something—anything—that could work as a wipe. We were kneeling with Baby Augie beneath my old honey locust tree.

"And I can't—I mean, we can't—I mean, she can't—"

"It's okay." Dean squeezed my hand.

"Really, Mary," he repeated, "it's going to be okay."

He wore a brown Izod polo shirt that matched his beautiful brown eyes. They were so warm.

So was his touch. All of it was too much. I began to cry.

"This was my house," I whispered to Dean, ducking my head so that my mother, who remained on her lawn chair throne next to the garage, wouldn't see.

"It still is," he said, gently rubbing my back.

"No," I said, shaking my head. I looked up at the house's familiar red siding and the yellow trim and the black shutters. I'd drawn them all countless times in kindergarten with a twenty-four-pack of Crayola crayons. "Not anymore."

The outside of the house was just the way I remembered it. But the feelings that the house conjured up within me had changed. The structure that had once made me feel solid and safe in the wake of my parents' divorce, my father's temper, now made me feel unspeakably sad. Those walls that had once sheltered me from the chilly elements of Wisconsin winters were the same walls that had swallowed my mother whole.

"God, Dean," I whispered, sniffling. "I just want to go home."

Later that night, Dean and I sat in a booth across from my mother at Ben Venuto's, my mother's favorite restaurant in Beaver Dam. After our day in the hot sun of her driveway, my mother insisted that she wanted to treat us to a good dinner. And the Italian establishment, which featured a bar and a large pizza oven, was what my mother declared was hands-down "the best restaurant in town."

Dean and I had hired a babysitter, a local high school student my old band director had recommended, to take care of the boys at the hotel so that we could dine alone with my mother. The outing was intended to give all of us a moment to collect our breaths and to talk in sentences that weren't interrupted by the inevitable wail of a child.

At first, the dinner was a lighthearted affair. My mother peppered me with questions about my class reunion, which had taken place the night before. She delighted in the details of who I'd seen, how they'd looked, who'd married whom. From the reunion, she went on to address her other favorite topics: the countdown to a new school year, the coming season for the Packers, her excitement over the fact that a Wisconsin native —Timothy Dolan— was on track to be New York City's next cardinal.

Dean and I smiled and listened and added to the conversation when appropriate. But when my mother at last paused, I decided to make my move as Concerned Daughter. "Mom, I've been doing a lot of thinking about you and the house."

"Don't do that," my mother said quickly as she reached for her soupspoon. "Why don't you let me worry about my house and you worry about yours?"

I licked my lips, ignoring her attempt to change the subject. "Mom, how would you feel if maybe Dean and I helped you find someplace else to go for a couple of months? Maybe an apartment? Someplace brand new that you could try out temporarily—to see if you liked it?"

This was a new idea Dean and I had been floating. My mother and my uncle were making some headway on the house, but the progress was painstakingly slow, due in large part to my mother's presence. If she moved out temporarily—and allowed a professional cleaning crew to come in—we could likely turn the house around in just a couple of months. We'd been in touch with old family friends—Gail and Charlie Fakes—who owned a series of apartment buildings as well as an assisted-living facility in Beaver Dam. They were open to the idea of offering my mother a short-term lease at a reduced cost. Moving someplace clean, we reasoned, might enable her to clear her mind, part with some of the baggage that was literally and figuratively weighing her down. And it would enable us to help her make the house again a clean and safe place in which to live.

"A new apartment?" my mother asked, with a tone that suggested she was both offended and intrigued. "Who's going to pay for that?"

"Dean and I could help," I said gently. "And it's not like it would cost that much."

"What do you mean by 'not that much'?" my mother asked defensively. "I don't have that much."

Discussing money with any parent is tough. But it had become increasingly difficult to do with my mother since the fall of 2007, when my brother lost his job at a prominent Houston law firm. By early 2008, my mother was sending my brother and his wife monthly checks. Shortly thereafter, she started sending two or three checks a month. Then came the additional mortgages she took out on the house so that she could send him still more money.

I knew my mother's finances were tight. That's why she adamantly refused to retire even as she approached her seventy-fifth birthday. I also knew money wasn't the primary reason my mother was reluctant to leave the house.

"Mom," I said, putting down the fork that I'd been using to pick at a plate of salad. "Forget the money. Why won't you leave the house?"

"I won't leave because I want you and your brother to have a place to come home to," she said. "That house is your safe haven. It's your nest egg."

At this, I pushed my plate away from me. "A nest egg? A safe haven? Mom, are you insane?"

"I'm not insane," said my mother calmly, studying her cheese soup. "I'm sincere."

I leaned over the table, staring intently at my mother.

"Mom, you haven't let me into that so-called safe haven for ten years. I've been here in Beaver Dam for three days and you wouldn't even let me in the front door today. Not even to change your grandson's diaper! That's not a 'safe haven.' That house is a fucking albatross."

"That house is your home," said my mother, wiping her mouth gingerly with a napkin.

"Was," I said, fighting back tears. "*Was*. It *was* my home. But now it's not. You wouldn't even let me show Roman my room today."

"I didn't know it meant that much to you," my mother said. Her tone was sincere. It broke my heart to hear how sincere she sounded. It was so confounding. She was so brilliant and in control one moment—and then, at moments like this, she sounded like a seven-year-old.

"It does mean a lot to me, Mom. All of my awards—all of my old dolls and toys—I'd love to show them to my son. I'd love to see them for myself. But I can't—because of your situation."

"What situation?" my mother asked. Again, the tone was innocent, like that of a child.

"The hoarding," I said at last in a whisper. I marveled at my timidity. I'd proudly and loudly said "fucking" to my mother's face moments ago at a public restaurant. But when it came to "hoarding"—the dreaded H word—I whispered.

"I don't know what you're talking about," my mother said, reaching again for her napkin.

"Don't you?"

"Mary," Dean said softly, speaking at last. He reached his hand under the table to hold mine. "It's okay—maybe we should change the subject."

"No, Dean," said my mother softly. "It's not okay. I know what Mary's getting at. I've seen those reality shows on TV. Those hoarding shows. That's what you're talking about, isn't it?"

I nodded in surprise. She'd seen the shows? She watched something other than *Law and Order*?

"But you need to know," my mother continued, "that those

shows are nothing like me. That's not my situation. I just haven't had time to pick things up. I've just been . . ."

My mother paused and searched for the right word.

"I've just been . . ." she said, her voice trailing off once more.

"I guess I've just been tired. No, I'm not like those shows at all."

I nodded. She'd seen the shows. She'd seen the piles of filth. She'd seen the hoarders in denial, the families in tears. But she'd failed to see herself in any of it.

The room began to spin. I was a grown woman. Over thirty. Mother of three. And for a moment I felt as though I hadn't escaped from Beaver Dam after all. It was exactly the same—except different. My mother and her hoarding still made me feel embarrassed, powerless, unbearably sad. But now I no longer had the delusions I'd had when I was younger, that she'd one day clean up for my wedding, that I'd one day spend Christmas with my children in the home. I was faced with the grim reality that the situation was only going to get worse because now I realized that my mother was never going to see she had a problem.

"I—I'll be right back." I stood and made my way to the bathroom. I waited until I was safely in a stall before breaking down in tears. My brilliant mother—known for her empathy, always lauded for knowing who in a classroom full of children needed hugs or support, how to bolster confidence in the most insecure of young charges—seemed to know herself least of all.

Dean and I remained in Wisconsin for three more days. But we were never invited back to the house. It was just as well. My mother was happier—less anxious—when we gathered at hotels. And in the end, so was I. So it was only appropriate that we spent the last night of our visit at Milwaukee's Pfister Hotel, the grand hotel where we'd stayed for our wedding, the lodging my mother adored above all others.

We had named Augie in part after the beloved hotel. His middle name is Pfister. And to honor Master Augie's arrival in his namesake, the hotel pulled out all the stops, upgrading us to its famous Governor's Suite—a grand two-bedroom, three-bathroom suite—and preparing a four-tiered wedding cake for Baby Augie that was wheeled into our room with great pageantry.

My mother delighted in all of this. Fresh from the house piled high with debris and mice and bats and chipmunks, she reclined on the couch in the suite's giant living room, directly in front of the largest of the suite's three enormous televisions—looking, of course, for *Law and Order*.

Dean and I treated her to a room-service steak dinner that night and bought her favorite wine as an early birthday present. As we made the transition from dinner to dessert, she surprised us by being the one to bring up the house.

"I've been thinking a lot about what you said the other night at Ben Venuto's."

"You have?" I asked, surprised. Dean and I exchanged glances.

"I don't know what it is about the house. You know—I always had such great plans for it. I wanted to put a back deck behind it so we could watch the sunset. Add a sliding glass door so that we could get a nice cross breeze. Make at least one bathroom wheelchair accessible for when Mother and Daddy visited. I even hoped they might move in with me after they left the Pine Patch instead of going to that assisted-living facility.

"I would have liked that."

She talked, looking not at me and Dean, but at the flowers the room service team had delivered with our meal.

"I thought about putting another window in the dining room. I even thought how nice a swimming pool might be."

I nodded, remembering how she had talked about this when our next-door neighbors, the Swanbergs, put their pool in when my brother and I were still in elementary school.

"I always wanted to do something to make the house mine."

"But, Mom, the house has always been yours."

"No," my mother said, still looking at the flowers as she shook her head. "Your father picked it out. He picked the state we'd live in, the town, the house. He picked everything. I just followed his orders. He picked the paint, the wallpaper, the trees we planted in the yard. He made all of it his. Even when he left—"

She paused, her voice breaking off.

Then, drawing in her breath, she finished her thought: "He made it his."

I nodded sadly, realizing that some of this mess was starting to make sense. When she got out of the convent, she had nothing. When my father left her in a house he'd picked out, she still felt like she had nothing. So she filled the house with things she had bought, things that, cheap and messy though they were, were hers.

"I always thought I'd get around to fixing it up," she continued. "But then you and Anthony left. And then Mother and Daddy died. And then—well, then I got tired. And then things got out of control.

"When you don't pick things up for a while, it's hard to know where to begin."

"We can help you with that now," said Dean, his eyes growing moist. He reached his hand across the table in search of hers.

I nodded vigorously. "That's all we want."

"It would be nice to have a place that I picked out. That was mine. I just don't know if it's too late."

"It's not too late," I said, shaking my head. "You're not trapped."

I remember her using those same words to me—when I worried about the financial crush of losing my job at CNN immediately after getting saddled with that stupid condo in Atlanta. Now I was giving her a dose of her own advice.

"You're never trapped," I said.

"I guess not," my mother said softly. "You know, Mary, you've asked me so often over the years why it is your father seems to behave so much nicer—so much more empathetically—to distant relatives and perfect strangers than he sometimes seems to act toward you and me and your brother."

I nodded. I'd asked her to explain the phenomenon to me for decades.

"I've been thinking a lot about that lately, too. This is what I've decided: When your father left, he wanted to get rid of every part of his life that made him feel trapped. You and your brother and I—we made him feel trapped. That house made him feel trapped. Don't ever lose sight of the fact that he loves you. When he acts the way he does toward us—it's just because he couldn't stand how trapped all of us as a family unit made him feel."

My mother paused and took my hand.

"Does that make sense?"

A tear rolled down my cheek, and I nodded, remembering him happily loading his things into that pickup truck with his gay friends the day he moved out and pulling away without looking back at the mess he'd left behind.

"Yes."

I squeezed my mother's hand. "But just because Dad got to escape from feeling trapped by that house doesn't mean that you can't. You can escape, too, Mom."

"I wish you were right," she said, squeezing my hand in return.

When Dean and I returned to New York, our lives kicked back into high gear. Fall was approaching. That meant back to preschool for our older boys and an increasingly hectic work schedule for Dean and me. In my case, the crazy work schedule was dictated by the intense battle brewing between *Good Morning America* and our archrival, the *Today* show. After years of being narrowly beaten in the ratings race for number one morning show, we at *GMA* were at last within spitting distance of taking the top spot. It was all hands on deck.

Some mornings I started work in the studio at four A.M. Some evenings I stumbled home after midnight. I wrote, I scripted, I pitched stories, I oversaw shoots. And in between shoots and interviews, I continued to breast-feed—dutifully pumping milk for Augie at the office during those hours when I couldn't nurse him directly. Add to that the demands of raising the older boys—of taking part in helping on parent days at their co-op nursery, and taking them to and from the pediatrician and music classes—and my plate was full.

But I wasn't about to give up on my mission. Soon—very soon—we would extricate my mother from her mess of a house. We could save her, I told myself repeatedly. On that last night at the Pfister, she had seemed open to help, receptive. We were on the verge. I just knew it.

There were signs of hope: that fall, she allowed her sister Kathy and her brother Mike to fly out to Beaver Dam for a weekend to help Uncle Al tackle her living room, dining room, and kitchen. At last, she was letting more loved ones in. Literally and figuratively.

"It was just like those hoarding reality shows," Uncle Mike would later recount. "I watched the shows to do some homework and, walking in, that's exactly what we saw."

"It was heartbreaking," Aunt Kathy said. "I had to keep trying to tell myself to view the process as some kind of archaeological dig and not dwell on the fact that she'd been living like that for so long."

The trio of siblings filled trash bag upon trash bag. In just two days, hundreds and hundreds of pounds of newspapers, magazines, remnants of takeout meals were at last laid to rest. But there were casualties. My mother snapped when she discovered that a poetry collection she'd been writing—and kept stored in a dirty kitchen drawer laden with debris—had been tossed by Al.

"The drawer was full of junk. I thought it was all junk," Al said, defending himself.

My mother was devastated. Decades ago, her own mother, Aurelia, had thrown out all of her old plays and short stories when she'd joined the convent. My mother was crushed to find them gone when she returned to the Pine Patch. Now her writing had been destroyed again.

Back in New York, I tried to further advance our mission to rescue my mother by tracking down a pair of hoarding experts. One was a university professor, the other ran a hoarding clinic. In a series of telephone calls, I conferred with them about my mother.

"Your mother is hardly alone," the professor assured me during one particularly lengthy chat. "But remember—if you're looking for a magic bullet when it comes to hoarding, there isn't one."

He warned me repeatedly of the hazards involved in trying to "cure" a hoarder by cleaning a house in his or her absence, against his or her will—or of doing any kind of dramatic cleanse or purge of what the rest of us deemed "junk."

"Hoarding comes from all kinds of places. You don't want your mother to resent or hate you for your efforts—since those efforts might make her feel unsafe and even more vulnerable. She'll wind up turning against you. And then you really won't be able to help."

"Be patient," he implored. "Just get her to get some help. From someone. She needs to start that process of talking and realizing and healing."

I took the advice. During subsequent phone calls with my mother, between talk of the kids and our jobs and the weather, I addressed the matter head-on. "Mom, what about seeing a counselor? Remember how you used to get so much out of seeing Dr. Graupner?"

Kenneth Graupner, a Beaver Dam–based psychiatrist, had seen my mother through the divorce and her years of depression that followed. Were it not for Graupner and her near-daily visits to St. Peter's to pray, I'm not sure that my mother would have survived those dark days in the 1980s.

"I know," my mother said wistfully. "I wish he hadn't retired. I just don't know who to see . . ."

Her voice trailed off.

"It could be helpful," she conceded. The fall had been a trying time for her. She was terribly worried about my brother. His marriage had broken down irretrievably, and now that the divorce was final, he was living in a motel in Dallas, away from his children.

"I could help you find a good therapist," I offered, my tone hopeful. "I could make some calls and get some recommendations."

"I know, honey. But why don't you be the daughter and let me be the mom? I'll ask around at church."

Her tone wasn't harsh. Just tired.

"Promise?"

"I promise," she said before hanging up.

Two weeks after she made her promise, *Good Morning America* sent me to London to cover the engagement of Prince William to Kate Middleton. For five days, I staked out Buckingham Palace, interviewed Princess Diana's wedding dress designer, enjoyed the celebratory mood of all of those Brits thrilled for a new generation of royals finding love.

GMA had given me many wonderful opportunities over the years, but the royal assignments—those were my favorites, in large part because of my mother.

Like so many mothers the world around, Anne Diener Pflum woke her daughter early on the morning of July 29, 1981, to watch Lady Diana Spencer become a princess. I loved every moment of it: the dress, that train, all the pageantry. My father had already left us for greener pastures. But in the living room that early morning, all that mattered was the fairy tale unfolding before our eyes. I'm not sure who was more excited by all of it—me or my mother.

Over the years, my mother remained a loyal Diana fan. To her, Diana was something of a kindred spirit. Both of them, my

mother liked to remind me as we pored over *People* magazines
bearing her photo on the cover, were victims of circumstance—
marrying men who would never love them, then working like
mad to make their bad marriages somehow work.

"I wish I could have been there," said my mother wistfully as
we chatted about London in late November after I returned.

And I wished she could have, too.

"I'm going back to cover the wedding in April," I said. "You
should try to come then."

"I'll have to work," my mother reminded me. "But what an exciting life you live. I so often wish I'd gotten to live your life when
I was young. I really would have liked that."

"You still can," I reminded her. "There's still time."

"I don't know," said my mother wearily. "But the thing is, I get
to do something even better. That's what I realized when I went
to Mass tonight."

More than forty years after leaving the convent, my mother
still did not feel that her day was complete without going to Mass.

"I realized, after Father's sermon, that far better than having
any of those adventures I'd dreamed of having for myself is getting to watch you living such an exciting life. You're doing what I
only dreamed of doing when I was growing up. When I was your
age—well, when I was your age, I wasn't happy. I get to watch you
being happy. At the end of the day, that's all any mother wants—
for her children to be happy. You'll see."

In December 2010, Dean and I made plans for the holidays.
We would drive to the Midwest and meet my mother there. We
were excited for the New Year. This would be the year of overcoming hurdles, making miracles happen, I told myself. 2011 would
be the year we'd get my mother out of the house.

We rented a car for our journey, arranged for my mother to
spend the night before we met up at the Pfister, and began to pack
our bags.

On December 15—a Wednesday—Dean and I sat in our kitchen, finishing up a late-night dinner after tucking the kids into bed. I wore the white Vera Wang nightshirt my mother had given me for Augie's birth. I'd worn it nonstop in the months since his arrival, but the shirt had held up well. It was my favorite nightgown, and I stroked it contentedly as I sat with my arms crossed, talking with Dean about what we should buy the boys for Christmas.

We were just preparing to make our way to the bedroom when Dean's cell phone rang. I looked at the clock. It was eleven P.M.

"Should I answer it?" he asked.

"It's a 920 area code," I said, confused. "That's Beaver Dam."

My heart leaped into my throat, and I grabbed the phone from him.

"Hello?"

"Is this Dean?" asked the woman on the other end of the line.

"No—it's his wife, Mary."

"Is this Mary Pflum?" asked the voice.

"Yes," I said hesitantly.

"I'm calling from Beaver Dam Community Hospital. Your mother, Anne, was admitted earlier today—and I'm calling because she recently flatlined."

"She what?" I asked, my voice shaking.

"I'm afraid your mother expired."

I pitched forward in that Vera Wang nightshirt—that snow-white perfection of a nightgown—and struggled to breathe. My mother—my touchstone—was gone. And I hadn't gotten a chance to say goodbye. Worse, she'd died before I could save her.

Chapter 12
A New Beginning
May 2012

I stood in the living room of our Upper West Side apartment, my heart racing. We were late. Or about to be. And there was so much to do. I had to find Roman's shoes. They were lost. Under a dresser somewhere. Or maybe he'd left them in the laundry room again?

We had to pick up the cake from the bakery. We'd ordered it just that morning. Fingers crossed that it would be ready for the three o'clock pickup we'd requested and that they'd spelled the name right. I cringed, remembering how a different bakery had misspelled Augie's name on his big day—and had declared, "Congratulations Angie!"

And then there was the church. We had to get there. In just thirty minutes. Our guests would be waiting for us.

But before any church or any cake, there were more important matters to attend to: the dress. I had to get her dressed.

I'd already slipped into my white dress—well, my off-white dress. I'd scored the short-sleeved eyelet number at the Nanette Lapore sample sale last week. The baby wasn't even sitting up and already she was hitting New York City sample sales with me. She'd watched from her position in her Baby Bjorn carrier as I picked through hanger upon hanger on the jam-packed clothing racks. I'd almost settled on a red dress when I found the ivory dress. It had me at hello. Its short sleeves had delicate little bows and its cloth-covered belt showed off my slowly-but-surely-getting-back-to-normal figure. And its color *was just right. But better than any white dress I would wear today would be what I had in store for Piper.*

My hands shaking, I reached over Piper, sprawled out on the changing table, and pulled the white linen gown off the hanger that I'd hung in the window the night before. The garment was just as breathtaking as I'd remembered. It was long—extending more than three feet. It had the loveliest touches of lace down the front, at the hem, and on either wrist of the long, billowy sleeves. And it had the fairy dust of love and Ireland sprinkled throughout it. For more than seven years, the dress had hung in the closet, waiting for her. At last its time had come.

Undoing the last of the little buttons lining the back of the dress, I gathered the inches and inches of material together into two hands and slipped it over Piper's little head. Next came the hard part: turning her over onto her tummy so that I could close the same buttons I'd just unbuttoned. The buttons were so little, so delicate, so like my new daughter.

Unlike the boys, Piper didn't mind spending time on her tummy. She seemed to embrace the chance to look at the world from a new perspective.

Then, turning her back over, it was time for the finale: the little bonnet trimmed in ribbon and lace that matched the rest of the dress.

I couldn't believe my luck. After three boys, I'd given birth to a baby girl. And every day when I awoke and turned from our bed to her, sleeping in her little bassinette beside me, I marveled at her beauty. She had the softest wisps of dirty-blond peach fuzz on her head, yummy little toes, big brown eyes that reminded me of—well, that reminded me so much of her.

As I finished tying the ribbon on the bonnet, the tears fell down my cheeks.

The snow-white dress fit Piper to a T, making her look like something out of one of the JC Penney Christmas wish books I used to covet as a child—like a perfect little baby doll, with porcelain skin and a little nub of a nose. There was only one problem with the moment.

"What's wrong?" asked my father. He'd flown in from Florida two

nights before and, hearing me sniffling, had entered the living room,
his white dress shirt untucked over his khakis and two mismatched
little socks clutched in his hands. He'd been trying to dress the boys and
had apparently stopped at their feet.

"Does the dress not fit?" Dale Pflum asked.

I shook my head, trying to will the tears to stop. But I failed miser-
ably, and the tears fell harder.

"Then what's wrong, sweetheart?" he asked again, his voice growing
concerned.

I shook my head once more. "I miss Mom."

I've had many "love at first sight" moments when it comes to
white dresses. But only one happened outside of the U.S. In
November 2006 in County Cork, I fell in love with the white
christening gown my daughter, Piper, would eventually wear for
her baptism.

At the time of the dress sighting, I was six months pregnant with
my oldest son, Roman. I had been sent to Ireland to cover a story for
Good Morning America and had managed to convince my obstetri-
cian that, pregnant though I was, it was an assignment I couldn't
turn down. County Cork was where my grandmother's ancestors
had come from. Her grandfather—my great-great-grandfather—
had farmed its soil before setting sail for New York in the late
nineteenth century. With a baby growing inside of me, I wanted
more than ever to become one with my roots. In the end, my doctor
agreed, signing the note to Delta indicating it was safe for me to fly.

It was a wonderful journey, full of traipses through lush green
fields, boat tours that boasted stunning views of picturesque towns,
and that fateful meeting with The White Dress. I spied it on the
second-to-last day of my journey, situated behind a store window
not far from where the crew and I were scarfing down a hurried
lunch. The ensemble was elegant and timeless—something that
my great-great-grandmother might have worn a century before,

and something that my great-great-granddaughter could easily wear a century from now. I was in love.

As was the case with all of my pregnancies, I had elected not to find out whether I was carrying a boy or a girl, so I was in the "gender dark" on that day in 2006. If the baby I was carrying turned out to be a boy, I knew I would likely dress him in something more masculine on the day of his christening. But if the baby I was carrying was a girl or if I eventually birthed a girl, well then, this was the dress.

The family gown I'd been baptized in as a newborn—the one my father had worn before me, and his mother before him, and my great-grandmother before her—had been retired in the late 1990s after one of my cousins had elected to mount and frame it as part of a 4-H project that won her a blue ribbon at the county fair in my father's Indiana hometown. It was time for me to start a new tradition, and this dress was it.

As it turns out, the dress would go unworn for six years. When Roman turned out to be a boy, I dressed him on the morning of his baptism—and later his younger brothers, Creedence and Augie—in a little white linen suit and matching hat that made him look like a Pillsbury Doughboy. The dress—*the* dress—would wait. It would wait for Piper Anne Peterson, who made her debut on February 10, 2012.

My mother's passing had happened some eighteen months before the christening. And in that time, the gaping, gushing wound that her death created had, bit by bit, begun to heal. But when I saw Piper in that dress for the first time, the fragile scab fell away—and the sore called Grief bled anew. For a moment, it was as if my mother had died all over again.

After the call came from the hospital announcing my mother's death, I sat with Dean at the kitchen table, wondering what to do. I had never planned a funeral before. But most people haven't until death comes knocking.

My first shell-shocked call that night was to my brother. I tried once, twice, three times. He didn't answer. I tried to call my former sister-in-law, who had divorced him just a few months prior. She said she'd keep trying him at the budget motel he'd moved into. Then I called my mother's sister Kathy and my uncle Al. Both seemed a strange combination of stunned, yet not entirely surprised, before telling me they'd call their other siblings. Finally came the call to my father. When he answered, I heard the familiar music in the background, loud with a techno beat. He was at a bar. I'd heard similar music when, in my single days, I'd accompanied him on his outings with his friends. I heard the voices around him. They were laughing.

"It's Mom," I said.

"What's wrong?" he asked.

"She died," I said.

"She what?" he asked, straining to make his voice heard over the music.

"She's DEAD!" I yelled, the tears spilling down my cheeks.

"Hang on," he told me. "I'm going to have to call you back."

In the moments after his abrupt hang-up, I imagined my father sharing the news with those around him—his friends, many of whom, like him, had married women before coming out of the closet. Many had left their wives—and any children and remnants of their straight lives—forever. My father was among just a handful in his group of newfound BFFs who maintained any ties with former wives and children. Would they be empathetic? Or think that my mother's death should be viewed as a source of relief for him?

My father would eventually call me back, but later admitted he remembered little of the night or of our conversations, including his offer to help me and Dean with the funeral arrangements. When it came to that, we were very much on our own.

All deaths are hard. But sudden deaths are especially so. And sudden avoidable deaths are perhaps the worst of all.

It turns out that my mother had been admitted to the hospital on the day of her death because, upon arriving at work that morning, she hadn't felt well. She'd had some shortness of breath and dizziness. And my mother being my mother, she didn't want to worry anyone. So rather than ask anyone from her school to call an ambulance, or to come with her, and rather than call me or Al or any friends from church, she'd driven herself the seventy minutes back to Beaver Dam to see a local doctor filling in for her regular physician, who eventually suggested she go to the hospital for what he described as "routine tests."

"Why would I want to worry you?" I would later imagine her asking, had she lived to phone me. "You had work and you had the kids to look after. I can take care of myself."

At Beaver Dam Community Hospital, the only hospital in town, she'd been left unattended in her room after the tests— even though she'd told the nurse that she was dizzy and even though she had a history of falls owing to her bad knees. The rooms had recently been redone with shiny new faux wooden floorboards that were slippery when dry. They were part of some grand hospital redesign, I would later be told, that a new hospital administrator had worked tirelessly for the better part of two years to complete.

My mother didn't like hardwood floors. Any hard floors bothered her. She preferred carpeting—owing, I suppose, to all those hard floors at the convent that she'd spent hours shining and waxing and kneeling upon.

"Carpeting," she murmured with a roll of the eyes when she saw the hardwood floors in our Manhattan apartment, "is underrated. Give me a thick rug over the most expensive hardwood floors any day."

But my mother's anti-hardwood opinion mattered little to the Beaver Dam Community Hospital staff, particularly on the evening of December 15. It was shift change when the nurse finally brought her back to her room after her tests, and the countdown to Christmas was on. The nurse who was supposed to be minding my mother, I was later told, left. And a new nurse was slated to come on duty. But until she did, my mother was alone. Consequently, no nurse was there to catch her fall—or to even hear the fall. Records indicate that twenty minutes—maybe more—elapsed between the time my mother was left alone and when she was discovered in the room unconscious and bleeding on the floor—her glasses broken and her face badly bruised from the force of her head hitting the unforgiving floorboards.

By the time the mousy-voiced nurse called me two hours later, my mother was dead, and staffers were telling me she'd died from "unknown" complications. They'd failed to transfer her to the ICU until it was too late. They'd failed to call me when she did finally reach the unit. They'd failed to track down her emergency contact numbers. And when they eventually did call, after she'd already died, they failed to tell me she'd suffered a fall that had left her unconscious and bleeding. They told me only that she'd "expired," describing her passing the same way the DMV described my old driver's license—something in need of renewing.

Small-town hospitals forget that small-town funeral homes often have relationships with bereaved family members. So when Todd Michael, the young funeral director with whom I used to ride the school bus home, called to talk to me about my mother a few hours after her death, he gently pushed me to learn more about the nature of her death.

"What did she die from? Did they tell you, Mary?" His tone was kind, tentative, concerned.

"I—I don't know. They were vague."

Todd paused.

"Did they tell you about the cut? The broken glasses?"

"The what?"

I held Augie in my arms. It was early in the morning—four or five o'clock. It was dark. He was nursing while I cupped the phone to my ear. Dean and I had tried to get some sleep after making our round of calls to family members but had managed to doze for little more than an hour.

"Your mother was so nice. She always used to stop in to see me when I was doing yard work in front of the funeral home," Todd said. "She deserved better than this. Mary, I'm so sorry. Did they bother to tell you why your mother died with a black eye? With your permission, we need to call the medical examiner. You need a full autopsy."

And so—while I juggled the tasks of penning an obituary, calling her friends, sorting through that horrible suffocating grief—we began the task of launching an investigation into my mother's cause of death.

Dean held my hand through all of it. It's often said that couples grow stronger—or discover their fissures and flaws—in the wake of death. I was fortunate in that we grew immeasurably tighter, operating in the aftermath of my mother's death more as a single, unified unit than we ever had before.

Together, we searched for the priests I knew my mother would want to give her a final send-off. In the years since my parents' divorce, my mother's relationship with the church had grown increasingly complicated. She continued to love the sacraments and the idea of the church. She attended Mass on a near-daily basis. But more and more, she questioned and frowned upon— even openly disliked—the words and attitudes of priests. The old fire-and-brimstone variety rankled her. And those who were too young and judgmental—too absolute in their beliefs, who didn't recognize the gray in the world—bothered her as well.

She preferred priests who were kind and wise and aware that most of the world isn't painted in shades of black and white.

Among her favorite priests during her later years was a pair of brothers, sons of her longtime friend Mary Bergin from Beaver

Dam. Unlike other Beaver Dam natives, Mary Bergin never turned her back on my mother in the wake of her very public divorce. Her sons, Father Jim and Father John, were, like their mother, intelligent and kind. And when I tracked them down in Iowa and Boston, respectively, I was relieved that they would say the funeral Mass together.

Putting on my producer hat in planning my mother's funeral helped me immeasurably as I dealt with the pain and shock that is grief. The tears came frequently but fell at a more controlled rate when I was able to view the funeral as a production—and my mother and her memory the star of the show I was helming. At every turn, I asked, *What would Anne want? What would make Anne happy?* The happiness that had eluded her in so many facets of her life had been beyond my control. But her final send-off? That was within my control.

Mom loved word games. So we prepared a crossword puzzle honoring her life for her funeral dinner. Among the queries: *Seven across:* Name Anne's favorite singer-songwriter (Answer: John Denver); *Nine down:* Name Anne's childhood home (Answer: the Pine Patch).

Anne worshiped Indiana cooking and pies. To satisfy those loves, we arranged to serve at the funeral dinner a dozen Wick's Sugar Cream Pies—a staple of Indiana potluck dinners.

And she'd long talked about her desire to be buried with Kermit the Frog—the embodiment, she'd always said, of a kind soul who forever tried his best even when the deck of life was stacked against him and even though he didn't always succeed. I made certain that the first of the items that the superintendent of my mother's school district collected from my mother's classroom to bring to the funeral home for us was her beloved Kermit the Frog stuffed animal, which she'd loved sharing with her young students. The smiling green creature was ultimately placed on the pillow of her casket, beside her head.

But there were things that proved more difficult to find than a beloved stuffed animal. Perhaps the hardest task I faced came when Todd Michael asked what we wanted my mother to wear for her burial. I looked at Dean as Todd asked the question and dissolved into a heap of tears.

"We'll figure it out," Dean told me, hugging me to him.

"But her clothes—her clothes—"

I cried harder, unable to finish my sentence. My mother had purchased some nice dresses in her final years—notably the dress she wore to my wedding. The dress complemented her figure. And more importantly, it made her feel good about herself.

But the dress had been left to corrode in that monstrosity of a house.

I shuddered to think of the kind of damage a few years' worth of mold and dust and moths and mouse droppings had done to the fabric. If my mother was to look nice in that open casket she'd always wanted, I needed to find something new for her to wear.

There are many reasons I will always love my best friend from childhood, Kim. But I will never love her more for any one thing than for taking me to find a new dress for my mother to be buried in. It was no easy task. My mother at the end of her life took comfort in few things other than food—and so had ballooned to a size 20 in the wake of mushrooming depression. The size posed a challenge. Beaver Dam had no stores that offered dressy clothing in plus sizes. And even nearby Madison—a forty-mile drive—offered spotty selections. Our best bet, Kim told me, was to journey to Baraboo, Wisconsin, home to what was considered the best plus-sized dress shop in all of southeastern Wisconsin. It's where my mother had found the dress for my wedding. And it's where we hoped we would find her final dress.

For more than ninety minutes, Kim gamely drove us through dark, winding roadways and a freezing rainstorm to find the store, with Baby Augie tucked into his car seat in the back. Upon reaching the store, the three of us—Kim and I standing and Baby Augie in his stroller—found It, sandwiched in the middle of a rack crammed full of hundreds of dresses: a lovely periwinkle-blue dress that hung in elegant folds and had a simple sophistication to it.

"That's the one," Kim and I said, nodding in unison. My mother, we knew, would have approved. She would have clapped her hands and then patted each of us on the back.

The preliminary findings of the medical examiner suggested that Beaver Dam Community Hospital made a number of errors in the hours leading up to my mother's death, not the least of which was leaving a woman with a history of bad falls unattended. But the official cause of her death issued by the county was pulmonary embolism. I hated that hospital and I hated the nurses who had abandoned my mother in her time of need.

And just as I hated that hospital, I hated my mother's house. It had swallowed her whole in her final years of life, sucking from her most of the energy she had left. I wanted to take a sledgehammer to it—raze it to the ground. My way of dealing with the house was to steer clear of it entirely the week of the funeral. I avoided it like the plague, pretending it didn't exist. We set up temporary residence at the AmericInn Hotel, where we had stayed during our last visit to Beaver Dam. When we weren't there, we were at the funeral home. Or at the church. Or at the florist's. Anywhere but the house. I couldn't bring myself to go near the dwelling that, in my eyes, was draped in my mother's blood. I needed to focus on the funeral.

The funeral home the night of the wake was packed with mourners, many of whom waited outside in the frigid temperatures for more than thirty minutes to pay their final respects. I stood beside her casket, dressed in a black nylon dress that buttoned at the side, shivering not only because it was so cold outside but also because of the shock of it all. Dean kept his hand planted securely around my waist the whole time. The warmth of both his hand and the mourners brought me comfort throughout the evening. There were teacher friends with whom she'd bonded over IEP reports and a shared desire to help young students—sometimes against the wishes of frosty school administrators. There were old neighbors who told me they'd miss her car, her spirit, her wit. There were parents of young students who thanked me for her kindness and sobbed as they told me stories of her Herculean efforts to find ways for their speech-impaired and autistic children to better communicate. There were the friends she'd made when she first moved to Beaver Dam, waitresses who faithfully waited on her at her favorite coffee shop, even local McDonald's staffers who regaled me with stories about how my mother liked her coffee (hot!) and her pancakes (with extra pats of real butter!).

"Your mother was so kind" was the most common refrain. "She always made you feel good. Always asked how you were."

And then there were her siblings. All five of Al and Aurelia Diener's surviving children arrived in time for the wake—from all corners of the nation. Aunt Mimi had come from Rochester, New York. Aunt Kathy and Uncle Mike both flew in from Colorado. Uncle Al drove up from Illinois. And Aunt Patty flew in from her post in Beverly Hills. They huddled together as a unit: Al and Aurelia's flock, now minus one.

Patty was perhaps the most stunned by my mother's passing—and by the line of people waiting to view my mother's casket.

"How did she know all of these people?" she repeatedly said aloud, more to herself than to anyone else, as she walked around the funeral home. "Where did these people come from? Don't they have places to be? It's a weeknight."

Her hair, once platinum blond, was now dyed red.

She floated around the funeral home, peering curiously at my mother's teacher friends, and huddled in tight circles with her siblings and one other curious funeral-goer: my father.

Dale Pflum arrived for my mother's funeral anxious to find a role to play. He had divorced my mother more than twenty-five years before, so could no longer be considered anything resembling a widower. Still, he seemed to long to carve out for himself at the funeral home a position as an integral member of the family. The night of the wake, he frequently came to stand alongside Dean and me at the casket, greeting mourners as a host might greet dinner party guests. I was one part exasperated and one part amazed. I shifted uncomfortably, watching community members warily look my father up and down, puzzled—wondering whether to applaud him for coming to his ex-wife's side in the wake of her death, or to question his intentions. Many of my mother's old friends knew my father was gay. Neighbors had long memories and had witnessed some of my father's outbursts, lobbed squarely at my mother. Still, there stood Dale Pflum, holding court a few feet from her casket.

"Doesn't she look nice in that shade of periwinkle blue?" he asked mourners.

"Did you get a chance to sign the guestbook?" he asked others who had made their way past the casket.

"Thank you so much for coming," he said in a folksy drawl that channeled his southern Indiana roots. "It means so much to all of us."

My father was oblivious to the silent stares.

Still, it was clear he loved her. In his own way, he adored her. At times during that funeral week, I was pleasantly surprised by the level of respect and understanding my father had for my mother. It was never more evident than during our second night at the hotel. We were in the throes of funeral planning when he called me in my hotel room. "Mary Elizabeth, I can't sleep. I have to tell you something. There's a crucifix your mother had. I'm sure you knew nothing about it. It was a heavy pewter. It was— "

"From Father Vincent," I said, finishing his sentence.

"Your mother told you about it?" he asked, stunned.

"Yes," I said. "I didn't know you knew." I paused. "How important was he to her?"

"Father Vincent meant the world to your mother," my father said flatly. "She'd want to make sure to have his crucifix." He sighed. "She'd want to be as close to him as possible."

Then he hung up.

But other times during the funeral week, it wasn't love and respect that my father displayed. Sometimes it seemed he was my mother's sworn frenemy—that person who purported to love her while talking about her behind her now-dead back. One night, seated at a communal table in a hotel conference room we had overtaken for a family dinner, I listened, horrified, as my father regaled Aunt Patty with breathless disclosures about my parents' sex life and her lack of hygiene.

"You know, she didn't like to bathe for days at a time, which posed a problem in the bedroom," my father said.

I sat directly across the table from him, sandwiched between two of my confused boys, my mouth agape.

"How dare you!" I cried, fleeing the room in disgust, overcome by both tears and rage. If I couldn't protect my mother in life, I was damn well going to do it in death. Only when Aunt Kathy reprimanded my father, the way a teacher might correct a sixth-grade bully, did he bother to issue a faint apology.

"I'm sorry, Mary, if you misunderstood our conversation about your mother," my father later said, never meeting my eyes.

But more concerning than my father during the funeral week was my brother. For my poor brother, our mother's passing was one more devastating blow in the course of a soul-crushing year. In just twelve months, he'd faced divorce, repeated rejections for employment, the loss of a house—and now the death of our mother, his one constant champion.

My brother had never been much of a talker, but throughout the funeral week, his reticence took on a life of its own. One family friend described Anthony as ghostlike throughout the proceedings—present only for glimpses at a time before vanishing. At the wake, he opted not to stand at the casket. Instead, he hovered in the funeral home's kitchen, wearing a short-sleeved shirt instead of a suit. He shied away from the attention of family and friends, seeking out only a few for handshakes and hugs. If he clung to anyone that week, it was his children, but even from them, he kept a certain distance. While the rest of the family set up camp at the hotel, my brother sought refuge at my mother's house. He embraced the place I shunned. The smell, he said, was bothersome, and the mess was a challenge. But he wanted to be home, he said, in our home, our childhood home, away from the prying eyes of family members, whom he felt he only vaguely knew.

It made sense to me. If my mother's spirit was present anywhere, I knew it would be in her house. And just as my mother had long sought comfort in its four walls, so too would my brother use the house as a protective armor now. My mother would watch over him in spirit, and the house—that big, messy house—would protect him in body.

As the countdown to the actual funeral continued, the reality of losing my mother hit me in dribs and drabs—sometimes with the force of a semitrailer that rendered me unable to breathe.

One night just before the funeral, I woke Dean in our hotel bed, breathless. "I'm thirty-seven," I whispered, my head on his chest. I could feel my heart beating rapidly. I struggled to breathe as the panic took over. I looked at the Pack 'n Play cribs scattered throughout the hotel room. One held a snoring Roman. One held a sleeping Creedence. Augie slept in the swing we'd transported from New York in our rental car. I didn't want to wake any of them. But the fear—the agonizing terror—inside was too great to keep within.

"What if—?" I began to ask Dean.

I stopped midsentence and began to cry.

"What if what?" Dean whispered, pulling me closer.

"What if I live to be a hundred?"

Dean paused, rubbing his eyes. "I don't understand. What if you live to be a hundred? Wouldn't that be a good thing?"

I shook my head and began to sob quietly, struggling to muffle the moans with a pillow so that I wouldn't wake the kids.

"If I live to be a hundred," I said, shaking my head once more, "that would mean I would live more than half my life without her. I don't think I can do that. I don't know how I'm going to get through even two weeks without her."

Dean stroked my hair then, trying to provide what comfort he could. But there was only so much he could do. Without my mother—my moral compass—the world was darker, colder, and unspeakably scary.

The day of the funeral was a long, sad blur. I entered the back of St. Peter's, where I'd received my First Communion in that white dress all those years ago, half expecting to see my mother looking at her watch, telling me we needed to find a pew before Mass started—or else.

There were two eulogies given that day—one by the superintendent of my mother's school and one by me.

I told mourners of the Wonder Woman who was my mother: the one who angelically swaddled and rocked my infant son to sleep when I was overwhelmed by new motherhood, the one who courageously and selflessly raised my brother and me alone after a humiliating and debilitating divorce.

The words of my mother, the former nun who once coached both speech and debate, rang in my ears the entire time I stood at the lectern: *Keep your chin up. Keep your hair—that hair that needs to be cut!—out of your face. Keep your shoulders back. Above all, keep that voice low—and your pace slow.*

I faltered only once. My breakdown, thankfully, came at the end of the eulogy as I read:

"I miss you, Mom. And I still need you. So much. You went too soon and there won't be a day that goes by now that I won't think of you and miss you and long to pick up the phone to call and tell you something. But I thank you for being such a wonderful soul—an angel on earth. And I count myself the luckiest woman alive to have called you my mom."

After the funeral dinner—after the word games and sugar cream pies and presentation of videos honoring Anne—my mother's brothers and sisters wanted to gather at my mother's house. "Do you want to come?" they asked.

I silently shook my head. Perhaps they wanted to gather so they could grieve as a group. But they could have achieved that at the hotel or at a local restaurant. No, if they were headed to the house, it seemed they wanted to take in the scene of the crime as a collective unit. They wanted to see the hoarding. Why else would they go to a drafty, smelly house overrun with junk? My stomach turned at the idea of all of them struggling to step over the piles of stuff, straining to breathe the putrid air.

"Why didn't they all want to come to the house when she was alive?" I asked Dean, crying, as we took our places inside our frozen rental car. "I know they love her, but why didn't they come and visit when I was growing up? I would have killed for their company then. Killed for their help. If they care so much about the house now when she's dead, why didn't they care to see the house when she was alive?"

Dean shook his head.

"I don't know. Morbid curiosity, I guess. Even people closest to her have it."

I buried my head in the shoulder of his navy-blue peacoat, the same one he'd worn on our first date. Dean held me while I cried. My mother was gone. But she'd seen me find the love of my life, the man she'd never managed to find.

While my mother's siblings toured the house, Dean took the kids and me on a drive around Beaver Dam. The motion was precisely what the children needed to fall asleep after a long day of funeral proceedings. And the drive was what I needed to momentarily clear my head. Dean drove us out into the countryside surrounding Beaver Dam. We drove past Trenton, the elementary school that I'd attended. Situated deep in the country, it had sheltered me from my parents' personal problems and had been the place in which I'd fallen madly and passionately in love with reading and writing.

Snow covered the entire countryside. It had fallen early and hard that year—giving Mother Nature a clean white dress for my mother's funeral. And a white dress would cover my mother's casket when we buried her later in the week.

Figuring out where to bury my mother was no easy task. She'd lived in Beaver Dam for three and a half decades, yet her heart had never made the trek from Indiana. She'd never felt at home in Wisconsin. She liked many of the people—especially her teacher friends. But she'd never felt as if she belonged. I couldn't bury her there. Besides, I didn't want her to be alone, buried next to no one she knew and with none of her family members close by to bring flowers to her grave.

My father briefly tossed out the idea of burying her in Connersville, where he grew up. But Connersville was my father's home, not hers.

No, she needed to go home to Dunkirk. Fortunately, a plot was available in the cemetery where my mother's beloved parents, Al and Aurelia, were buried. Better yet, the available plot was situated beside my mother's father. In death, at last, she would have her daddy's undivided attention.

Our rental car pulled into Dunkirk on the morning of the twenty-fourth of December, Christmas Eve. I had not been back since my grandmother's memorial service a decade before. Not much had changed since. Now, as then, the town remained small. Tired.

The community that had bustled when my mother was a girl and when her father had helped run the glass factory had slowed to a crawl in the eighties and nineties. Portions of the downtown were now boarded up, and many homes featured the telltale signs of a depressed economy: cars parked on front lawns, siding falling off houses. Faring better was St. Mary's, where my mother had made her First Communion. It remained a sweet little church, neat and warm and cozy. And then there was the Pine Patch. It still looked lovely, under the care of its new owners and their young children. Many of the trees had been trimmed—some had been removed. But it remained beautiful.

Father Bates, the priest who had married my parents all those years ago, was on hand to greet me at the cemetery, located just outside of the town, as we pulled in.

"Mary, so good to see you," he said, wrapping his gloved hands around my winter coat. It was a frigid day.

I'd reluctantly asked Father Bates to say the final blessing for my mother before she was lowered into the frozen ground. It was my father's idea. And since I didn't know any other priests in the area—and the Bergin boys couldn't make the trek to Indiana—I agreed. Now old and frail, Father Bates walked with a cane. He had retired not long ago. Would my mother have smiled at the idea of his presence at her burial? Or would she have cringed—noting that it was he who had introduced and married my parents and ushered her into another painful chapter in her life? I prayed that she would have smiled good-naturedly, arguing "the more the merrier" for her final send-off.

Noticeably absent from the cemetery when Dean and I arrived with the boys was my brother. No one had heard from him that morning, and no one knew where he was. Was he still in Wisconsin? Had he stopped in a hotel the night before?

Reaching into my purse, I fumbled with the cell phone and made the call. He didn't answer the first time. Or the second time. But the third time I hit the *send* button to call, he said, "Hello."

His voice was hollow. "I'm lost," he said. And I knew he meant it in more ways than one.

I guided him to the cemetery entrance with verbal directions as best I could. But when he arrived, driving his old minivan that used to take his kids to soccer practice, he looked no more found than when he was driving around Dunkirk. The reality of my mother's passing appeared to be hitting him—and on Christmas Eve, no less.

The burial was relatively quick. Fighting back tears, I recited the lyrics to my mother's favorite song, "Back Home Again in Indiana." They were more than appropriate for the occasion, as it was a long-awaited homecoming for her and a reunion with the place she'd been happiest, particularly when her parents were still alive.

> *Back home again in Indiana,*
> *And it seems that I can see*
> *The gleaming candlelight, still shining bright,*
> *Through the sycamores for me.*

We played the John Denver tune—"Annie's Song"—which she had so adored and which had last been played for her at our wedding.

And then came the time to say goodbye. I shook with disbelief as I stroked my mother's coffin with a mittened hand. Snow covered the cemetery. A bouquet of pine branches and pinecones covered the casket. It would have been beautiful if it hadn't been so sad.

Dean wrapped his arm around me as I said my final prayers.

But my brother had no one to wrap his arms around. His children had gone home with his now ex-wife to Texas to spend the holidays with her new boyfriend. And while he had told me repeatedly that he was doing all right in the wake of our mother's death, I could see by the slope of his shoulders as he pitched his head over his knees, studying the snow-covered ground, that he was not faring as well as he'd said.

I reached for my brother's shoulder at the same time that my father's first cousin David, a lifelong farmer who had made the drive from Milton, Indiana, did so.

"It's going to be okay," David said to Anthony, his tone a sweet mixture of matter-of-factness and compassion. David had always been my mother's favorite member of the extended Pflum family. While some other family members shifted uncomfortably in my mother's presence in the wake of my parents' divorce, David had done the opposite, making it a point to talk to my mother at family gatherings, to offer her an arm to help her in and out of cars or up and down stairs, even to ask her to dance.

"Some people," my mother always said, "were just born with the kindness gene—and David was one of them."

But while David tried to tell Anthony everything was going to be all right, it was far from it. Our mother was gone, and the mess of her house remained.

We spent Christmas Day on my father's boyhood farm, trying to provide for the boys something resembling a normal holiday, replete with a tree and presents. But by the end of the week, we were back in Beaver Dam, and I was faced with the new challenge of setting foot—at last—into the home my mother had kept me away from for a decade.

Pulling into the driveway on the morning of December 29, I

sat in the passenger seat while Dean drove, concentrating on my hands in my lap. I couldn't bring myself to look at the house. The kids were back at the hotel with a babysitter. There was no way I could let them see how their Oma had spent her final years.

"Are you ready for this?" Dean asked, leading me up the icy driveway and up onto the front step where Kim and I had spent countless hours in summers gone by, wondering whom we'd marry, what life outside of Beaver Dam might have in store.

I shook my head.

It was all familiar—the yellow door, the black knocker, the shrubs that lined the front of the house. At the same time, it was all so strange. I held my breath as I turned the front doorknob and stepped over the threshold.

"Welcome," said my brother from his post on the futon he'd placed in the middle of the living room, directly in front of the Best Buy TV Dean and I had bought my mother three years before. He was watching ESPN but stood now to greet us. "Whaddya think of the place?"

I couldn't speak. All I could do was smell. Or try to keep myself from smelling. The noxious combination of odors swimming around me made me want to hurl. It wasn't just the underlying scent of yucky—that smell that reminded me a bit of a stuffy, rancid barn. It was also the competing smells of Lysol and a knockoff version of Pine-Sol that my brother had used in the days following the funeral to try to mask the odor. The conflicting smells were too much. I felt the vomit burn in the back of my mouth and began to gag. How could she have lived like this? How could I not have found a way to get her out of this?

"You okay?" asked Dean.

I nodded but I felt anything but. I reached for a Kleenex in my coat pocket to cover my mouth, then worked to do what I did in particularly nasty gas station bathrooms: stop smelling. I

breathed in through my mouth, exhaled through my mouth—
willing myself to not allow my nose to enter the equation.

The house was much the way I remembered it from my last time
home. Yes, my uncle had made significant inroads in clearing the
debris from the main floor. Now I could see at least patches of
the floor. But there were still piles upon piles of stuff everywhere:
stacks of unopened mail, at least a dozen disposable cameras that
had been used or half used but had yet to be taken to a photo
processor, old key chains with no keys, boxes upon boxes filled
with filthy coins that had likely been rescued from the bottoms of
my mother's purses and coat pockets and never made their way to
the bank. There were Christmas ornaments still sealed in plastic
boxes, children's clothing that had clearly been intended for my
children or my brother's kids at some point but had never been
mailed, an old tape recorder, an ancient slipper that had lost its
mate, and a collection of toys from McDonald's Happy Meals
still in their plastic wrappers.

But I didn't care about the main floor. I wanted to see my
bedroom. I wanted to go back to where I'd spent all those hours
studying, and practicing my clarinet, and playing with my dolls,
and dreaming of a life beyond Beaver Dam.

Steeling myself, I made my way to the staircase. As I reached
for the banister, I gasped. This was the section of the house my
uncle had yet to touch. And it showed. There was clothing everywhere. It looked as if a dozen washing machines had thrown up
all over the steps, hurling their contents down the stairs: blouses,
slacks, sweaters, towels, undergarments, and rugs. I don't know
how my mother had managed to get through all the riffraff during
her last months in the house, or if she had even tried. Mixed in
with the clothing were dozens of random items: unopened boxes
of baking soda covered in dust and an old collar we'd used for
Blackie.

Using the banister for leverage, I pulled myself slowly but

surely to the top of the steps. I was in the process of swimming toward my childhood bedroom when I heard Dean's voice. It was urgent.

"It's your brother," he whispered from halfway up the stairs. "I think you should come down here."

I made my way down the stairs, stepping on an unopened box of Band-Aids and a pack of new but dust-covered panty hose as I went.

The living room door stood propped open, and the bitter cold of winter flew into the house. It felt oddly good—the cold air a strong antidote to the yucky smells of the house.

Out on the front walk, I found my brother struggling with the coffee table that had stood watch over the living room window for nearly four decades. He tossed the table into the snow-covered front yard angrily before returning to the house to take dining room chairs. The throws grew increasingly angry and deliberate. I screamed as he hurled the largest of the chairs, the one with arms that had always been situated at the head of the table, into the flower bed where we'd grown the tulips I'd posed in front of on the morning of my First Communion all those years ago.

"What are you doing?!" I yelled, running outside.

My brother didn't answer. He fixed his gaze back on the house, in search of new furniture to throw.

"What the fuck are you doing?!" I repeated, louder this time.

My brother ignored me. He turned and brushed past me, returning to the interior of the house.

I had never understood my brother very well. But I knew enough to know that this must be his way of mourning.

I looked to Dean for guidance. But he shrugged his shoulders, his hands jammed into his pockets.

A moment later, my brother was back, this time with the ancient green-and-white Castle typewriter that had sat in my mother's dining room for as long as I could remember. She'd used it to help me type my college applications since we'd been unable to afford a computer.

Anthony pivoted his body atop the front stoop, the way he used to when he threw discus on the high school track team, then hurled the typewriter into the snow.

"You can't do this," I told Anthony, crying. "This was Mom's. This was ours."

"This," Anthony said angrily, "was a mess. It was always a mess. And I'm sick of it."

And there it was: the realization that miles may have separated us for years, that he may have seemed to have tuned out the problems for two and a half decades, but that our struggle with this mess—this hoarding—was something that would always unite us.

"Still—it was hers," I cried. "This was—"

My voice cracked as I saw them then—the old plastic-covered photo albums that I'd loved to pore over as a child. They were my parents' ancient wedding albums. Two of them. They used to be housed behind the heavy doors of the coffee table. But they'd taken flight when my brother tossed the table from the house. Now they lay in the snow. One of them had opened up to a page showing photos of my unsmiling mother in her wedding gown.

"You can't do this," I said, beginning to cry. "These were her wedding photos."

I ran to the albums then, bending to touch them gingerly, as if they were an injured patient that shouldn't be moved until the paramedics arrived.

"Her marriage is over. And so is she. It all sucks." My brother's voice was wooden. As hollow as the now-empty coffee table.

"It doesn't matter," I said, crying. "I want these."

I scooped up the photo albums, trying to wipe them dry with my black wool coat in the process. Then I reached for the type-writer. It had been thrown hard. But I didn't care. She might have tried to write some of her last poems—the ones that had been destroyed—on the thing. I had to try to save it.

Dean bent to help me lift it.

"I'll put these in the car," he whispered. "You should get back inside. Take anything else you absolutely have to have. Get it now."

He looked from me to my brother. "With the way he's acting, I wouldn't count on anything you want remaining here for long."

I bit my lip and nodded. We'd rented an already-packed SUV for the week. I knew there wasn't much room in the car. But there was just enough.

Wading back up the stairs, my heart beating, I reached it at last: my room. It was my childhood oasis, where I'd done all of my studying and playing and crying and dreaming. Now it was covered—smothered—beneath a layer of thick, sooty dust. I wanted to take it all in. To linger on the trophies and the diplomas and the awards and the dolls. Oh, how I had loved those dolls! Mandy and Ballerina and Strawberry Shortcake. But I couldn't linger. There wasn't time. All I really needed was them. The white dresses. Our white dresses.

Looking past the *Gone with the Wind* artifacts still on display on my walls, my beloved bulletin board still hanging there, stepping around an old rocking chair and over the filthy carpeting, littered with mouse droppings, I reached the closet.

I held my breath and moved the right-hand closet door to the left so that I could see the clothes within.

"Please," I said softly to myself. Then, more loudly, "Please, God, let them be here."

Moments later, in the back of the closet, on the far right end of the closet rod, pushed up against the wall, I found it: my First Communion dress. It had hung there in a place of honor every day for nearly three decades and remained remarkably—

miraculously—white within the room coated in that layer of impenetrable dust. The closet had served as a sort of protective armor for it. The semitransparent sleeves remained pretty, the lace on the bodice delicate and unspoiled.

But that was just one white dress. There should be more. There had to be more!

I went through the closet again—past the spider-covered yellow shawl I'd worn when I was four, the ivory cardigan full of holes thanks to all the moths.

I didn't see any more white. I felt my heart pound in my chest anew, the beads of sweaty panic begin to form on my forehead. But wait!

There on the floor, peeking out of a dust-covered dry-cleaning bag, I saw a flash of something white.

Could it be? It was! It was my high school graduation dress. The dress had remained in a once-translucent plastic dry-cleaning bag all these years. Through the now cloudy plastic wrap, I could see that the dress was intact. No bats or mice or moths had eaten away at the starchy white material. The lace still looked like something Daisy Buchanan would have loved.

Hugging both dresses to me, I ran to retrieve the rest. From my bedroom, I swam through the clutter of the upstairs hallway to what had once been my mother's room. I could barely make my way through the doorway. There were clothes, lamps, old rotary telephones with their endless spiral cords, laundry baskets piled five feet high. This was the room that had remained untouched for the better part of three decades. My mother had started her hoarding here when my father left, allowing this room to rage out of control when he'd moved out, as some sort of silent protest or cry for help. This was where the cancer of hoarding had started before spreading to every crevice of the house.

The room's two closets—a his and a hers—had remained largely untouched since he'd packed up. In hers, there still hung a little girl's dress, orange and white with a dash of lace. It was purchased for a shower, intended for some friend's child, thirty-plus years ago. It had long since faded. The dress would never be gifted—just as the room would never be cleaned.

But never mind the dress—I had interest in only one part of the room: the old green trunk that had long stood against the front wall. It was a beloved relic of my mother's graduate school days at Ball State. I had always loved examining the trunk's contents as a child, as it was the place she'd taken to storing our baby clothes. I struggled to push the clothes and old bathroom rugs that covered the trunk to the side so that I could open its lid wide. And there inside I found it—just where I'd found it decades before, when I was a princess-obsessed five-year-old—my mother's wedding dress. It was still in the blue cardboard LS Ayres box in which it had been shipped to her, folded up in a rectangular heap. I pulled the box to me, crying. The satin remained rich, the train long.

I had them: the three things that I couldn't live without; three white dresses that helped to define me and my mother.

I turned to see Dean watching me, concerned, from the doorway. He'd followed me, swum his way up that fabric-covered stairway, and studied me now with those big brown eyes.

"You ready?" he asked, looking at the tears streaming down my cheeks.

"Now I am," I said, holding the dresses up to show him. I handed them over to him as I struggled to exit the room, tripping over an old broken black-and-white television set in the process.

The dresses made it home to New York intact—but my heart did not. It would take weeks of long cries and endless talks with Dean over tall glasses of wine before I started to process all that had happened when my mother "expired."

Work helped, as did the boys, whose sloppy kisses and constant demands took my mind off the gaping sore that was my grief.

And then—that spring—came the news that was the best medicine in the world: I was pregnant.

I didn't know for certain that I was pregnant with the boys until I peed on sticks that ultimately turned blue. But when I became pregnant with Piper, I didn't need any sticks. That quickening in my tummy—that soreness in my breasts—was unmistakable from day one. It was May in New York. The weather was warm. The air smelled sweet, at least sweeter than New York air usually smelled. And on our wedding anniversary—the anniversary of the day I'd worn that white nightgown of a Vera Wang gown—I knew, without a shadow of a doubt, that I was expecting. The discovery was a gift from my mother, I'd like to think.

Nine months later—after struggles to clean up my mother's house—she arrived: a perfect little reminder of the joy that life serves up to balance the sadness. When the doctor pulled her from me at New York's Mount Sinai Hospital after just a couple of minutes of pushing, I looked at her in total wonder.

"I don't understand," I told the doctor, eyeing Piper in confusion. "What's wrong with that little boy?"

Accustomed to seeing only naked baby boys, I looked the baby up and down in search of a tiny penis.

"It's not a boy." Dr. Kurtz, the father of five boys, laughed. He raised Piper up higher in the air so that I could get a better look. "You have a daughter."

I screamed and reached for her.

"It's Piper!" I shouted as I held her in my arms for the first time. "It's Piper Anne!"

Coming up with the name was easy. We'd loved the name Piper—a nod to my Irish roots—from the time we'd been dating. Aurelia Arvin Diener would have been proud. And Anne? Well, what else would we call her? Piper was my mother's gift to me. Of course she would bear her name.

During my pregnancy with Piper, I had been worried I would

be filled with renewed searing grief when the baby was born—that the hormonal shift that comes with postpartum would kick me into a deep state of depression and I would be consumed once again by all that I had lost. But Piper's arrival did just the opposite: she filled me with a sense of calm, peace, contentment where there had been none before.

I missed my mother dearly. That would not change. But in Piper I felt as if I had her back. Dressing Piper up in girly dresses, reading to her my mother's favorite poems, I felt Mom's presence. I knew she was there, somewhere.

And then that day—putting Piper into that girliest and most ceremonial of dresses—her christening gown from my journey to County Cork—my heart filled anew with love and with grief. How my mother would have loved to have seen her on that day, to have caressed that linen on the skirt, to have helped me tie the ribbon on her bonnet.

My father tried to dry my tears.

Piper continued to watch me from her post on the changing table as my father wrapped an arm around me.

"Your mother would be so proud of you," he said reassuringly, bending to kiss my cheek.

In the wake of my mother's death, he was working hard to be a good grandfather and a source of support to me. To my boys, he was a hero. With me, there were still rough patches. I'd hung up the phone more than once when he'd said something inappropriate about my mother's housekeeping. But in coming to see me for Piper's baptism—in standing here with me now—I knew he was waving the white flag and asking for the sort of forgiveness Anne would so readily have offered, as she did all those years ago when he came out.

"It's going to be okay," he said, watching me with the baby. "You know that, don't you?"

He was crying now, his salty tears mixing with mine as they

dropped onto the white lining of the changing table. This past year had not been easy for him. He mourned my mother in a way different from me. Even after he'd left the marriage, my mother remained his confidante. Often he called her at night just to talk. Now that she was gone, she wasn't there for those evening calls and he was a bit lost. And, I think, haunted.

Piper looked up at the two of us, her little smile now taking on a look of confusion as she watched me whimper.

I nodded, taking my father's hand in mine and looking at Piper reassuringly. My father was right. It was going to be all right. Piper's eyes studied mine, drank me in. Then she sighed and smiled and did that little kick with her feet that infants tend to do when all is right with the world.

I heard my boys laughing in their bedroom as they played with the new cars Opa had brought them from Florida. I heard Dean's key turning in the lock as he returned from his run to the corner deli to buy flowers for the house. He was humming the tune he always hummed when he was in a good mood. And I realized in that instant that all that I had—all the amazing love and stability enveloping me in my New York City apartment—was something that had long eluded my mother. Anne Diener Pflum had worked tirelessly to give me all of those things that she'd been denied in childhood, in the convent, in marriage, in that house. In me, in Piper, she had at last fulfilled her greatest dream. I had lived to realize the "happily ever after" in which she had believed, for which she had long prayed.

Taking a deep breath, I felt my mother standing beside me for the first time since her death, her arms tightening around me, her laugh filling the air.

"You're a good mother, Mary," my father said, touching a finger to Piper, whose eyes remained fixed upon me. "You know that?"

"I know," I said, smiling now. "I learned from the very best."

Afterword

June 2014

Three years after the death of my mother, I am still trying to make sense of the twists and turns of her life.

Time has healed some wounds. But scars—and questions—remain.

The process of cleaning out the house in Beaver Dam only recently concluded. For the first six months after my mother died, my brother volunteered to lead the efforts.

"I need a place to stay," he told me with a resigned shrug. He had yet to land another job, and in the wake of his divorce, he needed something to focus upon.

"Are you sure?" I asked. "We can hire someone."

"Mary, I'm sure," he said.

Armed with hundreds of Hefty garbage bags and rubber gloves, he dove into the house, making the basement and main floor his top priorities.

Some of the cleanup wasn't so bad, he told me. But some of it gave him nightmares.

"Mary, it's bad," he told me on the phone one night. "I don't care about the live mice. I can take care of those. It's the dead stuff that's gross. Yesterday I found what was left of a bat."

"God, Anthony," I said, taking a seat, "why do you think she wouldn't let us get her out of there?"

"I don't know," he said. "Maybe she somehow felt safe in the middle of all of that crap."

My brother deemed most of the furnishings and onetime keepsakes of the house—the books, the clothes, the dishes, the toys, the lamps—beyond the point of repair. Heartbreakingly, my mother's treasured classics that had sustained her during some of the loneliest hours of her childhood—the first-edition volumes of *The Wizard of Oz*, the beloved *Little Women* and *Little Men* and the Bobbsey Twins—were among the carnage, consumed by ravenous mice.

But hidden in and around the trash were treasures. Photos. Scrapbooks. Letters.

"Who was Father Vincent?" my brother called to ask me one day.

"Mom loved him," I said. "She used to pray with his crucifix. Why?"

"He must have had some power over her because the only thing that Mom seemed to bother to keep organized are letters from him."

Anthony went on to describe the collection of dozens and dozens of handwritten letters that he'd unearthed. They'd been placed neatly in an upright position in a box, sorted carefully according to date.

"Everything else in the house is total chaos and she's got a Dewey decimal system going for this guy's letters," my brother said incredulously. "It's like those things were the only things that mattered."

I nodded. "I'm guessing that to her they did."

"You want them?" Anthony asked.

"Absolutely!"

When I received the letters, I was stunned. Though yellowed, they were just as my brother had described them: in pristine condition, devoid of mouse droppings or that awful smell that filled the rest of the house. The notes—some written by Father Vincent during his time at Oldenburg, others penned by him during his time in New York—chronicled my mother's final months as a nun and her first painful years out of the convent. All were windows into his deep affection for my mother, whom he alternately referred to as Anne and Annie. Never as Sister.

One of the letters was set aside. It appeared to be the most well worn, and presumably most often read. It was the letter in which Father Vincent asked my mother to rethink her decision to marry my father.

I'm not sure when my mother last saw Father Vincent. Was he one of the reasons she always liked to return to Indiana? Did she pay visits to him after the divorce? I'm not certain. What is certain is that he was on her mind right up until the end of her life.

When my brother was badly burned in a brush fire behind my mother's house in the summer of 2011 and rushed by MedFlight to the burn unit at University Hospital in Madison, I made a hurried trip home to Wisconsin.

"I'm sorry about the house," he said from his hospital bed. His legs were covered in second- and third-degree burns he had sustained.

"Forget about the house," I said, sitting beside him. "Let's torch the house. Let's firebomb the thing."

"You don't mean that," he said.

The thing is, I sort of did.

After all the pain and suffering the house had caused first my mother and now my brother, I would have loved to call in a wrecking ball and a crew of bulldozers to raze the house to the ground. But that, I knew, would have broken my mother's heart.

In the end, while my brother recovered from his injuries, I hired a pair of professionals to finish the job. Our mission: to sufficiently clean up the house so that it could be sold to a new family. It was a daunting task.

The remains of the house were something of a time capsule.

As we sifted to the bottoms of the mountains of stuff, the years peeled away. On the tops of the piles were things my mother had purchased and periodicals she'd read toward the end of her life in 2009 and 2010. Mixed in with the newspapers were legal pads filled with to-do lists, half-written letters, poems, even prayers she'd penned in her familiar scrawl. Below that top layer of the piles came newspapers and receipts and mail from 2008, 2007, 2006, and earlier. At the bottom of the stacks were newspapers that dated back to the mid- to late 1990s, around the time when my brother and I had left the house and my mother's parents moved into the assisted-living facility. No one will ever know for certain what triggered my mother's hoarding. What is certain is that once it got under way, it took on the force of a mighty river, consuming everything in its path.

The cleanup took months. By day, I continued to piece together stories for *Good Morning America* about presidential elections, live weddings, extreme makeovers. By night, I bathed and fed and read to the kids. And during every moment I could find in between— late at night and early in the morning and over lunch hours and traveling to and from shoots—I worked the phones, checking in with cleaning crews, ordering the delivery of Dumpsters, calling local hardware stores in search of items for the house: faucets, window treatments, toilets, bathtubs. Eventually, a new house took shape, replete with new floors, new kitchen appliances, new paint.

In the end, we managed to sell my mother's house—and the newly restored yard—in April 2013. The buyers were a young couple who hailed from large families and were anxious to start a family of their own. In the house, they said, they saw "lots of possibilities." My mother would have been thrilled.

Dean and I flew out from New York for the closing, along with Piper. It was a beautiful day, the kind my mother would have loved. After a long winter, temperatures had climbed up into the sixties, the sun shone, and in the front yard, the pointy green spikes of tulip plants poked through the earth, preparing for the sorts of blooms that had graced the yard on the morning of my First Communion.

Walking through the house for a final time, I was overcome with a sadness for what might have been—what should have been—for my mother. Now, in its refurbished state, there were no stacks of newspapers, no horrific smells. Instead, there were gleaming floors, new appliances, and a feeling of airiness. This is how she should have lived, if only she'd allowed us to help.

The investigation Dean and my brother and I launched into the cause of my mother's death was ultimately deemed inconclusive. And though we received tips from hospital staffers on duty the night of her death, indicating my mother was not cared for properly, the malpractice attorney we consulted advised us against going further.

"The state of Wisconsin deems senior citizens completely worthless," he told us after reviewing my mother's case for months. "Even with a compelling case, they've put a cap on how much money any older person's life is worth. New laws mean you're looking at a maximum thirty-thousand-dollar payout even if a judge and jury think your mother died because of bad care. You'll spend three or four times that much getting the case ready for trial. At least."

He was disgusted, he told us, by the anti-senior laws. So were we.

Our focus shifted from getting even to remembering and honoring my mother.

To that end, we speak of her often, visit her grave in Dunkirk, include her in our nightly prayers.

My father has mourned her loss mightily.

"She was special," my father says often. "So very special."

Still, he's moved on. Last fall, he flew to New York to legally marry his partner, Javier, a Latino bank teller he met at one of his favorite bars in Florida. Javier was with him the night I called to tell my father that my mother was dead. Dean and I agreed to serve as witnesses for the weekday-afternoon ceremony at city hall, then later took my father and his new husband to Little Italy for a post-wedding dinner.

The most heartbreaking part of losing my mother so suddenly—and so soon—is knowing my children will never know firsthand the wonder that was their grandmother. They'll never listen to her quote from Shakespeare or "The Hound of Heaven." They'll never see her wonder at the sun setting over a lake or at the first star in the night sky or at a great big pile of colorful autumn leaves, her observations one part wise and one part childlike. They'll never watch her grow excited at the sight of crop dusters tipping their wings over fields of peas, flocks of geese flying south in the fall, tiny buds bursting into enormous peony blooms in the spring. Perhaps hardest for me, they'll never get to see her so heartily and enthusiastically lead by example a life of unwavering faith.

My mother liked to marvel at miracles, look for them in her everyday life, but she failed to realize she was a miracle in her own right. Time and again in her life, she managed to believe in God, in a Holy Spirit, in a divine truth, when there was no seeming physical or rational reason for doing so. In her darkest hours, over and over, she forgave those who hurt her most. And she loved. Not just a little bit. But a lot. With all that she had within her. And not just for part of her life, during those few-and-far-between times when things were going well. She loved mightily throughout all of her life, especially when things were at their worst. That's when she hugged hardest. And longest.

The church that had beaten her down to the depths of her despair in Oldenburg somehow, inexplicably, remained a sanctuary for her. Through loneliness and medical maladies, through a devastating marriage, through the stench of a decaying home, it was what she clung to, her chosen shelter in the storm of life.

Some might call that level of faith blind and ignorant. And in the wake of recent church scandals, many have. But here's the thing: my mother was okay with that. She liked to look beyond what man had made wrong with the church to what she believed pure and unadulterated faith could make right.

Once in my senior year of high school, when I didn't want to attend an early-morning Mass with her, I snarled, in typical teenager style, "What's your deal? Why do you love a church so much that doesn't love anyone? It rejected you when you left Oldenburg. It rejected you when Dad divorced you. How can you still love it so much?"

My mother stood at the foot of my bed and thought long and hard. "That's a good question," she said. "I guess for me, how can I not? At the end of the day, the church I see isn't about cold people making mean rules and bad decisions. For me, it's about the other stuff. The good stuff."

In piecing together the story of my mother's life, cleaning out the last of that house, it occurred to me that I had never been to Oldenburg, where she'd prayed so hard and where she'd been so hurt. So one recent June morning, during a visit to relatives in Indiana, I loaded the kids into the car and took the twisting road to the little town in southeastern Indiana where she'd pledged her life to the church.

Magnificent steeples still define the town. Now, in addition to fields and orchards, the community is surrounded by little coffee shops and cafés. In the center of it all stands the convent—still made up of a series of imposing buildings—surrounded by neatly manicured lawns.

The sister who answered the door when I rang the bell sported short gray hair and a stern expression upon her face. She smiled at Piper, situated in my arms, and frowned at the squirming boys, who sat arguing at my feet. There was no habit in sight. The nun before me wore civilian clothes—a sleeveless shirt and cotton slacks—that she'd paired with a cross that hung around her neck. The enormous habits of my mother's generation had been retired, slowly but surely, after Vatican II.

"Who are you here to see?" she asked, looking me up and down.

"I'm here to learn more about my mother," I said, straining to make my voice heard over the boys and their screams. My two-year-old and three-year-old both wanted the same Hot Wheels car. "She used to live here," I explained.

"What was her name?" asked the sister suspiciously, fingering the cross that hung around her neck.

"Anne Diener," I said, stumbling as Augie attempted to pull me down to my knees so that I could help stop the fight.

"That doesn't sound right," said the sister, narrowing her eyes. She glared at Augie and began to close the door. "You'll have to call back. Tours must be scheduled at least a week in advance."

"Sister Aurelia Mary!" I cried, reciting the name my mother had adopted as a nun. "Her name when she lived here was Sister Aurelia Mary."

The sister stopped abruptly.

"Sister Aurelia Mary? What year was she?"

"Late fifties?"

"I knew your mother," she said, nodding. "She was smart. Extremely smart."

She looked intently at me, then at the children, and after hesitating for a moment, motioned us inside.

For the next hour, the sister showed me around Oldenburg's Mother House, the chapel, the dining room, through all the places where my mother lived and worked—and suffered. I marveled at the floors on which we walked. Beautiful marble, they gleamed in the sunlight that shone through the enormous windows. I wondered if they gleamed as a result of women like my mother who had knelt to meticulously clean them for hours and days on end.

The chapel appeared untouched, a magnificent shrine of white, defined by its massive altar and equally massive pipe organ.

So this, I thought, looking at the pews and old kneelers, is where my mother prayed mightily for a sign from Mary, Mother of God. This is where she thought she'd been told by heaven to leave, and to go out into the real world to have a daughter.

On a pair of walls leading up to the convent's dining room, there were portraits, some of Mary, some of Christ, and many of unsmiling nuns. The nuns in the photos wore the sorts of habits my mother had worn: large, severe veils and yokes that appeared to swallow them whole. I studied the faces. The eyes that peeked out from all of that fabric appeared, more often than not, cold and unhappy.

"Those are the Mother Superiors," my guide explained.

Some wore glasses. All looked stern. Which of these women, I wondered, told my mother to simply pray away her illnesses? Which one ordered my mother to wear those rags for her shameful exit? Which ones on this wall had behaved cruelly in the name of God?

I knew my mother would forgive them. That was her way. But knowing how Oldenburg had scarred her—knowing how the years of youth she'd lost here had haunted her—I wasn't so sure if I could do the same. They'd crushed her. They'd put her in a place so dark, so low, that she never fully recovered.

Beneath the photos of women on that wall of nuns hung a photo that made me smile. It was a photo of a man. A priest. He sported dark hair, a kind smile, and twinkling eyes that reminded me a little bit of Bing Crosby in his turn as a priest in *Going My Way*.

"Who's that?" I asked the nun, squatting with Piper to inspect the face more closely.

"You wouldn't know him," said the nun curtly. "He's long gone. That's Father Vincent."

Of course it was, I thought. I laughed aloud.

"What's so funny?" the sister asked.

"He was a good friend to my mother," I said.

My mother had described at length Father Vincent's kindness. His dark eyes. His great big hugs. She had failed to tell me he was handsome. His was the one smile on a wall of frowns, the only one who looked like he might have been having a good time. Of course my mother had sought him out.

At the close of the tour, I sat at a round table in the convent's dining hall, a glass of lemonade the sisters had offered me in my hand and Piper on my lap. The sister who had been guiding the tour had disappeared for a moment and now reappeared, a small, fat book clutched in her hands. Taking a seat opposite from me, she pushed the book across the table.

I gasped as I caught sight of the handwriting on the cover. It was my mother's familiar scrawl.

"What's this?" I asked, confused.

"Your mother made this for the convent when she was here," the sister explained. "It's part of our archives. I'm afraid we need to keep it, but I thought you'd like to see it before you go."

My hand trembling, I took the book from the sister. This was just like my mother. She loved to make scrapbooks. She'd made one for my and Dean's engagement, one for our wedding, another when Roman was born. Of course she'd made one for her convent days. Scrapbooks were my mother's way of commemorating life— her means of satisfying the frustrated journalist within.

Opening the book, I saw that she'd scrawled a dedication to Oldenburg. Within the pages, she'd written out passages of favorite poems to accompany the black-and-white snapshots of her fellow novices and the Oldenburg grounds. There were pictures of religious statues, photos of beloved flowers.

I managed to keep my emotions in check as I looked through the book. But then I spied an image of her in that white dress.

I caught my breath. She looked so young and pretty and thin. And so very sad. I gently touched my index finger to the page, my lip quivering.

"Are you all right?" the sister asked, leaning over the table.

"My mother always loved white dresses," I said, beginning to cry. I looked to my mother's face—to that white dress—to steady me, then held Piper tighter, using the back of her dress as a make-shift handkerchief. "That never changed."

"That's quite typical in the church," the sister replied dismissively.

"No," I said, shaking my head. "There was nothing typical about my mother. For her, white meant—"

I paused, looking for the right words.

"—so many possibilities."

Acknowledgments

It takes a village to write a book. Such was the case for *White Dresses,* a collection of essays I never intended to become a book. But Patty Dann thought otherwise. Patty is not only a consummate teacher and gifted writer, but she is also a wonderful person and friend. I was fortunate to take Patty's Life Stories class in Manhattan's Westside YMCA, where my children attend preschool. At the time, I thought it would be fun to take a writing class while my kids were in session. Little did I know that an in-class essay I would write about my mother would strike a chord with my classmates, who saw something in my words that I didn't. They encouraged me to write more. And I did. My thanks go out to Patty for guiding me so patiently and to all of my Life Stories classmates—particularly Lisa and Irene—for their feedback, support, and candor throughout the writing process. My thanks go out, too, to the Westside YMCA for maintaining such a wonderful writing program and a gifted arsenal of instructors.

I am eternally grateful to Jin Auh and Andrew Wylie of the Wylie Agency for guiding me through the publication process. Thank you for your patience, advice, and insights at every turn. You are my heroes, literary and otherwise.

My hat goes off to Lisa Sharkey at HarperCollins. For as long as I have known Lisa, she has impressed me with her passion, her drive, and her golden gut. Lisa has always had a knack for spotting a great story, for recognizing a diamond in the rough. I am honored and thankful, Lisa, that you took the time to read my story and took a chance on *White Dresses*.

Thank you to Amy Bendell for being such a wonderful editor. From the very beginning, you "got" *White Dresses* and understood my mother and her many losses. Thank you for helping me to take that first version to the next level and beyond. Thank you, too, to Dani Valladares for your attention to detail in the editing process and helping to make later versions of the chapters sing. And thank you to Mumtaz Mustafa for crafting a beautiful book cover.

I would additionally like to thank the rest of the *White Dresses* "dream team" at HarperCollins: Zea Moscone, Heidi Richter, Trina Hunn, Alieza Schvimer, Molly Birckhead, and Jennifer Hart. You all are not only extremely talented professionals, but also lovely people.

My mother loved her siblings. And I do, too. Thank you for taking the time to talk to me by phone this past year, to help me better understand portions of my mother's life and your shared childhood. My mother always described you as a brilliant bunch—and she was right. I would like to especially thank Uncle Al, who provided so much support to my mother physically and emotionally the last few years of her life and gave her a sense of belonging and acceptance she so desperately needed. You were the first to get back into the house after all of those years. And instead of judging my mother harshly for what you found, as my mother had feared, you loved and accepted her as a sister and a human being even more. I can never thank you enough. I would also like to thank my mother's first cousin Bob Furge for all of his time and family insights.

I would like to thank the teachers in my life who took the time to encourage me over the years. So many of you helped me more than you know by offering kind smiles and warm hugs when I was at my most vulnerable. Special thanks go out to Edie Pondillo for calling me a writer and imploring me to chase my dreams, even if they were different from everyone else's, and to Jerry Anderson, who never stopped believing in me, even when I threatened to stop believing in myself. And a special salute goes out to Trenton Elementary School, for being the most magical shrine of learning an aspiring writer and budding journalist could ever want. You are gone but not forgotten, and the copious amounts of (very real) fairy dust your rolling country hills provided me and so many others will live on forever.

Finally, I must thank the love of my life: my husband, Dean. I once asked my mother how I would know when I had found the right man to marry. She told me there would be two telltale signs: an inability to stop thinking about him and the knowledge that being around him made me a kinder person. As always, she was right. I am such a lucky woman to be married to my best friend and biggest cheerleader. Dean supported *White Dresses*, and my complicated family, from the very beginning. He read through numerous drafts, dried lots of tears, and, most importantly, made me laugh along the way. To Dean: thank you for being a wonderful son-in-law to my mother, an amazing and giving father to our four wonderful children, and my knight in shining armor in every sense of the term. I love you WAMHAS.